RIGHTS, PERSONS, AND ORGANIZATIONS

RIGHTS, PERSONS, AND ORGANIZATIONS

A Legal Theory for Bureaucratic Society

Meir Dan-Cohen

University of California Press
Berkeley Los Angeles London

3/1986
Genl

University of California Press
Berkeley and Los Angeles, California

University of California Press, Ltd.
London, England

1 2 3 4 5 6 7 8 9

Library of Congress Cataloging in Publication Data

Dan-Cohen, Meir.
  Rights, persons, and organizations.
  Revision of the author's thesis (doctoral)—Yale
Law School.
  Includes index.
  1. Associations, institutions, etc.—Law and
legislation—United States.   2. Juristic persons—United
States.   3.   State, The.   4. Law—Philosophy.   I.   Title.
KF1355.D36   1985   346.73'06   84–28038
ISBN 0–520–04711–7   347.3066

    Part III and some segments from Chapters 2 and 4 were
published with minor changes as an article entitled
"Bureaucratic Organizations and the Theory of Adjudication,"
85 *Columbia Law Review* 1 (1985).

To my mother and father

Contents

Acknowledgments

This book began longer ago than I care to admit, as a doctoral dissertation submitted to the Yale Law School. At that stage, I greatly benefited from a well-balanced blend of criticism and encouragement provided by my two readers, Guido Calabresi and Leon Lipson. The manuscript has since undergone numerous revisions, for which many friends, colleagues, and students are in part to blame. I cannot possibly list them all, but since partial justice is better than none, I should mention, with deep gratitude, the contributions of William Barnes, Melvin Eisenberg, Ruth Gavison, Robert Post, Edward Rubin, Philip Selznick, Martin Shapiro, M. B. E. Smith, Hugh Spitzer, Christopher Stone, and Jan Vetter.

My main intellectual debt, which I acknowledge with particularly great joy and affection, is to Bruce Ackerman. As my thesis supervisor, he accompanied this project from its inception and through all its stages. In the meantime, he has become a dear friend while remaining an inspiring colleague and a much revered teacher.

Susan Hollander, my research assistant during the final revision, was of great help in organizing and supplementing the notes. Laura Bergang, Sandra Evans, Susan Lucibelli, and Janice Walker have all not so much typed what I had actually written as they have steadfastly transposed my rambling approximations into recognizably English words.

My last thanks go to my wife, Hana Rosyner-Cohen. Since I do not always find public displays of marital emotions altogether wholesome, I feel bound to exercise self-restraint in recording here my gratitude to her. I should simply say that if it weren't for her help, this book would not have been written. It is, of course, left to the reader to judge how much of a loss that would have been.

Berkeley   M. D.-C.
June 1984

Introduction: On Legal Theory

This book is an essay in legal theory about the law's treatment of large-scale bureaucratic organizations that pervade modern industrial societies. Every scholarly work, however, is perforce also an implicit methodological statement on the discipline that it practices. But whereas in many cases that statement is best left implicit, this would not, I think, be a good policy in the present case. Contemporary legal scholarship is marked by a high level of diversity of goals and disagreement concerning basic methodological commitments.[1] Given such an unsettled background, it may be better to preface this essay with some explicit methodological comments. By briefly explaining what I mean by legal theory, I will try to locate this study in the broad spectrum of legal scholarship, which will help to clarify both its aspirations and its inherent limitations.

Legal scholarship, broadly conceived, can be divided into three main methodological branches (or "ideal types"), each with its own particular rewards as well as its limitations and drawbacks.

The first branch consists of legal scholars who often think of themselves as "academic lawyers" and who view themselves as participating in essentially the same enterprise as practitioners and judges, and use very similar methods to theirs. In this view, scholars, practitioners, and judges all contribute to the articulation of legal doctrine by confronting and offering resolutions to particular legal problems. This variety of legal scholarship aims for and often attains immediate relevance. The measure of its success is the adoption of its preferred solutions to doctrinal problems by the other participants in the enterprise. However, compared to those other participants, the academic lawyer is at a clear disadvantage. Unlike the contribution of his more practical partners, his is necessarily one step removed from the action. He often acts as a kind of

1

deputy-judge, presiding over moot courts, or a shadow lawyer writing mock briefs for hypothetical or past disputes. The academic lawyer is thus in a certain sense resigned to the essentially secondary role of a kibitzer of the legal profession.

This self-inflicted modesty is bound up with the academic lawyer's activist ambition. His academic credentials give him little advantage in the kind of enterprise that he undertakes. No body of systematic, organized, articulated knowledge can decide particular cases. The rigor of any systematic and disciplined body of knowledge must be purchased at the cost of some simplification, some idealization—in short, some distortion of the real world. This is especially true of the social world, where complexity is at its peak and scientific knowledge at its lowest. Good decisions require wise deciders: judges and lawyers who can complement scientific analysis with intuition, insight, and common sense. By trying to operate on the level of reality, where common sense, intuition, and the like are major actors, the academic lawyer is forced to abandon the realm of abstraction, simplification, and generalization, where alone scientific progress and intellectual rigor can be attained.

The second group of legal scholars hold a diametrically opposed conception of their tasks. They align themselves with one or another of the human and social sciences, and they study law from the external perspective provided by their chosen discipline. These scholars (legal anthropologists, legal historians, legal sociologists, etc.) bring to bear on the study of law the complete theoretical and methodological paraphernalia of their respective disciplines. But as they "seek sheer insight, for insight's own sake, into any legal culture, past or present,"[2] these scholars by and large abandon any deliberate effort or ambition to directly influence the course of law.

The third conception of legal scholarship, which I call legal theory, stands somewhat midway between these two more extreme views. Law, as an academic discipline, is viewed by practitioners of legal theory as an applied science that is somewhat precariously poised between the *is* and the *ought*. Though the task of the legal theorist is not the systematic elaboration of human aspirations (this is the domain of the political and moral philosopher), and though she or he does not directly contribute to the body of empirical knowledge (the way that natural and social scientists do), the legal theorist seeks to combine the insights attained in these two realms of scholarly endeavor in order to construct or criticize legal institutions. Legal theory thus suggests an internal, normative study of the law, striving to contribute to the development of legal doctrines, concepts, and institutions. However, the legal theorist's unique contribution is not by way of substituting *her* considered judgment for that of the lawyer or the judge, nor does she merely try to match her wisdom against theirs. Instead, she operates on a level of abstraction, generality, and simplification on which alone she can find bodies of systematic knowledge that can be brought to bear on legal matters.

This simultaneously expands and constricts the sources from which the legal theorist can draw. On the one hand, the legal theorist must try to integrate the insights of various academic disciplines and explore their implications for the legal pursuit of some goals suggested by this or that body of normative thinking. This is a far cry from the occasional, quite erratic, interdisciplinary frolics attempted by the lawyer or judge—where limited time prevents a systematic confrontation with alien vocabularies and techniques. On the other hand, the legal theorist is not allowed to rely in her writings on rhetoric, intuition, and common sense as freely as a judge or a lawyer routinely do. While common sense rather than logic may indeed be the lifeblood of the law,[3] the legal theorist must reverse priorities.

This increased commitment to rigor and precision permits legal theory to play a critical, explanatory, and constructive role within the general legal enterprise. It is critical when it exposes the latent presuppositions (factural and normative) implicit in existing legal practices. It is explanatory when it unites various practices and relates them to a social or to a normative theory, which lends them coherence and meaning. It is constructive when it suggests new institutional arrangements and legal devices for the achievement of some ends. But legal theory can serve these goals only at the price of immediate relevance. It can offer only a partial view of the legal problems with which it deals. It cannot be more complete and truer to the richness of social reality than is the body of knowledge contained in the various disciplines on which it draws. The conclusions and recommendations of legal theory must therefore remain partial and tentative. To be applicable to the solution of problems, they must be filtered through or supplemented by the common sense and good judgment of a wise practitioner fully cognizant of the details of the specific legal issue. The first sin of legal theory is accordingly to presume that it can offer a blueprint for actual decisionmaking and be a substitute for judicial and lawyerly wisdom.

Both the promise and limits of legal theory are well illustrated by *law and economics*, a branch of legal scholarship that clearly belongs in that category. That law and economics fits my description of legal theory seems sufficiently clear. It consists precisely in the combination of ideas from normative philosophy—some form of utilitarianism—with the insights and methodology of a social science, that is, economics.[4] The result is a powerful tool for the analysis and elucidation of legal doctrines and institutions. The field of law and economics has had considerable success in the critical, explanatory, and constructive missions of legal theory. Along the way, it has introduced into legal scholarship an unprecedented degree of rigor and precision, bordering, when using mathematical formulae, on the obscene.

Besides its impressive achievements, law and economics also demonstrates the limits and dangers that inhere in legal theory. It cannot be more powerful or comprehensive than the microeconomics on which it relies. The goal it postulates for the law—efficiency—is only a pale shadow of the goal of social welfare or utility from which it is derived, and even these broader goals artificially impoverish the wealth of goals and ideals actually pursued within any legal system. All this only marks the obvious limits of the economic analysis of law. The limits turn into dangers when some practitioners in the field, overcome by hubris born of success, not only imply that theirs is not merely a partial, simplified, and highly artificial perspective on the law but also presume to provide the lawyer with final answers, substituting their expertise for her wisdom.[5] This is when the theoreticians arouse the justified ire of the more practically oriented lawyers, who criticize their "tunnel vision," their amorality, and insensitivity.[6] If, however, law and economics is seen as a form of legal theory, aspiring to no more than the limited ambitions implied by this characterization, such accusations would be simply beside the point.

So far, I have dealt with the role of legal theory within the law. The example of law and economics can serve to illustrate another benefit that may be expected from this branch of legal scholarship.

By bringing various disciplines to bear on legal issues, legal theory may hope not only to elucidate those legal issues but also to make an indirect contribution to the disciplines on which it draws. An examination of the legal implications of various disciplines and theories may sometimes sharpen the understanding of practitioners in the different fields of their own subject matter. By engaging, in this way, in an active dialogue with other disciplines, legal theory makes legal scholarship into a kind of intellectual laboratory in which conclusions and implications of other disciplines are put to the test of social reality.

As an essay in legal theory, this study shares the aspirations and is subject to the limitations of that methodology. To see this more specifically, let me first give a short overview of my project. My starting point is the commonplace that America today (as well as other industrialized nations) is a society of organizations: large bureaucratic organizations have come to play a dominant role in almost every area of social life. This central societal feature has not been fully integrated into social and specifically legal thinking. Not that lawyers or legal scholars are blind to the existence of organizations. After all, they deal with them all the time. But whereas lawyers do recognize organizations as legal actors, they often tend to refer to them as if they were indistinguishable, from a legal point of view, from another familiar kind of "legal person," namely the individual human being. Legal discourse often applies a unified normative vocabulary to both individuals and to organizations. Concepts, institutions, doctrines, and attitudes that originated in an individualistic context, and whose applicability to organizations is at best questionable, are frequently used indiscriminately and unreflectively to deal with organizations as well. The use of a unified normative vocabulary that is oblivious to differences between individuals and organizations allows the law to deal with various organizations within an essentially individualistic framework, without fully confronting organizational realities and exploring their potential legal implications.[7]

This failure is by no means total. In many legal areas, especially in those in which the presence of organizations is particularly massive (as it is, for example, in corporate or antitrust law), lawyers are paying increasing attention to the organizational phenomenon.[8] Indeed, even more traditional and predominantly individualistic areas of law have responded in various ways to the growth (both in size and number) of organizations. For example, though the same body of contract law generally applies to individuals and organizations alike, a special branch—contracts of adhesion—has grown in this area to accommodate some particular features of standardized contracts that are typically drawn by bureaucratized business enterprises.[9]

However, the two parts of this composite picture—the many instances in which an individualistic normative vocabulary is applied to organizations, and the disparate and rather ad hoc legal responses to organizational realities—both point to the same void: the absence of any shared normative conception of the organization. One task of such a conception would be to lend unity and coherence to the varied ways in which the law has in fact responded to organizational realities. More importantly, such a normative conception would provide a common ground from which the issue of the adequate legal treatment of organizations can be confronted in those areas in which the law ignores those realities. The present essay is a step toward filling that void.

Two recent intellectual developments make this step possible. One is the progress that has been made in acquiring systematic knowledge and in theorizing about organizations. In Part I of this book, I draw particularly on organization theory in order to suggest a conception of the organization which can serve us in normative, specifically legal discourse. The challenge that I hope this part meets is to provide a conception of the organization which is not modeled on nor reducible to the individual actor, and which is yet an entity that is a fit subject for legal ordering. The discussion in this part attempts to demonstrate that even without espousing holistic views, and without forsaking the ethical and the ontological individualism of the liberal tradition, the treatment of organizations as distinctive, irreducible social and legal entities can be made intelligible.

The second intellectual development that underlies this study is the recently renewed interest and consequently growing literature in normative moral and political philosophy, and the extensive application of this literature to the law. As a result, we are now in an improved position to discuss the philosophical foundations of various legal fields and institutions. This development is both an invitation and an opportunity to try to devise some general moral principles that should guide the law in its treatment of organizations. This is the task of Part II. Using the conception of organization developed in Part I, I try in Part II to make sense of the ascription of rights to such an entity, and explore what types of rights such an entity can be plausibly said to possess. I do so by examining the validity of organizations' legal claims from the point of view of two dominant strands in present-day American normative philosophy which I call the paradigm of autonomy and the paradigm of utility. The analysis of organizations' legal rights which ensues is a product of the joint operation of these two philosophical orientations in determining the grounds for and the extent of the appropriate legal protection of various organizational claims.

The resulting theory of organizations' rights is then used as a basis for discussing, in Part III, the theory of adjudication. I argue there that organizational litigants radically transform the nature of that central legal institution. The normative conception of organizations developed in the first two parts helps us to appreciate and better understand that transformation. Finally, in Part IV, I deal with an organization of special social, political, and legal significance: the state. My main point there is that as part of its individualistic outlook that often leads the law to ignore the distinctiveness of organizations, the law also tends to adopt an individualistic political theory that exaggerates the uniqueness of the state both as a singular locus of impersonal repressive power and as a legitimate executor of the popular will. The result of such views, I argue, is detrimental to the law's protection of fundamental individual rights. Furthermore, the great expansion of modern government and the bureaucratization of its branches permit us to apply to the state the general organizational perspective that the present study elaborates. I conclude accordingly with the suggestion that it is sometimes fruitful to analyze various governmental legal claims in terms of the same theory of rights which applies to other, nongovernmental organizations.

This sketchy survey should suffice to indicate how this study intends to practice the methodology that I have called legal theory. Moreover, as an exercise in legal theory, this study is sure to suffer from all the shortcomings of its methodology. The normative landscape within which the argument is cast has been schematized,

simplified—and inescapably impoverished. My examination of
organizations' rights takes place entirely within the liberal tradition. And even this tradition is represented in highly simplified and
abstract form, in terms of the by now familiar juxtaposition between utility-based moral theories and rights-based theories. Furthermore, I use these clusters of theories as the stated but un-
examined premises of my argument. I feel justified in doing so by
the nature of my undertaking, which is to articulate a normative
conception of organizations that is viable in terms of dominant
modes of present legal discourse. My examination of the legal
treatment of organizations is thus conducted from an internal point
of view. That is to say, it tries to unravel the implications for the
normative status of organizations of currently acceptable forms of
legal argumentation and rhetoric. This definition of the enterprise
permits me to take at face value the philosophical positions on
which my argument rests, without subjecting them to critical evaluation. My theory of organizations' legal rights cannot, of course,
be more important or any sounder than the normative theories
from which it derives. And my brief includes no express warranty
concerning the importance and soundness of those normative theories. Instead, by being explicit about the normative premises of
the argument, the methodology of legal theory as I attempt to
practice it puts readers in a good position to assess for themselves
the merits of those premises and of the conclusions to which they
lead.

Similar qualifications must apply to the theoretical (as distinguished from normative or practical) sources that underlie my
discussion of organizations, especially in Part I. My proposed con-
ceptualization of organizations relies heavily on organization theory, a field which, as its own practitioners readily admit,[10] is at
quite a preliminary stage. Moreover, by being general and abstract,
my proposed conception of organization does not do justice to the
great diversity of organizations and to the important differences
among them. Still, such a general and abstract conception is, I
believe, useful as a counterweight to the ingrained habit of thought
that is led by either anthropomorphism or reductionism to assimilate all organizations to individual legal actors.

The weaknesses, inherent in legal theory, of thinking about legal
problems by deductive reasoning from explicit theoretical and nor-

mative premises will thus be certainly reflected in this study. I hope, needless to say, that some of the promise of this methodology to which I have previously alluded will be realized too. But the general observation that I have made about the limited ambitions of legal theory must be emphatically reiterated. Like legal theory in general, this study does not purport, and should not be expected, to generate blueprints—specific practical proposals for immediate applicability. Its conclusions are strictly valid only within the hypothetical, artificial, simplified universe within which they are derived. Indeed, by promulgating theories of the kind that I am about to suggest, one assumes the risk of merely offering one set of blinders as a substitute for another. More likely, in the competition with rival theories, the contenders may ultimately just cancel each other out. Still, even this would not make such theorizing altogether futile. As competing theories cancel each other out, they may sometimes open up a space, or they may create a clearing, within which practice can proceed with a somewhat greater degree of open-eyedness and a somewhat diminished opportunity for blunder or bad faith.

Part I

The Distinctiveness
of Organizations

Chapter I

Changing Conceptions
of Organization

A FAILURE IN LEGAL ONTOLOGY

I will begin by briefly restating the two observations that motivate this study. They are both familiar points, and they do not require additional elaboration. The first is that contemporary American society (like other industrial societies) has undergone during the last hundred years an "organizational revolution"[1] that made it into an "organizational society"[2] in which "every major social task has been entrusted to large organizations—from producing economic goods and services to health care, from social security and welfare to education, from the search for new knowledge to the protection of the natural environment."[3] Central to this development is the increasingly dominant role played in the American economy by large corporations. Even though the measurement and extent of economic concentration are still debated, the proposition that a substantial segment of the American economy is dominated by large corporations can be safely asserted on any sensible notion of what *substantial* and *large* mean in this context.[4]

The second observation is that despite these developments, the individual human being remains the paradigmatic legal actor, in whose image the law is shaped and then applied to corporations and other collective entities.[5] To be sure, the claim that the individual is the paradigm legal actor need not deny the notable instances in which lawyers are fully cognizant of organizational realities. But as I have already indicated,[6] such cognizance finds legal expression mainly when the organizational reality thrusts itself upon the lawyer's attention with special force, as it often does in legal areas (such as Corporations and Antitrust) that deal almost exclusively

13

with organizations.[7] The special attention paid to organizations in these and other instances has not, however, penetrated legal thought nor permeated legal practice in general. In the absence of special circumstances to alert lawyers to the organizational identity of the legal actor, the paradigm is likely to prevail, and legal discourse is likely to lapse into its uniform individualistic mode. Thus, we find that the discussion and the operation of legal institutions (such as adjudication), legal rights (to property, for example), and legal doctrines (such as strict liability in torts) often fail to explicitly acknowledge the existence of organizations. Legal discourse proceeds instead in those instances with a uniformity that implies that there is only one kind of legal actor: the individual human being.

It must also be emphasized that the point is not that the law fails to recognize organizations as legal actors. Quite to the contrary. The battle for the legal recognition of organizations (especially corporations), which was once waged with great zeal and clamor,[8] was won long ago: we view it now as a matter of course that organizations can be legal actors, bearers of rights and duties. But there is an element of paradox in this victory. The legal personality of corporations (and other collective entities) has been firmly established, but at the cost of ignoring them as *distinctive* social and legal phenomena. By using the ambiguous concept of "person," applying it to both individuals and organizations, the law has assimilated the organization into its preexisting individualistic framework.[9] This linguistic twist frequently allows lawyers—scholars and practitioners alike—to maintain the uniformity of legal discourse on the tacit assumption that the magic term *person* can successfully comprehend both individuals and organizations. Consequently, for many legal purposes the differences between an ordinary human being and American Telephone and Telegraph (or, for that matter, General Motors, or the AFL-CIO) are deemed irrelevant.

Just to state this strange equation is to indicate the apparent implausibility of the law's characteristic mode of accommodating large organizations. My first task is accordingly of a diagnostic nature: I will try to identify some possible conceptions or mental images of organizations which may have led to and can still sustain this accommodation. Such a diagnosis will help us in constructing a sounder basis for the law's treatment of organizations.

The philosophical debate over the nature of collective entities is marked by a perennial dispute between holistic and atomistic views: roughly between the view that fully acknowledges the reality of collective entities and denies the possibility of completely reducing that reality to a description of individuals and their interrelations, and the view that collective entities are constituted by and are therefore reducible without loss into individuals and their interrelations.[10] These conflicting views of organizations contribute, no doubt, both to the explicit debate over the legal personality of corporations and to the more tacit background conceptions that in fact shape their actual legal treatment. Yet, in so participating (overtly or covertly) in legal discourse, both of these opposing views of the nature of collective entities tend to assume very simple versions, which converge on the individualistic legal conception of those entities.

In its simplest form, the holistic attitude exploits a seductive metaphor that has a grip on the legal imagination: that of the natural person. This metaphor at once captures the unity and reality of the corporation (or other organizations) as well as its fitness for legal personhood as the bearer of rights and duties. I will call the use of the metaphor of person as the expression of the holistic view of organizations *personification*.[11] There is an equally simple picture of collective entities which expresses the opposite, atomistic view. In this picture, corporations (or other collectivities) are seen as being essentially mere clusters or aggregates of individuals. The normative status of any collective entity is identical with the normative status of the individuals that compose it. I will call this simple version of the atomistic view of collective entities *aggregation*.[12]

It is easy to see that when the two main opposing views on the nature of collective bodies (holism and atomism) assume the forms of personification and aggregation respectively, they converge on the same normative implications. Both personification and aggregation are conducive to the assimilation of organizations, for normative purposes, to the individual human being. Whether organizations are perceived as essentially *like* persons (as they are in the case of personification) or essentially as clusters of persons (as in the case of aggregation), they share the normative status of persons, and should be treated likewise. Accordingly, the opposition (which marked much of the debate over corporate legal personality) between the belief in the "reality" of collective entities, on the one hand, and viewing them as mere "fictions," "figments of the imagination," on the other, is of little practical moment when these opposing views assume the forms of personification or aggregation, respectively.[13]

My next diagnostic step focuses on the organization on which the legal conception of organizations is primarily modeled: the corporation. In the following section, I will attempt to establish a link between the attractiveness of both personification and aggregation as modes of comprehending organizations and a certain picture of the corporation which is a composite of particular theories that prevailed at the time when corporate legal personality was in its formative stage. After briefly sketching that picture, I will draw an alternative one which expresses the changes that have since taken place in those theoretical perspectives. The new image of the corporation, it will be seen, is less conducive to an individualistic approach, either through aggregation or through personification, than the old one was. The movement from the old image of the corporation to the new is therefore a step away from an individualistic conception and in the direction of recognizing corporations as distinctive entities. In the final section of this chapter, I will show that parallel changes to those that occurred in our understanding of corporations have also taken place in regard to other organizations. Associating in this way personification and aggregation with an obsolete picture of corporations and other organizations implies the need for a different conception of those entities, one that is more in tune with their realities as presently understood. I will suggest such a conception in the next chapter.

THE CHANGING IMAGE OF
THE CORPORATION

Three main fields converge to create our image of the corporation: law, economics, and sociology. What one saw when one looked at the corporation during the first quarter of the century from all three perspectives could be accommodated within an individualistic framework with some plausibility.

As conceived by neoclassical microeconomics, the corporation is not all that different from the individual *qua* economic actor as he is perceived within the same theoretical framework.[14] Replace the individual's utility frontier by the firm's production frontier, and the economist can derive basically the same expected behavior and analogous theorems. More specifically, the firm is portrayed as having a well-specified, single goal—profit maximizing—with respect to which it reaches optimal decisions. These decisions are, furthermore, uniquely determined by the market conditions in conjunction with the firm's production frontier. Remarkably, none of the attributes of the firm as an organization enter this scheme. Specifically, dimensions such as complexity and size are completely absent. As far as this economic theory is concerned, the firm could easily be replaced by a single individual manufacturer, with no consequences for the theory whatsoever.

The basic image of the corporation within traditional legal theory is that of a group of businessmen—or entrepreneurs, as they were once called—who get together for a mutual venture. The corporation is basically only a mode of conducting business by the shareholders. They are the rightful owners in a most meaningful way: they both exercise authority in the corporation and reap the benefits. To this basic conception of what is essentially a kind of partnership, legal concepts of agency and trust were added to account for the role played by other actors in the corporation. These legal extensions do not, however, upset the initial pattern; rules of agency and trust merely allow the law to see to it that officers and other functionaries do what they are supposed to do: maximize profit for the sole benefit of the shareholders.[15]

The third component of the traditional image of the corporation is the Weberian model of bureaucracy.[16] The Weberian conception of the corporation as an hierarchical structure, rationally pursuing a single goal (or a small set of well-specified and consistent goals), comports with both the economic theory of the firm and the legal theory of the corporation, and allows one to maintain the personification implied by the former and the aggregation supported by the latter. Merely conceive the entrepreneur (who is both manager and owner) at the top of the hierarchical pyramid, as Weber himself explicitly does: "It is the peculiarity of the modern entrepreneur that he conducts himself as the 'first official' of his enterprise, in the very same way in which the ruler of a specifically modern bureaucratic state spoke of himself as 'the first servant' of the state."[17] With the owner-entrepreneur at the top, the corporation mechanically carries out his will and serves his interest, which is, in accordance with the economic theory of the firm, the maximization of profit. The Weberian model of bureaucracy thus enhances the individualistic view of the corporation by making it seem plausible to identify the entire structure with its "head": there is always a single person at the top of the hierarchy who wields all the power and reaps all the benefits, the rest of the structure being a mere mechanical elaboration of that person's will and interests.

The microeconomic theory of the firm, the traditional legal theory of the corporation, and the Weberian model of bureaucracy all combine to a conception of the corporation which lends some plausibility to a view that treats the corporation indistinguishably from individual human actors. Furthermore, insofar as these theories still exert influence today, the continuous viability of the myopic view of the corporation is also partially explained. Major changes have, however, occurred in the fields discussed above, and in conjunction they convey a radically different image of the large corporation. The relevant developments in economics, legal theory, and organization theory are all well known, and a brief sketch should therefore suffice.[18]

The natural place to begin the drawing of the new picture of the corporation is the classical work of Berle and Means, *The Modern Corporation and Private Property*, published in 1932.[19] Research done since then confirms the radical separation of stock ownership from control in the large corporation which these authors have emphasized.[20] The dominant figure in the older theory of the corporation, the entrepreneur, who both owns and runs the enterprise, has been replaced by a professional, hired, self-perpetuating management.[21] The idea that the shareholder owns the corporation has lost much of its credibility. "These views," writes Professor Blumberg about the changes in the legal theory of the corporation, "reflect the changing position of the shareholder in the large public corporation from part owner to investor."[22]

But the significance of the individual shareholder to the corporation is on the decline even in his capacity as investor. As noted by Berle[23] and confirmed by later studies, a significant proportion of the investment funds at the disposal of large corporations is either self-generated or supplied by institutional investors such as banks, investment companies, insurance companies, and pension funds.[24] It should be noted that in the case of these institutional investors the *only* shareholders are organizations, while the individual claimants, whose money (e.g., savings, pension funds, insurance premiums) is invested by these organizations, are mere "second-order" investors with no proprietary claim attached to their investment.

Just as the corporation attains in this way relative independence from the individual shareholder, the shareholder, too, becomes less attached to a particular corporation. As portfolio theory recommends, the investor's shares are likely to be diversified across many corporations.[25] Such a pattern of shareholding severs the direct correspondence between the fortunes of any particular corporation and the interests of an individual shareholder.

The decline in the role and status of the shareholder in the large corporation has permitted another change in the legal view of the corporation: advocates of corporate "social responsibility" assert that the corporation serves a variety of constituencies, which include, in addition to shareholders, employees, customers, and the community at large.[26] In this view, the corporation can no longer be identified with a single homogeneous group of individuals. Its decisions and activities are the resultant of and are responsive to a complicated set of interests and conflicting claims.[27]

This is also part of the image conveyed by the post-Weberian developments in organization theory which have badly shattered the neat Weberian pyramid. "The 'pyramid' headed by the single all-powerful individual," writes James Thompson, "has become a symbol of complex organizations, but through historical and misleading accident. The all-powerful chief can maintain such control only to the extent that he is not dependent on others within his organization; and this is a situation of *modest* complexity, not one of high degree of complexity."[28] The organization is instead portrayed as a coalition of groups of divergent claims and interests, engaged in a continuous process of bargaining with one another.[29] The final action and the overall performance of the organization can

be characterized as "political resultants"[30] of these complex bargains as well as other processes of group decisionmaking, rather
than the expression of the will or wisdom of any particular individuals.[31] With its focus on bargaining relations and on decisionmaking processes, this view depersonalizes the organization even
more than does the Weberian model. While the Weberian model
preserves at least one individual, the one occupying the top of the
hierarchy, as a human locus of power and responsibility, the modern view dissolves the structure of authority into a dispersed network of impersonal processes.[32]

The separation of ownership and control and the organizational
conception of corporations have also greatly influenced economic
theory.[33] Managerial theories of the firm explicitly challenge the
monolithic picture painted by the older economic theory. They
focus instead on the conflicting motivations and interests that underlie corporate decisionmaking, and on the frequently self-serving
decisions reached by corporate officers.[34] If the firm is no longer
dominated by a self-interested profit-seeking entrepreneur, it is no
longer obvious what should motivate a single-minded policy of
profit maximization.[35] The firm is accordingly depicted as pursuing
various other objectives such as growth, increased volume of sales,
management returns, stability, and others.[36] These various goals
need not be consistent with one another, and their contradictions
may be resolved by a sequential attention on the part of the corporation to different goals at different times.[37] Furthermore, the
notion that the firm's choices are uniquely determined by the conjunction of market conditions and its production frontier has been
largely discarded in favor of a greater acknowledgment of the role
of uncertainty and the importance of economic size,[38] which together leave to the large firm considerable room for discretion.[39]
The way in which this discretion is exercised and corporate decisions are made is in part determined by information constraints
and by the internal structure and operating procedures of the
firm.[40]

Just as the old picture of the corporation, taken by itself, contains
elements that may support personification and aggregation as viable conceptions of the corporation, so the contrast between the old
picture of the corporation and the new conveys vividly the point
about the diminishing capacity of those conceptions to capture the

reality of the corporation and provide a sound basis for its normative status. When a corporation can no longer be identified with a relatively homogeneous group of shareholders, when its behavior can no longer be portrayed as the inert mechanical execution of an owner's will, and as our attention is drawn to its distinctive organizational properties and processes, the posture of simply equating the corporation via personification or aggregation to a natural person loses whatever surface plausibility it might once have had.

FROM CORPORATIONS TO ORGANIZATIONS

The corporation is, no doubt, the most conspicuous organization treated as a "legal person," and as such it often serves as the legal paradigm of a collective entity. Yet most of what we said about the large corporation applies, *mutatis mutandis*, to many other organizational types, such as membership organizations. The temptation to extend to these organizations, through personification and aggregation, an individualistic treatment is founded, as in the case of corporations, on outdated and oversimplified conceptions of organizational realities.

As we have just seen, the plausibility of aggregation is undermined in the case of the corporation in part by recent developments in legal theory which dethrone the shareholders as owners and relegate them to the status of "beneficiaries," shared by other groups of individuals as well. Thus the corporation is rendered "ownerless." In the case of most other types of organizations (the trade union or the university, for example), there isn't any such group of owners in the first place: these organizations are "ownerless" in the strictest and most formal legal sense. The absence of legal owners does not, however, save such organizations from the dangers of aggregation. Their membership naturally assumes the cognitive role that shareholders play in the legal perception of the corporation. The membership organization, one might think, can be identified, for normative purposes, with the group of its individual members: isn't a trade union, after all, so many workers joined together?

The negative answer can be derived both from sociology and from economics. The obvious starting point for the relevant sociological perspective is still Robert Michels's classic *Political Parties*.[41]

The iron rule of oligarchy, inaugurated in that study, has long since become a cliché; but becoming a cliché does not disprove a proposition.[42] The pertinent part of Michels's thesis is short and merits quotation:

The party, regarded as an entity, as a piece of mechanism, is not necessarily identifiable with the totality of its members, and still less so with the class to which these belong. The party is created as a means to secure an end. Having however become an end in itself, endowed with aims and interests of its own, it undergoes detachment, from the teleological point of view, from the class which it represents. In a party, it is far from obvious that the interests of the masses which have combined to form the party will coincide with the interests of the bureaucracy in which the party becomes personified . . . . By a universally applicable social law, every organ of the collectivity, brought into existence through the need for the division of labor, creates for itself, as soon as it becomes consolidated, interests peculiar to itself. The existence of these special interests involves a necessary conflict with the interests of the collectivity.[43]

This description shifts the focus of attention, when thinking of a membership organization, from the group of individual members to the permanent, self-perpetuating bureaucratic apparatus that constitutes the organization. Members, in this view, are relegated to a secondary position as resources or beneficiaries of the organization.[44] But they can no longer be realistically identified with it.

The observation that members are a resource for the organization needs some elaboration. It is a widespread assumption among organization theorists that "whatever else organizations seek, they seek to survive."[45] For that purpose, organizations need the human and financial resources provided by their members. Though this may seem to establish a necessary link between the membership group and the organization, this is not necessarily the case. In his book *Political Organizations*,[46] James Wilson describes some recent developments with respect to membership organizations which parallel the growing independence of corporations from shareholders that we have previously described. "The rise in recent decades of large private foundations and of massive government grant programs," Wilson argues, "has provided major new opportunities for the maintenance and enhancement of organizations that, left to their own devices (which is to say, left to the interests of their members), would face decline or even extinction."[47] As a result, we are faced with the curious phenomenon of the membership organization that has virtually no members: "Indeed, for some associations 'members' exist only as an historical artifact, as symbols of 'private' legitimacy, or as grounds for claiming a representational function. The essential contributors have increasingly become the professional staffs and their counterparts in the foundations or government agencies that provide funds, and the relevant incentives are those to which staffs and agencies respond."[48] The specter of a membership organization with no members dramatizes the centrality to the concept of the organization of the permanent structures, the ongoing apparatus, to which different groups of individuals are only contingently and problematically related.

An economist, Mancur Olson, offers in his well-known book *The Logic of Collective Action*[49] an argument that can be used as another line of attack on the adequacy of aggregation as an account of membership organizations. An aggregationist view would describe the evolution of a trade union, for example, as starting from several workers who get together to achieve certain common goals, and who then gradually and incrementally increase their numbers, until they become the kind of large trade union that we actually face. The point of such an incrementalist evolutionary story is to emphasize that no discontinuity occurs in the gradual transition from the initial small group of labor activists to the large trade union that finally emerges, and hence that there can be no qualitative difference of any normative consequence between the two.[50] However, according to Olson's theory, the picture of individuals who willingly and spontaneously join each other in increasing numbers to achieve a common goal misses a crucial feature of large organizations. The goals of many important membership organizations, such as, for example, a trade union's goal of improving safety conditions at the workplace, are "public goods": if achieved, they benefit nonmembers as well as members. Joining the organization therefore makes little sense for most self-interested potential members: the individual costs of membership (fees, time, etc.) are most likely to outweigh each member's marginal contribution to the attainment of the desired goals. As a result, each person will figure out that, without participating, he or she is likely to have practically the same share, for free, in the public good that is provided anyway by the organization. This, Olson points out, is only true of large organizations. In small organizations each member counts: each member's contribution may be crucial to the achievement of the collective goal, thus making membership consonant with the individual's self-interest. Olson concludes that the difference between a small and a large organization is not merely quantitative but qualitative as well: in the large organization, unlike the small one, membership cannot be expected or explained merely in terms of the individuals' mutual interest in the collective good sought by the organization. To attract members, the large organization must rely either on coercion or on the provision to members of some *selective incentives*, that is, benefits that are tied to membership.

This account of the large organization rejects aggregation as even a hypothetical description of its emergence. Membership, in the case of the large organization, presupposes organization, rather than the other way around: for there to be a large membership group, there must be in the first place an organization that will be willing and able to coerce or "bribe" individuals into membership.

Olson's argument has a further implication for the nature of large organizations. Once members are recruited either through coercion or through selective incentives, their relation to the organization cannot be seen as primarily related to and contingent upon its pursuit of collective goals. The same considerations of self-interest which would have prevented members from joining the organization in the first place, unless coerced or "bribed," also argue against active participation in the internal decisionmaking of the organization: the costs of such participation to the individual member are again likely to outweigh her benefit from her marginal contribution to the pursuit by the organization of its stated goal. The result, in the language of another economist, is that there is little incentive for members in large organizations to exercise "voice" in order to remedy deviations by the organization from its pursuit of its stated goals; and at the same time, they may have good reasons (e.g., coercion, "bribes," or loyalty) against the exercise of "exit."[51] This familiar extension of Olson's economic perspective on the large organization gives further support to the view that emphasizes discontinuity between positions and actions of the organization and the wills or interests of its membership.

So understood, the bureaucratization of the large membership organization has also a chilling effect on a brand of personification which seems to have had little impact, at least within the Anglo-American liberal tradition, and which we can therefore mention only in passing. It is the idealist vision of the association as a living person endowed with a real will of its own which is the product or the expression of the associative wills of its several members.[52] Whatever one's initial inclination to perform the leap of metaphysical faith necessary for the adoption of this vision, that inclination must be greatly diminished in the case of organizations by the realization that a permanent bureaucratic machinery is interposed between the members and their supposed "collective identity" in the form of an organization.

Chapter II

What Is an Organization?

PERSONIFICATION, AGGREGATION, AND THE "WHAT IS AN ORGANIZATION?" QUESTION

In the preceding chapter, we identified personification and aggregation as two putative mental constructs conveying simplified pictures of the organization which permit us to maintain in the organizational society an essentially uniform mode of legal discourse. However, once the large corporation is disassociated from its shareholders, the membership organization is no longer identified with its members, and the thorough bureaucratization of these entities is recognized, the great oversimplification involved in both personification and aggregation becomes apparent. Neither of these two models offers a plausible picture of the organization in which its normative status can be securely grounded. Yet even as we discard personification and aggregation for their simplemindedness, we should be guided in our search for an alternative conception of organization by some important and valid messages that they contain.

As the representative of the "holistic" attitude toward organizations, personification captures, but exaggerates and misstates, the commonsense belief, embedded in ordinary language and common practices, in the unity and the reality of organizations. It conveys the triple insight that organizations are commonly the objects of meaningful predication; that this predication is possible and meaningful apart from and in the absence of any detailed knowledge pertaining to individual constituents of the organization; and that in many cases *the same* predication is equally appropriate for organizations and for individuals. To the question, for example, "Who manufactures the Mustang?" all of us (who know something about American cars) would confidently answer: "The Ford Motor Company." Our confidence would not be diminished by our utter ignorance about the specific role played in the production by various people, machines, and processes; and our answer would be as intelligible and as correct as would be the assertion that Phyllis Doe manufactured that car, had she in fact spent her life doing so. The exaggeration, however, consists in the implication of the person metaphor that since organizations have some global properties similar to those of individuals (e.g., both are in principle capable of manufacturing cars), they must therefore have all the properties relevant to the individual's moral and legal status.

So also in the case of aggregation. Reflecting the "atomistic" element in our commonsense conception of organizations, it correctly insists on the critical dependence of organizations, both phenomenally and normatively, on the actions and interrelations of individual human beings. However, by equating organizations to a homogeneous group of individuals, aggregation vastly understates the extent and the significance of the complexity and inscrutability of that dependence.

There is a third important insight, one that is shared by both personification and aggregation. They both represent a belief in the need for and the primacy of some cognitive picture of the organization as a precondition for determining its normative status in law and morality. The assertions (or the tacit beliefs) that the corporation is "really" just like a person, or that it is "ultimately" just a bunch of shareholders, while embodying misleading pictures of the corporation, are nonetheless on the right methodological track: we must make *some* pre-legal cognitive peace with the phenomenon of the organization before we can intelligibly tackle the question of its appropriate normative treatment. In this respect, the approach signified by both personification and aggregation is diametrically opposed to the view that "lawyers as a rule have no concern with the structural differences underlying the various kinds of legal persons, as that is a question of sociology."[1] Rather, this approach is in keeping with H. L. A. Hart's famous formulation of "the minimum content of natural law."[2] Some universal features of legal systems, Hart contends, can be explained in terms of basic attributes shared by all human beings and reflected in the law. The attributes he lists are those of aggressiveness and vulnerability ("men are both occasionally prone to, and normally vulnerable to, bodily attack"); approximate equality; limited altruism; and limited understanding and strength of will. These attributes, together with the "minimum purpose of survival which men have in association with each other,"[3] account, according to Professor Hart, for some of the basic institutions and characteristics of all legal systems. My present concern is not with Hart's specific list of human attributes, but rather with the general point he makes about the link between the law's conception of the attributes and characteristics of the legal actors and basic normative features of the law. Insofar as organizations have different properties from individuals, this difference, once acknowledged, may turn out to be of legal relevance and require a correspondingly different legal treatment of organizations in areas where hitherto they have been treated equally.

An effort to get acquainted with the organization and to draw some mental picture of it would seem, therefore, the obvious starting point of any normative, specifically legal investigation concerning organizations. Yet it is Hart himself who raises strong objections to precisely this enterprise. Before we proceed, we have to confront and try to surmount this hurdle. We should do so not only out of deference to the eminence of the originator of this objection but also because removing such a conspicuous obstacle from our way will help clarify the direction in which we're headed.

In his much celebrated inaugural lecture entitled *Definition and Theory in Jurisprudence*,[4] Hart urges us to give up "the ever-baffling form of question": "What is any association or organized group?" and substitute for it the following: "Under what conditions do we refer to numbers and sequences of men as aggregates of individuals and under what conditions do we adopt instead unifying phrases extended by analogy from individuals?"[5] If we conduct such an investigation, Hart anticipates, "we shall cease to talk about group-personality (and indeed individual personality) as if it were a single quality or set of qualities. For we shall find that there are many varieties of widely different conditions (psychological and others) under which we talk in this unifying personal way. Some of these conditions will be shown to be significant for legal or political purposes, others will not."[6] Two different objections to posing the question "What is an organized group?" can be distinguished in this passage: one based on an ontological view and the other based on an empirical guess.

Let me begin from the latter point. The investigation of conditions under which we apply "to numbers and sequences of men" "unifying phrases extended by analogy from individuals," Hart argues, though important, should not be viewed as a search for an elusive "personality of the organized group," because of the great variety and divergence of the conditions we are likely to find. This, it should be noticed, is an empirical hypothesis which may but need not be true. This objection to the attempt to provide a unified definition or description of organized entities should accordingly be removed if it turns out that there is in fact a significant convergence or uniformity in the conditions under which we use "unifying phrases," and if it furthermore turns out that these recurrent sets of conditions are systematically "significant for legal or political purposes." This, however, is precisely what one would expect to be the case in the organizational society. The very existence of a body of study called "organization theory" suggests that we can identify at least one field in which there is a significant uniformity of identifiable conditions for the application of "unifying phrases"—namely, the field densely populated by formal organizations.[7]

Hart's other objection to the question "What is an organized group?" may be based on his opposition to the ontological stance toward collectivities implied in the language in which this question is formulated. Asking what *is* a collective entity and what are its properties implies an ontology committed to the separate and irreducible existence of such entities. But in this case Hart's objection pertains to the form of the question; it does not affect the nature of the investigation to which it leads. The investigation is meant to unpack and account for expressions such as "The University expressed its gratitude" (Hart's example) and "The Ford Motor Company manufactures the Mustang" (my example). If the conditions under which these and many other similar expressions can be correctly and intelligibly used are sufficiently uniform (as we assumed they are in responding to Hart's other objection), little of practical significance seems to me to turn on the form in which the question that leads to their discovery is cast. Hart does not, after all, seek to deny the intelligibility of such "unifying phrases" as we commonly use with respect to collective entities. The issue he raises concerns only the proper way to characterize the enterprise of elucidating such phrases for normative purposes. Should we include in the description of this enterprise reifying references to the collective entities by asking: What is an organization and what are its normatively relevant properties? Or should we rather exclude such language from the description of the enterprise, asking instead: What are the normatively relevant conditions under which "unifying phrases" are properly used?

The choice of description will indeed be conditioned by one's ontology, but it will make little practical difference. As long as we are entitled to use "unifying phrases" in practical contexts (an entitlement Hart does not challenge), and as long as we are agreed on the intellectual agenda, which is to identify cognitions that underlie and shape the normative use of such phrases, little seems to me then to turn on the ontological characterization of the enterprise. For legal purposes, which are of course eminently practical purposes, I see nothing objectionable in asking the question: What is an organization and what are its normatively relevant properties? But my willingness to revive the question banned by Hart is, in part, due to his own argument against it: he has clarified, for me at any rate, that this question can be always recast as a question about the normative implications of the conditions for the proper use of "unifying phrases," thereby allowing us to proceed in practical matters while evading difficult ontological commitments.

ORGANIZATION THEORY AND THE DISTINCTIVENESS OF ORGANIZATIONS

With this obstacle removed, we can now pose the question "What is an organization?" with greater clarity and confidence. In answer to this question, I will seek some unified conception of organizations which captures our main cognitions about them, and which will provide a workable foundation for their sound legal treatment. The place to look for such a conception, I have already indicated, is organization theory (broadly conceived). However, as everyone familiar with this field knows, "organizational theory" is a misnomer; there certainly is no such thing as a unified theory of organizations. The field does not even contain a number of competing theories: hardly any of the various statements, research projects, and hypotheses in this field has attained the level of generality and rigor, nor does any of them enjoy the degree of scientific consensus that would warrant the appellation "theory" in any but the most rudimentary sense.[8] Nonetheless, the research that belongs to the field of organization theory, rudimentary and provisional though it may be, is an important repository of (more or less) systematic observations about organizations. In trying to divine from them a unified conception of the organization, I will focus on eight essential properties, or rather clusters of properties, that recur in various descriptions and definitions of organizations. Accordingly, organizations that are the subject matter of organization theory (and of the present study) can be described as *large, goal-oriented, permanent, complex, formal, decisionmaking, functional structures.*[9] In discussing these clusters of organizational properties, I will emphasize how each of them supports and explains the ordinary habit of referring to organizations in global, nonreductionist terms, thereby contributing to a conception of organizations as unified and distinctive phenomena. This discussion will set the stage for a picture, or rather a motion picture, of the organization which will be presented in the next chapter and which will serve as the basis for the normative analysis in Part II.

Structure

The most obvious starting point for any comprehension of the unity of the organization is the idea of structure.[10] This implies the existence of a (more or less) fixed and perceptible pattern or order, which, in the case of the organization, is susceptible of representation, at least in broad and rough outline, in the form of an "organizational chart." The relation between the idea of structure and a unified conception of the organization is straightforward and can be easily understood on the familiar analogy of the relation between a car and a heap of its disassembled components. The analogy with the car can be further exploited for bringing out two other aspects of the idea of structure: first, that the organization's performance (like that of the car) depends on its structure; and second, that the structure is amenable to deliberate tinkering and change. These two related ideas combine to make the organization a "manipulable sructure": its internal order may be modified with an eye to bringing about desirable changes in its performance.

Permanence

By permanence I mean the fact that "organizations can persist for several generations . . . without losing their fundamental identity as distinct units, even though all members at some time come to differ from the original ones."[11] Permanence is reflected in the nature of two important functions that take place in the organization: memory and planning. Looking at an organization at any point of time, t_2, we find that its current actions and decisions are influenced by events at a prior time t_1 (due to memory) and a later time t_3 (due to planning).[12] However, because of the nature of permanence, which divorces the identity of the organization from the identity of any particular individuals, the personal composition of the organization may be altogether different at t_1, t_2, and t_3, so that none of the individuals related to it at an earlier time is still related to it in the later point in time. The operative time span of the organization (operative in the sense that events within this time span influence the organization's decisions and actions) does not coincide with that of any particular individual or group of individuals, but rather extends both backwards and forwards beyond that of particular individuals.[13] We might call this property of organizations, born of their permanence, *temporal independence*.[14]

Decisionmaking

The focus on decisionmaking as a central and essential organizational activity draws attention in the first place to the crucial importance that *information* plays in organizational activities. The idea of decisionmaking implies the capacity to perform such functions as gathering, registering, recording, decoding, and disseminating information. It is sensible to impute these information-related functions to the organization (rather than to some specific individuals) because the total information that leads to a certain decision (or action or product) is not normally possessed by any single individual nor is it straightforwardly related to the combined knowledge possessed by a number of identifiable individuals. What information is gathered, to whom it is disseminated, how it is decoded, and how it is combined and brought to bear on the final outcome critically depends on the structure of the organization, on the presence or absence of particular units or positions in it, on the relevant standard operating procedures, as well as on the presence of "noise" that introduces an element of randomness into the processing of information.[15]

Furthermore, speaking of an organizational decision presupposes the existence of some organizational *preferences*. Here, too, it is sensible to impute the preferences to the organization itself, on the ground that even though the organizational preferences are ultimately the product of some individuals' preferences, it may be utterly impossible to account for the organizational decision in terms of the latter. Two lines of argument discourage the effort to reduce the organization's preferences (as embodied in its decisions) to their individualistic constituents. One line is based on the coalition view of the organization, which depicts decisionmaking as essentially a bargaining process among various groups with divergent and often conflicting interests. Decisions are accordingly characterized as the "political resultants"[16] of these complex bargains, determined in part by logrolling and strategic behavior.

More generally, the difficulties, both practical and conceptual, in aggregating individual preferences into a collectively rational choice are studied and demonstrated by social choice theory.[17] Arrow's famous impossibility theorem, proving that under some plausible assumptions no voting procedure is available to translate individual preferences into transitive collective orderings, is a prime example of my present point.[18] A group's decision this way rather than the other thus may not reflect the actual preferences of the group's individual members but result from nothing deeper than the accidental (or manipulated) arrangement of the agenda. A similar message is contained in Thomas Schelling's book *Micromotives and Macrobehavior*,[19] which examines various ways in which rational behavior on the part of individuals results in a pattern of group conduct that is irrational or suboptimal.[20] His thesis can be stated in reverse, and thus support my point about the relation between individual preferences and collective behavior: from observing a certain collective position or decision, we can not confidently deduce the underlying individual preferences or motivations that generated it.

To portray organizations as "intentional systems"[21] possessed of "organizational intelligence" may be a cogent way to express the dual message that organizations make decisions infused with cognitive content, which are, at the same time, the product of widely dispersed informational sources and diffused individual interests and attitudes, all mediated by structures, processes, and chance in ways that defy translating or tracing the organizational decision into its individual sources.

Size

The designation of organizations as *large* pertains both to the scale of their operations and to the high number of individuals that are involved in carrying out those operations.[22] Both of these dimensions of size bear on the arguments that follow. The main significance of the large magnitude of the resources processed by an organization is that it greatly increases the social importance of organizational policies and decisions, as well as the importance of external (e.g., legal) policies and decisions that pertain to the organization. The large number of individuals involved in the organization's operations contributes to the anonymity and thus to the impersonality of the organization. It also suggests a divergence of views and individual interests which implies a discontinuity between the *organization's* interest or point of view and those of any particular individuals. Finally, recall the discussion in Chapter 1 of the importance of size for the incentive structure in membership organizations, and the qualitative difference that it suggests between small and large organizations.[23]

However, the main importance of organizational size for our present purposes lies in its two most prominent structural correlatives: the large organization is typically both formal and complex.[24] I will comment on these properties next.

Formality

Formality[25] appears already as a central feature of organizations in Weber's model of bureaucracy. It is there linked to the key concept of "office," which describes a set of prescribed duties, responsibilities, and expectations attached to every role within the organization. The organization is constituted by formal offices and rules connecting them. People are secondary, in that they merely fill the offices, enacting their formal requirements and carrying out specified rules and fulfilling preexisting expectations. As I indicated before, however, this view leaves at the top of the pyramid someone who is a human locus of power and responsibility within the bureaucracy.

Chester Barnard, who has inspired much of the modern developments in organization theory, paints an even more impersonal picture of the organization. Organizations, according to Barnard, are "nonpersonal," in that they do not consist of persons (or other "things" such as machines, etc.) but rather of "activities" or "forces." These forces are given off, in part, by persons, but the persons themselves are not, strictly speaking, constituents of the organization.[26] Barnard mediates between this conception of organizations and the role that individuals in fact play within them by his notion of the "dual personality" of individuals who participate in organizations—"an organizational personality and an individual personality."[27] This psychological aspect of the formality and the impersonality of the organization was later taken up by Simon in his classical book *Administrative Behavior*,[28] and further developed by him in terms of "loyalty" and "identification."[29] These concepts are meant to account for people's attachment to organizations and for the observed change in their behavior and attitudes once within the organizational context.[30]

The formality and impersonality of the organization render it, we may say, *impermeable*. By this I mean the difficulty that events and actions, directed at and affecting the organization, may have in "getting through it" and affecting in similar ways particular individuals. In other words, impermeability here stands for the proposition that there is a distinctive sense in which events (actions, orders, law) can be said to affect the organization which is not easily and straightforwardly reducible to a comparable impact on individuals *qua* individuals.

Complexity

Organizational complexity is a property that designates the large number of interdependent sub-units that constitute the organization and interact in various ways.[31] We have already seen that when we speak of the organization's decision or action we are referring to the end product of a long and complex set of interactions, decisionmaking processes, bargaining games, authority relations, operating procedures, and other activities and processes in which both humans and machines participate.[32] The complexity of the large organization joins its formality and impersonality to give it a quality of *opaqueness*.[33] The organization may be described as opaque in the sense that its complexity makes it hard to "see through it": it is difficult to trace the decisions and acts of the organization to particular wills and actions on the part of particular individuals. Thus the organization's actions are impersonal in a distinctive way—they are not the direct reflection of individual decisions and actions.[34] Opaqueness stands in marked contrast to the Weberian model of bureaucracy, where the end product (whether decision or action) can, at least in principle, be traced through the clear structure of authority, up to the person at the top of the pyramid.

Functionality and Goal Orientation

The characterization of organizations as *functional* structures is best discussed in conjunction with their characterization as *goal-oriented*. In this way, both the relatedness of and the difference between these two attributes can be best appreciated. By saying that organizations are functional structures, I refer to the instrumental conception of organizations according to which organizations' "distinctive characteristic . . . is that they have been formally established for the explicit purpose of achieving certain goals."[35] Conceived as an instrument, the organization's actions and decisions are always amenable to assessment and legitimation in the light of its stated goals.[36]

While holding to the instrumental conception of organizations, organization theory also depicts them as goal-oriented, by which I mean the emphasis that is often laid on the inability to fully explain organizational behavior in terms of the stated, legitimizing goals. Instead, organizational actions and decisions are frequently better understood by imputing to the organization self-serving or "reflexive" goals, which are not necessarily derived from or conducive to the attainment of its stated goals.[37]

A number of mechanisms have been suggested as accounts of this "goal displacement," i.e., organizations' propensity to deviate from the pursuit of their stated goals.[38] First, this phenomenon may occur as a result of the activities of interest groups that are formed within the organization and exert influence on its decisions, and that are "frequently concerned more with preserving and building up the organization itself than in helping it to serve its initial purpose."[39] Secondly, goal displacement can be a product of the tendency of individuals and units within the organization to adhere strictly to rules and to pursue blindly their sub-goals in ways which in the aggregate may lead the organization to a deviation from its stated goals.[40]

Next we find Professor Selznick's description of a typical reason for goal displacement:

> Running an organization, as a specialized and essential activity, generates problems that have no necessary (and often opposed) relationship to the professed or 'original' goals of the organization. The day-to-day behavior of the group becomes centered around specific problems and proximate goals which have primarily an internal relevance. Then, since these activities come to consume an increasing proportion of time and thoughts of the participants, they are—from the point of view of actual behavior—substituted for the professed goals.[41]

Finally, for reasons we mentioned in describing organizational decisionmaking processes, the goals actually pursued need not be the product of a deliberate decision by any particular individual, nor need they necessarily reflect any individual's interests, but may rather be a consequence of systemic functions and dysfunctions generated by the organizational setup itself.[42]

The functional view of the organization as an instrument in the service of some individual or social goals and its view as a goal-oriented organism capable of assuming and pursuing goals of its own can be combined in the image of the organization as a "recalcitrant instrumentality."[43]

The twin concepts of functionality and goal orientation, as well as the notion of "recalcitrant instrumentality" which they suggest, should be viewed as dynamic and relative. They are dynamic in the sense that both the stated, legitimating organizational goals and the patterned deviations from their pursuit (i.e., the "actual" goals) can change over time. Furthermore, as time goes by, some goals can move from one category to the other: what has begun as a patterned deviation from the pursuit of a stated goal (and thus as an "actual" goal) may later come to be perceived and embraced as an explicit, stated goal of the organization. The concepts of functionality and goal orientation are also relative, in the sense that what counts as a legitimating goal and what as a mere dysfunction is to a certain extent relative to the observer and to the normative scheme of interpretation that he brings to bear on the organization. The main point, however, is that at any given point in time and within a particular normative scheme, organizational behavior is amenable to analysis and interpretation in terms of the organization's instrumental nature, that is, in terms of its pursuit of some predetermined individual or social goals; as well as in terms of its goal orientation, that is, its propensity to develop and carry out patterned and directional modes of behavior which may or may not coincide with the imperatives of its stated goals.

CONCLUSION

An individualistic view of the organization naturally tends to conceal the various organizational properties that we have listed. Take functionality, for example. Equated to an individual, the organization can no longer be seen as a mere instrument whose existence is defined and legitimated in terms of some predetermined goals. Similarly, equating the organization with a group of individuals hides the possibility that the organization may in fact pursue goals that do not coincide with those of any such individuals. The same is true about the other properties that make up the proposed description of an organization. They all combine to shape a conception of the organization as an entity divorced from any particular group of individuals in ways that would be concealed by an individualistic view based on simpleminded reductionism. Let me summarize this conception. The permanence of organizations renders them temporally independent: they operate on a different time scale, in terms of both their memory and their planning, from that of any particular individual. Because of their complexity and formality, organizations are both opaque and impermeable: their acts and decisions are not the straightforward product or expression of any particular individual will, nor is the effect one's action has on an organization readily reducible to the effect that action may have on any particular individual. Being structures, organizations are manipulable: their performance is amenable to change through structural modifications. And finally, due to the nature of their decisionmaking function, organizations can be plausibly seen as intentional systems endowed with organizational intelligence.

These observations go some way toward accounting for the common perception of organizations as unified and distinctive social entities. This account steers a middle course, keeping clear of the mystery associated with holistic notions, without falling at the same time into the other trap of simpleminded reductionism. In this it draws on what may be one of the main implicit insights of organization theory. Rather than trying to fully reduce organizational phenomena into their individual constituents, organization theory explains, in essentially individualistic terms, our inability to perform such a reduction. Familiarity with the peculiarities of group decisionmaking, for example, leads to an individualistic account of the discontinuity between individual and collective rationality. By thus spelling out the grounds for and emphasizing the inevitability of the imputation of global properties to organizations, organization theory makes us somewhat more confident and clearheaded in using the ordinary holistic, reifying language we commonly apply to organizations. The intelligibility of such holistic terminology as we daily use need not accordingly depend on a metaphorical personification of the organization nor on some far-reaching metaphysical commitments.

Indeed, modern organization theory itself accommodates an important holistic strand which is compatible with and expressive of the picture of the organization that we have painted.[44] I have in mind the application to organizations of the vocabulary and imagery of cybernetics and general system theory.[45] In rough outline, the organization is portrayed by these vocabularies as a system whose interactions with its environment through "inputs" and "outputs" are critical for its survival and which is equipped with a "feedback loop": an informational mechanism that feeds into the organization the consequences for the environment of its "output." It thus allows the organization to constantly modify its actions and structure in an adaptable way, that is, in a way that will reduce conflict with the environment that might be detrimental to the organization and threaten its survival. If not taken too literally, the imagery of general systems and the related vocabulary of cybernetics embody quite adequately the picture of the organization as we described it in terms of impermeability, opaqueness, intelligence, etc. They also provide a convenient transition to the next step in my argument, which will take, as I have promised, the form of a short story.

Chapter III

The Story of Personless Corporation

PROLOGUE: IN SEARCH OF A METAPHOR

Metaphors, Organizations, and Legal Thinking

In this chapter, I propose to substitute one legal metaphor regarding organizations—that of the person—with another. Such a suggestion requires a preliminary justification. Given the dubious status of metaphors as intellectual tools, even readers who agree that the person metaphor is inadequate and leads all too easily to unthinking anthropomorphism may doubt that legal thinking about organizations will be helped by instituting another metaphor in its place. I will argue in this section, however, that such a move is warranted, because the juncture in which law and organizations meet is one where the cognitive need for a metaphor is particularly intense: both law and organizations have certain features that make them especially suited for metaphors. Given that the need for a metaphor is compounded by the meeting of law and organizations, the safest strategy by which to expose and safeguard against the pitfalls of one metaphor may be that of inducing another.

Though it is an open question whether metaphors play any essential, indispensable cognitive role,[1] it seems indisputable that whether bound to do so or not, we in fact rely on metaphors abundantly both in theoretical and in practical discourse, in ordinary language as well as in science. It is equally clear that metaphors are often beneficial. In theoretical matters, they can give us a grip on unfamiliar phenomena, open up avenues of thought (or research) about them that may lead to valid insight, and facilitate communication. The need for metaphors is felt more urgently in some theoretical contexts than in others. As Professor Boyd argues, the metaphor "is especially well suited to the introduction of terms referring to kinds whose real essences consist of complex relational properties"[2] providing us with what he aptly calls "epistemic access"[3] to such phenomena. The role played by metaphor in practical thinking is no less important. As Donald Schön has demonstrated in the context of social policy, the metaphors we use "select for attention a few salient features and relations from what would otherwise be an overwhelmingly complex reality. They give these elements a coherent organization, and they describe what is wrong with the present situation in such a way as to set the direction for its future transformation."[4] In this way, the use of metaphors in framing social policy problems helps perform the "normative leap from data to recommendations, from fact to values, from 'is' to 'ought,'"[5] "in such a way as to make it seem graceful, compelling, even obvious."[6]

However, the force of metaphors as cognitive and practical tools is also a source of their dangerousness. Their essential ambiguity and open-endedness, which enable us to capture unfamiliar and complex phenomena, and which may yield novel insights into them, may also cause mistakes and confusion. Metaphors do not contain a self-limiting or guiding principle, in the light of which only those points of analogy between the metaphor and its referent will be picked up which are fruitful and theoretically warranted. Consequently, metaphors can easily lead us astray by inducing false analogies. The assessment of the role played by metaphor in a particular context, especially in practical thinking about social problems, is often made difficult by the fact that the metaphor in question may be what Professor Schön calls a *tacit* metaphor; that is, one that shapes our perception and understanding in social matters without our being aware of the influence it exerts on our thinking.[7]

Law is a branch of discourse about social problems that is particularly prone to metaphorical thinking; it therefore accentuates both the value of metaphors and their dangers. First, law is practiced by generalists: it is dominated by professionals whose expertise is typically quite unrelated to the various social issues that generate legal problems and underlie legal decisions. Lawyers and judges must often operate on foreign intellectual terrain, attempting to get an ad hoc mental grip on unfamiliar and often complex realities that lie outside their professional ken. Metaphors, we have seen, are particularly handy in facilitating this difficult cognitive task.

Secondly, unlike many other social decisionmakers, lawyers typically cannot shrug away a problem or delay a decision until better understanding of the problem area is available. A legal decision must be reached as soon as the legal problem is duly presented. Accordingly, law must often live by whatever crude approximations of social reality are available. Here, too, metaphors may fill the epistemic gap between what is known and the knowledge that would be desirable for a sounder decision. Finally, legal rhetoric is bent on downplaying or hiding stark value judgments and blatant political choices. It is therefore likely to exploit the ability of metaphor described above to help in performing gracefully and inconspicuously the normative leap from *is* to *ought*.

Moreover, it is also apparent that the law's proneness to use metaphors is particularly acute with regard to organizations. Organizations are precisely the kind of entities "whose real essences consist of complex relational properties," with respect to which, it has been argued, metaphors are most needed. The cognitive need for "epistemic access" through a unifying metaphor is felt most urgently with respect to organizations because of their "ontological elusiveness": hovering between the abstract and the concrete, they evade our grasp by constantly invoking the opposing fears of reductionism and reification.[8]

Organizations and the Person Metaphor

All of this makes the law's reliance on a metaphor in dealing with organizations understandable. The choice of the particular metaphor that prevails in the law, that of a person, can also be readily understood. Treating the organization as a legal actor, capable of legal acts, bearing legal consequences, and generally endowed with rights and duties, presupposes certain features that would make such treatment meaningful. In particular, the organization must be thought of as being able to register legal obligations (that is, it must have a memory), and capable of following legal rules and of responding to legal incentives and disincentives. This means that it must "understand" legal norms, possess a degree of rationality, and be able to act on its understanding and rationality.

These features of the organization, necessary in order to make its status as legal actor meaningful, can be summed up by the term *intelligence*: to qualify as a legal actor, the organization must possess intelligence. This requirement is of course easily satisfied by the person metaphor. Since, as we have seen, the organization does possess the various functions that correspond to the above-mentioned elements of intelligence, the metaphor of a person as a way to describe the organization seems proper and satisfying: it at once provides a unifying familiar image of the organization, and expresses those features in virtue of which treating the organization as a legal actor makes sense.

The metaphor of person, however, also exhibits the typical dangers of metaphorical thinking. By inducing misplaced analogies between individuals and organizations, the metaphor of person easily leads to anthropomorphism: the attribution to organizations of traits and the adoption toward them of attitudes that properly pertain to individuals only. I have already alluded to some famous examples of the grotesque anthropomorphisms resulting from an explicit and excessive reliance on the person metaphor.[9] But such extravaganza aside, the person metaphor seems to exert its main influence in shaping our cognitions and attitudes concerning organizations as a tacit metaphor, embedded in ordinary linguistic usage. Recall the example of the common usage of referring to a ranking corporate official as the "head" of the corporation; there is but a short step (or "a graceful leap") from this metaphorical usage to the attribution to the corporation of the official's intentions, e.g., for the purpose of imposing on the corporation criminal liability. More importantly, by fitting organizations into an existing, individualistic, legal framework, the metaphor of person offers a simple solution to the problem of corporate legal personality. It thereby diverts attention from the distinctive features of organizations (such as those we enumerated in the preceding chapter) and from the normative implications of these features.

The Case for Another Metaphor

There are two ways to cure legal thinking from the distortion and myopia introduced by the person metaphor. One is to give up metaphorical thinking about organizations altogether. The uncovering of the tacit and unwelcome influence that the person metaphor exerts on our thinking in this area may be all that is necessary to free us from its grip. Free of metaphor, we should be able to confront organizational realities head-on, and explore directly their normative implications.

In implementing this approach, we might have proceeded directly from the analytical description of organizations in terms of their essential properties in the previous chapter to the exploration of the normative status of organizations in the next one. The preceding considerations about the role of metaphor in general and in the present context in particular may, however, breed some skepticism regarding the ultimate prospects of such strategy. Even if we set aside the view that the use of metaphor is a cognitive necessity in any strict sense, we may still doubt whether we can successfully exorcise the person metaphor by fiat or argument and recover from all metaphorical thinking in this area. Rather, the preceding general considerations may lead us to suspect that the person metaphor will in fact tacitly reassert itself, propelled by the cognitive and practical needs that have sustained it so far. A safer therapeutic strategy may be, therefore, to fight metaphor with metaphor: to introduce into the legal vocabulary and imagination a metaphor for organizations that will satisfy cognitive and practical needs while correcting for the inadequacies of the person metaphor.

Two criteria of adequacy must guide our search for such an alternative metaphor. First, it must convey a picture of the organization consistent with its description in the preceding chapter. Second, without lapsing into anthropomorphism, it must comport with and make intelligible the treatment of organizations as legal actors.

To make such an alternative metaphor more compelling, I will introduce it by using another argumentative device: an imaginary story about the possible evolution of an organization. The strategy is a familiar one. Essentially it underlies the aggregation view of organizations which we have previously discussed. The position that the normative status of an organization is identical with that of the individuals who constitute it can also be seen as the product of a simple evolutionary tale. To account for the large corporation, for example, the aggregationist begins with a few individuals joining together, each endowed with certain rights. The description then proceeds by incrementally increasing the number of individuals, seeking to demonstrate that this process of growth involves no qualitative changes that would justify treating the large collectivity differently from its individual components. On a grander scale, telling an imaginary evolutionary story is the method used by Robert Nozick to delineate the legitimate boundaries of the minimal state.[10] Similarly, in what follows I will tell an imaginary, though possible, tale about the evolution of a corporation.

THE STORY OF PERSONLESS CORPORATION

Act I

The beginning of the story is quite a familiar one. Long ago there was an entrepreneur—Rupert Personless was his name—who started a business of manufacturing small widgets. The business was going well, and after some time Rupert took several partners. They next decided to incorporate, and to call their firm after its founder: Personless Inc. The shares were first issued to the original partners, but within a number of years they went public. All this time, Personless Inc. was booming, opening new plants and hiring thousands of employees. Its profits were high, and it had a policy of paying low dividends to its shareholders, reinvesting most of its profits. As time passed by, Rupert Personless and his initial partners retired, and a professional management took over. By now the number of shareholders was so large and shares so dispersed that actual control over the appointment of top executives was in the hands of management. At this stage, the activities of Personless Corporation were varied. They included supporting political candidates who favored trade restrictions that would limit the import of small widgets into the U.S., or who steadfastly advocated the inviolability of property and other constitutional rights of corporations. Personless Inc. also contributed to the arts department of the local university ("people with better taste will better appreciate the beauty of the small widget," the chairman once said) and occasionally sponsored cultural programs on the public channel of the local television station. Up to this point, as you see, there was really nothing special about Personless Inc.; it was just your next-door, ordinary, large corporation.

Act II

Now our story becomes more exciting. The first step taken by Personless Inc. that marked it off from other corporations was its decision to buy its own shares. At first, even that was within the acceptable and familiar: American corporations (unlike English companies) often can, and sometimes do, buy and own some of their stock.[11] Personless, however, went further than any of its predecessors: it purchased its entire outstanding stock. It thus became an "ownerless" corporation.[12] This step, dramatic as it may sound, had little practical or legal effect on Personless. Its capital had been for a long time largely self-generated,[13] and its management was already in control and self-perpetuating.[14] From the law's point of view, Personless was now, as before, a legal person with the right to litigate and enforce its contract and property rights, and with duties to pay its debts, meet its supply deadlines, and so on.

The next step taken by Personless was no less dramatic and no more consequential. It completely automated its entire operation, and thus was able to fire all its workers. It had become not only an ownerless corporation, but also a fully-automated corporation.[15] This fact, again, had little effect on the manufacture of small widgets, nor did it alter the legal status of Personless in any important way.[16]

Personless did not, however, stop at that. The current managers, you see, were old and tired. They were particularly weary of the strife that attended every high-level appointment in the corporation. And the corporation, in its infinite complexity, was largely run by its computers anyway. Only they could handle the enormous amount of information and complex computation needed for making decisions, predictions, and plans. As a consequence of all that, Personless decided to become fully computerized: all the management functions, and all the decisionmaking processes, were ably programmed and delegated to the computers. When the last manager retired, no one replaced her. No one had to.[17]

Let us ponder for a moment this last step taken by Personless Corporation. First, we must note that, if successful, this step would not visibly alter Personless's operations. It will go on manufacturing various small widgets as before; its profits will be reinvested, as they used to be, in growth and expansion; it will even, in all likelihood, continue to support friendly politicians and worthy cultural events. To the outsider, who got used to Personless's computerized bills and automatically produced letters long ago, the change in management will hardly be noticeable. It is also important to notice that if the transition to computerized decisionmaking is successful, the legal status of Personless is hardly threatened by the change. It will still be capable of litigating its grievances, and the nature of its litigation will remain unchanged. True, the law may require occasionally that a human signature validate some legal documents. But such signatures are mechanically reproduced nowadays (as when a treasurer's signature is mechanically stamped on thousands of payroll checks of a large organization), making the requirement into a meaningless formality. The replacement of human managers by computers will, of course, make a difference with respect to those laws that impose personal duties and liabilities on officials. But these are not the laws with which we are concerned here. Our main concern is with the treatment of the corporation itself as a legal entity, and this, it seems to me, would not be significantly affected by the shift to computerized management.

The displacement of human management by computers would, I suggest, have little effect on both the actual operations and the legal status of Personless. But the question arises, is such a shift sufficiently conceivable, or does the last part of my story stretch credibility too far to make it of any real interest? Recent literature on artificial intelligence tends, it seems to me, to dispel such doubts.[18] Even if one does not share Herbert Simon's optimistic (pessimistic?) view that "there is every prospect that we will soon have the technological means . . . to automate all management decisions, non-programmed as well as programmed,"[19] the capabilities that computers already possess—such as the capacity for goal-directed, or "purposive," adaptation to a changing environment, that is, a capacity for "learning" behavior[20]—make the last stage of my story sufficiently credible and interesting for the present purpose.[21]

Act III

Readers who like their organizations animated by human beings, and therefore find what has so far transpired in the history of

Personless Corporation to be a sad story, may be relieved to hear that our story is after all bound for a happy ending. In the third stage of its evolution, Personless confronts economic difficulties which trigger a decision on the part of its computers to sell some of its stock to outsiders. The new shareholders, distrustful of machines, reinstate human managers. And finally, the new management decides to hire some employees who will listen to the music broadcast by the radios installed long ago by organization theorists of the human relations school.[22]

THE MORAL OF THE STORY

The story of Personless Corporation can, I believe, serve as a useful antidote to the twin tendencies to personification and aggregation that may underlie an individualistic legal view of organizations. Our focus naturally turns to the end of the second stage in the history of Personless, when no individuals at all are part of it. What we find there, in fact, is a machine endowed with artificial intelligence. This unusual machine can replace the person metaphor and serve as an alternative legal metaphor for the organization.[23] It combines, as an adequate metaphor for an organization should, both the notion of the instrumentality of the organization and the intelligence needed to make intelligible the treatment of the organization as a legal entity.[24] What makes this metaphor particularly credible and compelling is the fact that we were able to deduce it from the first—"normal"—stage in the history of the corporation, through gradual steps that are logically, technologically, and legally possible. We were able to strip the corporation of all individuals and yet preserve, both conceptually and legally, the identity of Personless Corporation as we knew it from its earlier and more conventional days. The intelligent machine, into which Personless Corporation has thus evolved, may therefore be a cogent way to think about corporations and other organizations. It supplies the needed unifying image of the organization, reflecting some of its essential properties, while at the same time guarding against the dangers of anthropomorphism which attend the metaphor of person.

While the metaphor of the intelligent machine is both plausible (as the story of Personless Corporation demonstrates) and, as I argued, superior to the metaphor of person, it is nevertheless just a metaphor. It is thus not meant to relieve us from confronting the reality of the organization. Quite the contrary: it is, indeed, one of the merits of the intelligent machine metaphor that it forces us to such a confrontation, since, unlike the metaphor of person, it does not allow us to ignore the reality of the organization by simply assimilating it to a prevailing individualistic framework.

The story of Personless Corporation is also an effective remedy against the second of the two possible grounds of the law's individualistic view of the organization, that is, aggregation. True, unlike the corporation described in the second act of our story, real-life corporations do contain individuals in various roles and positions. The relation, however, between the corporation and any group of individuals is a contingent rather than a necessary one. We have already indicated how the aggregationist obscures this fact by an incrementalist reasoning that starts from a small number of individuals and by gradual steps reaches finally the large organization. The "happy ending" of the Personless Corporation story, when individuals are once again made part of it, is meant to reverse that line of reasoning. The starting point for normative analysis may be not a group of individuals from which the organization slowly evolves, but rather an organization to which no individuals are attached (like Personless Corporation in its second stage). The analysis then proceeds by adding on various groups of individuals to this "personless" structure. This intellectual procedure guarantees better than its reverse that we pay attention to the distinctive normative features of the organization, while also examining in detail how these normative features are affected by the relation of the organization to this or that group of individuals. In addition, this procedure reflects correctly the temporal relation between individuals who belong to the organization and the organization itself. The existence of the permanent organization typically predates the membership in it of any particular individual. Individuals within organizations have characteristically joined and been socialized into an existing structure, rather than created or constituted one.

None of this implies that a line of reasoning based on the Personless Corporation story must necessarily lead to normative conclusions different from those arrived at from the opposite direction. It may be the case that after we add to the "personless" core of a given organization all the individuals who are in fact related to it, we will reach normative conclusions similar to those we get through personification or aggregation. All I have suggested so far is that the metaphor of person and the method of aggregation discourage a full exploration of the appropriate normative treatment of organizations, and that in the light of the theoretical perspectives on corporations and other organizations described above, such an exploration is needed. In the next Part, I hope to demonstrate that the suggested conception of the organization does in fact have some significant normative implications.

Part II

Organizations and Rights

Chapter IV

A Theory of Organizations' Rights

THE NORMATIVE BACKGROUND

In this chapter, I will explore the normative implications of the picture of the organization as Personless Corporation. More specifically, I will focus on the kinds of claims of right an organization ought to be able to make in law. I will assume without argument that legal rights ought to be interpreted as founded on considerations of political morality, or, more simply, that legal rights are, at bottom, moral rights (broadly understood). According to this view, the articulation, the elaboration, the elucidation, and the application of legal rights all require an understanding of and an appeal to some underlying moral considerations. The identification, though, of the relevant moral view is in general likely to be both difficult and controversial. Our present task is made, however, more manageable by the considerable work that has been done in recent years in investigating and articulating the moral underpinnings of contemporary American legal discourse.

In these theoretical writings, one comes quite frequently across descriptions of a normative dichotomy that is said to underlie and inform the law. Different writers have used different terms to describe the two poles of that dichotomy: fairness versus utility[1]; Kantianism versus Utilitarianism[2]; the paradigm of reciprocity versus the paradigm of reasonableness[3]; and the "moralists" versus the "economists."[4] While the terms used by the writers differ, and their conception of the two poles of the dichotomy may not wholly coincide, it is nevertheless possible to discern a common ground shared by all (or most) of these writers. First, they interpret American law as rooted in and shaped by the liberal tradition. Second, they identify within this tradition two competing philosophical strands or orientations, claiming (or implying) that American law (or at least some important parts of it) can be understood, and is in fact developed, in terms of one or the other.

According to one of these orientations, the law is primarily concerned with the ideal of social welfare. The main criterion for legal rules and the main guideline for legal decisions is, according to this view, the tendency of those rules and decisions to maximize social utility. The second orientation views the law as primarily committed to the ideal of individual autonomy. According to this view, the chief purpose of the law is to provide adequate protection to individual rights, understood as expressions and safeguards of the individual's autonomy, irrespective of the general societal consequences of such protection. I shall call these two basic orientations, according to their respective core values, the paradigm of social utility (or, for brevity, the paradigm of utility) and the paradigm of individual autonomy (or the paradigm of autonomy). In using the term *paradigm*, I follow, with some hesitation, both Professor Fletcher's[5] and Professor Barry's[6] usage in a similar context. I do not mean to put too much pressure on the term *paradigm* as used here; other terms—such as *models, approaches,* or *orientations*—would do equally well (or equally badly). The allusion to Kuhn,[7] though weak, is nevertheless appropriate. Utility and autonomy do designate two clusters of highly abstract sets of ideas and beliefs (not always fully articulated) which underlie, shape, and lend unity to the bodies of law which they serve to interpret.

While utilitarianism as a starting point for erecting comprehensive systems of politics and morals may well be, as some believe, on the decline,[8] it nevertheless maintains a considerable hold on the legal mind. The paradigm of utility has been revivified in recent years through that special blend of utilitarianism and economics known as welfare economics.[9] The application of welfare economics to major areas of the law has become perhaps the most distinctive, and theoretically explicit, expression of the paradigm of utility in current legal thought.[10] It is, however, the paradigm of autonomy that, as Brian Barry testifies, is currently "taking the offensive,"[11] not only in moral and political philosophy but also, perhaps somewhat more hesitantly, in legal thought. Despite the great divergence in many important respects that exists among the works that I mean to comprehend within the paradigm of autonomy, there are two important themes that they all have in common.

On the negative side is the rejection of consequentialism as a proper measure of the morality of an action. On the affirmative side, despite important differences, the various proponents of the paradigm of autonomy share a common starting point for the moral evaluation of actions and social institutions. This starting point, frequently expressed in Kantian terms,[12] is the conception of the individual as an autonomous moral agent, possessed of dignity and deserving of respect. This philosophical orientation embraces and seeks to elaborate the categorical imperative that individuals should not be treated as merely means to society's ends, but rather as ends in themselves. Conceived as autonomous moral agents, individuals have rights which define and protect their sphere of moral autonomy,[13] constraining what others may do to them even for the sake of society's welfare.

This simplified normative landscape will enable us to investigate the question of organizational legal rights posed at the beginning of this chapter. To do so, we need to fit Personless Corporation into the dichotomous normative universe just described, and find out what sorts of valid claims it can make within such a normative universe, in which every valid claim must at bottom rest either on individual autonomy, expressed in one or another individual right, or on social utility.

My conclusion will be, let me anticipate, that organizations can make valid claims both in the language of autonomy and in the language of utility. However, while their reliance on considerations of utility is quite uninhibited, essentially similar to the reliance by individuals on such considerations, their ability to rest their claims on autonomy grounds is much more limited. It is there, within the autonomy paradigm, that the conception of the organization as an "intelligent machine" assumes its main legal significance, dramatically constricting the moral vocabulary at the disposal of organizations compared to that available to individuals. Accordingly, insofar as the choice between arguments of utility and arguments of autonomy is legally consequential, organizations' valid legal claims will differ from those of individuals.

ON HAVING RIGHTS

Before we can engage in the normative investigation, some preliminary analytical distinctions must be made. By saying that *A* has a right, I shall roughly mean that *A* may make a valid claim for a decision in his favor, by way of redressing an injury that he sustained or being awarded some benefit (resource) which is his due.[14] *A* may have a right because of either of two reasons. A right may be recognized in *A* out of concern for *A* himself. In such a case, *A* has an *original right*. A right in *A* may also result from a concern not for him but for *B*. In this case, *A* will be said to have a *derivative right*. A guardian, for example, may be given such rights as are necessary for the effective execution of her role. She may, for instance, have a right to reimbursement for expenses incurred in carrying out her duties. This right is, according to our definition of having a right, properly described as *hers*: she may rely on it to solicit a decision in her favor, granting her a particular benefit. However, the reason for the right to reimbursement lies in the concern for the ward and his interests, and only derivatively in the concern for protecting the guardian's interests.

There are also situations in which *A* may rest a claim on a right without himself having one: *A* may either rely on *B*'s right or merely invoke *B*'s right. *A* can be said to *rely* on *B*'s right when, in virtue of some special relationship with *B*, he can cite the violation of *B*'s right as a reason for a decision in his (*A*'s) favor. A common legal instance of such a state of affairs is the institution of *subrogation*. It operates, for example, when *A*, an insurer, compensates *B*, the victim of an accident, and consequently becomes entitled to reimbursement from the injurer, on the basis of the victim's rights to damages. Relying on another's right (e.g., by way of subrogation) is different from having a right. One practical difference is that, in relying on *B*'s right, *A*'s claim is defeasible by all the counterclaims that would defeat the right in *B* himself. However, again as a practical matter, relying on a right comes quite close to having one, in that in both cases one can cite the right as a reason for a decision in one's favor.

The situation is different when one *invokes* a right. By this I mean the case in which *A*'s claim is not only founded upon a wrong committed against or a benefit due to *B*, but is also meant to solicit a decision in *B*'s favor. To return to our example of the guardian, she typically invokes and exercises rights which reside in someone else, (i.e., the ward) for that other person's benefit. In this case, the guardian's status with respect to the right is of a strictly procedural nature: the right is entirely *B*'s both as a theoretical and as a practical matter.

In order to apply this analysis to the case in which *A* is an organization, we must explain what it would mean for an intelligent machine, such as that into which Personless Corporation has been transformed, to make a claim for a decision in its favor, to sustain and redress a wrong, and to have a resource or benefit due to it—all notions which appeared in our definition of having a right. It seems to me that even as we strip the organization of individuals and expose its essential existence as a mere instrumentality, we can still intelligibly speak about its making claims on its own behalf, its suffering and redressing wrongs, and its getting benefits and resources. The most natural way of applying these normative expressions to an instrumentality is by relating them to the instrumentality's ability to discharge its functions. In the case of the organization, accordingly, these expressions can make good sense in relation to the organization's goals. The organization may be said to make a valid claim on its own behalf only if the claim is somehow linked, directly or indirectly, to one of the goals which define and legitimize the organization. Similarly, the organization can be said to be wronged only in the sense that it was impeded in the pursuit of its goals; it can benefit from resources only to the extent that such resources contribute, directly or indirectly, to the attainment of the organization's goals.*

For the organization to have rights *of its own* requires, according to this account, that these rights survive the various transformations undergone by Personless Corporation, and more specifically, that those rights persist even at the stage where that corporation is stripped of all individuals. As I have just indicated, such rights are claims whose validity depends on their relation to the goals of the organization. But this of course states only a necessary

---

*See the discussion of functionality and goal orientation on pp. 36–38 *supra*. As a conceptual matter, the "goals" mentioned in the text as mediating the application of normative expressions to organizations can be either "stated" or "actual" goals. For example, it makes sense to say that an organization was wronged either because it was hampered in the pursuit of one of its stated, legitimating goals, or because of an impediment to one of its actual though unstated goals. However, once a legal claim based on this alleged wrong is made, the frustrated goal that supports it must be stated. This may require the identification and the explicit articulation of what has hitherto been an actual but unstated goal. The making of a legal claim may in this way be the occasion for making explicit, and in this sense changing, the structure of the organization's goals. Whether the attempted articulation of a goal will succeed in supporting the claim will depend, among other things, on whether the putative goal fits into the broader social value system, as explained in the next paragraph in the text.

but not a sufficient condition of their validity. The second condition which must also be satisfied is that the goal to which a particular claim of right is related is itself legitimate, i.e., that it fits into the value system that informs the society within which the organization operates and that society's legal system.[15] In terms of the two philosophical orientations that I have imputed to the American legal system, this means that the normative status of the organization depends on whether its goals promote individual autonomy or contribute to the achievement of social utility.

The story of Personless Corporation did not end, you may recall, at the "personless" stage. Instead, the story went on, in its final act, to add to the corporation various groups of individuals, in acknowledgment of the obvious point that real-life organizations do, in fact, have individuals related to them in different roles. The relation between the organization and these individuals may give rise to another ground of validity to the organization's claims. Rather than (or in addition to) having rights of its own, in the sense explained above, there may be good reasons to allow the organization to *rely* upon rights which reside in some individuals so that those rights, even though not belonging to the organization, do as a practical matter operate in its favor. Similarly, the relationship between the organization and various individuals may allow the organization to *invoke* those individuals' rights, though the organization is neither bearer nor beneficiary of those rights.

ORGANIZATIONS' RIGHTS WITHIN THE AUTONOMY PARADIGM

I turn first to an examination of the claims open to organizations within the paradigm of autonomy. The core notion of this paradigm, it should be recalled, is the notion of a right, which expresses and protects a conception of the moral agent as an end in himself. I will call such rights *"autonomy rights"* (ARs for short).[16] These rights are commonly conceived of as noninstrumental and categorical. To use Professor Fried's definitions, a norm is noninstrumental "when its application is not contingent upon the agent's adopting some other independent end, which the norm will lead him to attain."[17] It is categorical insofar as it "displaces other judgments in its domain, so that other values and ends may not be urged as reasons for violating the norm."[18] More specifically, Professor Dworkin describes his concept of rights that are based on "the vague but powerful idea of human dignity"[19] as "the anti-utilitarian concept of a right."[20] By this he means that "if someone has a right to something, then it is wrong for the government to deny it to him even though it would be in the general interest to do so."[21]

In the light of our analysis, in the preceding section, of the different ways of possessing rights, we can now pose the question about the status of organizations within the paradigm of autonomy in greater detail and with greater precision in terms of the four following questions: Do organizations have original autonomy rights (OARs) of their own? Do they have derivative autonomy rights (DARs)? Can organizations rely on autonomy rights of some particular individuals? Can they invoke the autonomy rights of particular individuals?

The Organization and Original Autonomy Rights

The negative answer to the first question—that is, whether organizations can have original autonomy rights of their own—follows simply and straightforwardly from combining the ethical individualism of the paradigm of autonomy with our description of organizations in Part I.[22] As put by Charles Fried, "it is respect for persons as the ultimate moral particulars which is expressed by the contents of categorical norms."[23] The instrumental conception of organizations, expressed in their definition as "social units deliberately constructed and reconstructed to seek specific goals,"[24] and dramatized by the story of Personless Corporation, makes them unfit objects of the moral concern which underlies original autonomy rights. Seen as an intelligent machine, the organization is the antithesis of the moral person presupposed by the paradigm of autonomy.[25] While the Kantian notion of individual autonomy is closely linked to the perception of individuals as ends, formal organizations exist only as means. As such they are not equal members in the Kantian kingdom of ends, and they do not deserve or admit of the special kind of respect that gives rise to the individual's ARs.[26]

In all this I might seem to be belaboring the obvious, were it not that this point is persistently ignored by legal theorists, who ground their arguments in the paradigm of autonomy and yet deal with individuals and organizations indistinguishably. Against this background, the point made so far, though narrow in scope, is crucial to my argument and should be emphasized: within the paradigm of autonomy, organizations cannot make the same claims or have the same rights as individuals. The paradigm of autonomy is directly concerned with individuals only, and it provides moral grounds for legal claims made by individuals alone.

This negative and clear-cut conclusion does not, however, exhaust the possibilities of "translating" organizational claims into the language of individual autonomy. It still remains to be seen whether such a translation can be successfully carried out either by organizations having *derivative autonomy rights* of their own, or by their *relying* upon or *invoking* the autonomy rights of some individual. To facilitate such an examination, I will conduct it by considering three hypothetical cases, each representing a typical situation in which an organization may try to rest its claim in one of these ways on an autonomy right.

Invoking an Autonomy Right

Case 1: O_1, a journalists' association, brings an action against A, a governmental agency, for abridging the freedom of speech of R, a reporter who is a member in O_1.

We may summarily dispose of this way of citing an autonomy right by an organization. I see no great difficulty, nor great interest, in answering in the affirmative the question whether organizations can invoke ARs on behalf of some individuals. By invoking a right, the organization plays a purely procedural role: both as a theoretical and as a practical matter, the right invoked belongs to and benefits only a particular individual. Case 1 demonstrates this quite clearly. It involves the reporter's right to freedom of speech, which it can be plausibly assumed is an autonomy right.[27] Furthermore the organization in this case, the journalists' association, is genuinely concerned with the protection and the vindication of the AR involved: the journalist's right to freedom of speech. However, in this case the organization is not trying to redress a wrong done to itself. Assuming that the protection of its members' freedom of speech is one of O_1's goals, acting to remedy a violation of such a right is within the scope of its organizational activity. But the injury to be remedied is to the individual member. The organization itself is not wronged by restrictions on the members' freedom of speech. An injury to the organization would occur only if some restriction were imposed on its activity in trying to remedy the interference with the reporter's freedom of expression. Only such an impediment to the organization's ability to pursue its goals would qualify as a wrong committed against the organization. Furthermore, O_1 is not claiming a decision in its favor, nor is it expecting to be benefited by the decision. On the substantive (as distinguished from the procedural) level, the case can be seen as one in which the reporter is trying to vindicate her autonomy right to free speech, so that the question of the normative status of the organization does not arise at all.*

The Organization's Reliance on Individuals' Autonomy Rights

Beyond merely *invoking* rights, it may be possible for the organization to *rely* on the violation of some individual's original autonomy right. The injury to the organization, it can be argued, must involve harm to some particular individuals. That harm, in turn, may constitute a violation of those individuals' ARs. The organization's claim merely embodies such harmed individual interests, and consequently may draw support from the fact that individual ARs were violated. Furthermore, in light of the relation between the organization and the individuals associated with it, a decision in favor of the organization can be plausibly seen, one might think, as a way to vindicate the individuals' violated ARs. This would still fall short of ascribing rights to the organization itself. Yet, if the organization could easily and as a matter of course state its case within the paradigm of autonomy by relying in this way on some individual's OAR, the insistence that the organization has no ARs of its own would be of little practical significance. It is therefore important to examine in some detail a typical situation in which, one might think, the organization's claim may rest on the

*This indeed seems to be a distinction that courts implicitly draw when determining the standing of various organizations, especially in the environmental area. See, for example, *Sierra Club v. Morton* 405 U.S. 727 (1972); and cf. Professor Chayes's comments in A. Chayes, "Foreword: Public Law Litigation and the Burger Court," 96 *Harv. L. Rev.* 4, 8–26, especially p. 12 (1982), and sources cited there. Though the distinction is sound, it need not lead to the courts' conclusion in these cases. The question whether or not certain organizations should have standing to *invoke* environmental claims is, however, not my present concern.

violation of an individual's OAR. In analyzing such a situation, I will argue that the organization's attempt to draw support from the violation of an individual's AR is unlikely to succeed, and that this avenue to ARs turns out to be in most cases a blind alley.

Case 2: O_2, a large corporation, sues D for cutting off a cable that supplied electricity to its machines, bringing its production of widgets to a standstill. It alleges that, as a result, its shareholders suffered economic loss, it had to lay off a number of workers, and its managers became considerably demoralized.[28]

It should first be noticed that, unlike O_1 (the journalists' association of Case 1), O_2 does successfully point to an injury that *it* sustained: the interruption in the supply of electricity creates, no doubt, an impediment to the organization's goal of producing widgets. Consequently, O_2 does, while O_1 did not, ask for a decision in its own favor. O_2 is at the same time also seeking to remedy a situation harmful to the different individuals on whose plight its claim partially rests: restoring the flow of electricity and recovering the lost revenues will arguably benefit the shareholders, allow the rehiring of the fired employees, and cheer up management. In this way, O_2's attempt to establish a link between redressing its own injury and the vindication of some individuals' ARs may seem compelling. If so, Case 2 would count as an example of an organization's successful reliance on an AR.

I will, however, argue that this success is only apparent. Put metaphorically, my argument is that, because of its *impermeability*,[29] the organization serves as a kind of "moral buffer": harming the organization is not exhaustively reducible to the harming of particular individuals. More specifically, the harm done to the organization does not typically redound to a violation of any individual's AR. Consequently, a corporation such as O_2 will not be able to point to and rely upon any violated individual autonomy rights.

No One Harmed

The first line of attack against O_2's position challenges the implicit premise that the injury to the organization results in harm to some particular individuals. But the fact that the organization sustained an injury does not entail that some individuals were harmed too. A number of factors account for this apparent paradox.

One such factor is "organizational slack," a concept that designates the existence within the organization of considerable latent, untapped resources, which are normally not allocated to any productive activity.[30] A sudden adverse change in the organization's environment may trigger some of those latent and otherwise wasted resources, which will now be used to make up for the external injury. In this way, the entire "blow" may be absorbed by the organization itself and never be transferred to or even noticed by any individuals associated with the organization.

Related to the concept of slack is the following, narrower, observation: the large corporation's activities are typically cushioned by considerable funds which at any given moment of time allow the corporation to sustain a financial loss without it being felt by any individual. This becomes even clearer if we recall that the interests of such groups as consumers and employees are protected, in part, by market and contractual constraints, such that unless the loss to the corporation is above a certain magnitude, prices and wages will not in fact be affected by it. Similarly with respect to shareholders. Their interests mainly depend on the stock market. Because of the finite sensitivity of that market, only a loss to the corporation above a certain order of magnitude will be registered by the market and reflected in the price of shares. Dividends, like prices and wages, are frequently determined on a long-term basis, and in any event do not reflect every fluctuation in the fortunes of the corporation.

Furthermore, the shareholders of a large corporation are frequently other large organizations,[31] so that the individual shareholder may be several steps removed from the injured organization and therefore shielded by a number of organizations, each of which may absorb the loss in one of the ways described above.

Finally, an organization may sustain an injury although no individual is harmed, because of overlapping membership. The point is easiest to illustrate by the case of shareholders. We have already alluded to the increasingly common pattern of stock ownership recommended by portfolio theory, according to which individuals hold shares of a relatively large number of firms. In the extreme case of two firms, A and B, which have the same body of shareholders, an injury caused by B to A, even if it does affect the value of A's shares, may still benefit, on balance, all the shareholders, provided the injury benefited B more than it harmed A. The phenomenon of overlapping membership is not, of course, limited to the case of shareholders. The members of trade union T may also be members of local cooperative supermarket S. In a dispute between T and S, T may lose and S may gain (or vice versa), to the ultimate detriment of no individual at all.

The argument that no harm must befall any individual as a result of a loss (injury) incurred by a large organization puts a limit on the generalizability of Case 2. It can no longer be assumed, as a matter of course, that in each case of an injury to an organization some harm to some particular individual is entailed, lending thereby the necessary support to the organization's claim. Instead, in case of doubt, it may be incumbent upon the organization to point out who are the individuals whose interests were in fact compromised by the injury to it, and this may occasionally prove to be an insurmountable hurdle. Still, the main importance of the point I have now made is not practical but conceptual. That harm to an organization is not constituted by and need not result in harm to individuals dramatizes the distinctiveness of the organization as legal claimant and the discontinuity between it and the individuals who are associated with it.

No ARs Violated

Assume now, however, that this hurdle has been cleared, and that in fact O_2 can point to some individuals who were harmed as a result of the injury sustained by it. Further assume that the harm to those individuals is of a kind that under certain circumstances might qualify as a violation of their ARs—for example, depriving an individual of his job or taking some of his property. Even so, I will now argue, there are good reasons to believe that proponents of the autonomy paradigm would not count the harm caused to individuals in this way as a violation of their ARs. Consequently, such harm provides no support within the paradigm of autonomy (or, alternatively, provides only weak support) for the organization's claim.

The root idea, intuitively expressed, is that ARs do not protect individuals against any and all harms, but are only concerned with the protection of individuals against violations of their dignity and autonomy. By safeguarding individuals against being used, and abused, by others, ARs embody the ideal that human beings be treated by their fellows with concern and respect. The word *treated* should be emphasized. ARs can be said to owe their stringency to the special context in which they come into play: this is the context of interpersonal relations, within which one individual can be said to be *treating* another, that is, expressing his or her attitude, of respect or disrespect, to the other person. It is in this context, in which treatment occurs, that mistreatment, the expression of disrespect, is possible. ARs are accordingly directed only against mistreatment, that is, against harm that conveys disrespect for another individual. Harm inflicted or a due benefit denied can accordingly give rise to a claim based on an autonomy right only when they amount to mistreatment.

This general idea is expressed by Professor Charles Fried in the form of his notion of *directness*. Roughly, it describes the physical immediacy with which one person harms another. "Physical harm inflicted directly, personally as it were—in the language of the classical Roman law, *damnum corpore corpori datum*—provides a paradigm for the kind of relation between persons which is the subject of categorical prohibitions."[32] The notion of directness reflects the perception of the harm-inflicting transaction as an interpersonal relation and thereby tries to capture the special moral significance of this factor. "Direct harm," says Fried, "describes a wrongful relation between two particular persons, just because it so intimately involves their particularity."[33] The requirement of directness, however, is satisfied not only in the paradigm case where the harm is brought about through the physical proximity of injurer and victim; understanding the special significance of the direct harm within the paradigm of autonomy points to a possible extension of this requirement to harm which is intentionally inflicted. By intending to harm another person, such a person is singled out for treatment that fails to comport with the respect due to him. "Another person, who after all has the same capacity for reflection and the same concern to maintain his integrity, his person, as I do, has chosen to make my body, my person, a means to some end of his own."[34] Consequently, argues Fried, "planned results are the natural extension of direct results and intention of directness."[35]

The requirement of directness draws a sharp distinction between the intended results and the unintended side effects of one's actions. Only the former can make the agent responsible for the violation of the victim's AR, since only the agent's acts directly and intentionally aimed at the victim can express his relation to him, and therefore may fail to convey the respect that is required within that relation. This aspect of the requirement of directness is closely related, as Professor Fried points out, to the doctrine of double effect,[36] which asserts "that there is a morally relevant distinction between bringing about the death of an innocent person deliberately, either as an end in itself or as a means, and bringing it about as a side effect of something else one does deliberately."[37]

Proponents of the autonomy paradigm who subscribe to the view under discussion do not, of course, deny the relevance to the acceptability of one's actions of the side effects that such actions have on people towards whom the actions are not directed. But these ramifications enter the decisional (or evaluative) process only as part of the general weighing of consequences; they do not carry the categorical force of ARs. This point is summed up well by Professor Nagel as follows:

> The view that it can be wrong to consider merely the overall effect of one's actions on the general welfare comes into prominence when those actions involve relations with others. A man's acts usually affect more people than he deals with directly, and those effects must naturally be considered in his decisions. But if there are special principles governing the manner in which he should *treat* people, that will require special attention to the particular persons toward whom the act is directed, rather than just to its total effect.[38]

The element of directness is also present, though in an attenuated form, when harm is caused recklessly or negligently. When I step on your foot with my foot or run over your foot with my car, because I walk or drive carelessly, my mode of walking or driving bespeaks a general disrespect for humanity; but the physical impact concretizes my general attitude, making you the immediate object of it, and conveying to you my attitude in a most dramatic and painful way.[39]

The requirement of directness is not, however, satisfied when an injury is done or a benefit denied to an organization. When one deals with an organization, one's deliberate actions are directed toward *it*. One chooses the organization as the immediate, intended object of one's action: one trespasses upon the *organization's* property, cuts *its* profits, pollutes *its* waters, and so on. True, in doing so one can often foresee that consumers, shareholders, employees, or other individuals may suffer as a result. But these are *possible* side effects, not the direct, intended, inescapable objects of the action. These side effects must be taken into account by the actor, as well as be incorporated into any later evaluation of the action. But the role that such side effects play in decision and evaluation lacks the special categorical force that norms pertaining to the treatment of one person by another have. Put differently, in dealing with an organization, one is outside the domain of inter-personal relations where ARs come into play. One can of course still cause harm to individuals, and must bear responsibility for it, but one does not thereby mistreat them: actions toward an organization do not carry the insidious message of personal dis-respect that is the essence of mistreatment.

A similar conclusion can be reached on the receiving end of the relationship. From the point of view of the harmed individuals, their harm can hardly be perceived as being directly inflicted on their persons. Rather, they experience the harm as being mediated by the injury to the organization. They can scarcely feel the special indignation of being singled out and personally mistreated by an-other individual. Professor Fried's claim that "the individual [does not have] a right not to *suffer* harm as an indirect and unintended or accidental concomitant of another's purposes"[40] would thus seem to apply to every case of a harm to individuals that is a concomitant of an injurious act directed toward an organization. The requirement of directness, we may conclude, is not met in such cases.

These considerations attempt to spell out the point I expressed more intuitively and metaphorically when I said that the or-ganization serves as a kind of "moral buffer" that deprives harm caused to individuals as a result of the injury to the organization of some of the more insidious moral implications that such harm might otherwise have. Thus, in the case of an injury to an or-ganization, no categorical ARs are violated, and O_2 cannot fortify its claim by relying on such a violation.

Beyond Respect

This may be a good place to mention a cluster of ethical views whose subsumption under the paradigm of autonomy would seem forced, but which are sufficiently related to that paradigm and sufficiently important for our present issue so as to justify dis-cussing them at this point. I have in mind such attitudes as love, pity, and compassion, which many argue are (or should be) em-bodied in the law. Thus, for example, Professor Noonan believes that "the central problem . . . of the legal enterprise is the relation of love to power."[41] Similarly, Professor Kennedy is concerned with "the pity and fear aroused in us by the image of a fellow human being at grips with institutions of formal justice."[42] And finally, Professor Fletcher views excuses in the law of torts "as expressions of compassion for human failings in times of stress."[43]

It is obvious that attitudes such as love, pity, and compassion naturally have human beings as their objects. They do not directly apply to organizations, and they cannot therefore be invoked by them in legal argument in the same way they can be invoked by individuals. It is, however, less obvious, but also true, that organizations cannot reap legal benefits from such sentiments indirectly by relying on the claims of individuals to whom such sentiments do properly apply. The argument that denies the possibility of such reliance is similar to the argument from directness (or mistreatment) that bars organizational reliance on ARs. The notion of mistreatment on which the previous argument rests emphasizes the moral significance of the *particularity* of the interacting individuals. But whereas respect is in this context due to the particular individual, it is due to him or her solely in their capacity as autonomous moral agents, that is, as embodied wills. In other words, respect applies to the particular individual *abstractly* conceived. Love and compassion, by contrast, must be addressed not only to particular individuals, but must also address them in all their *concreteness*, as unique human beings. This is the view eloquently expressed by John Noonan when he says that "we can often apply force to those we do not see, but we cannot, I think, love them. Only in the response of person to person can Augustine's sublime fusion be achieved, in which justice is defined as 'love serving only the one loved.'"[44] This view also underlies what Charles Fried terms the *personalist argument*:

Now the personalist argument holds that some preference for known over statistical lives is justified by virtue of the fact that it is with known lives that we enter into relations of love and friendship, while to the abstract statistical lives we stand in relations defined by justice and fairness. . . . The reason for the preference would be that relations of love and friendship are personal relations, in which the parties to the relation are aware of each other as particular persons, as individuals, rather than as abstract persons having only such characteristics as make them the appropriate objects of duties of justice and fairness.[45]

Once again, it should be emphasized that the fact that the law deals with an organization should not obscure the obvious reality that any decision regarding the organization is likely (though not certain) to affect various individuals; nor is the present argument meant to diminish our concern for the interests of those affected individuals. But the organization does hide from sight the particularity and the concreteness of the affected individuals. Consequently, when an organization is the object of legal relations, no particular individual makes on us the claims to love, pity, or compassion that could otherwise single out an individual from the rest of affected humanity for *special* attention and concern.

The Measurement of Harm

Assume now that, despite the arguments to the contrary, the harm to the organization does involve the violation of some individuals' ARs. Even so, I will now argue, the organization can draw only weak support from reliance on such a violation. The argument rests on a central tenet of the host of moral theories subsumed under the paradigm of autonomy: their commitment to the uniqueness of the individual as "the ultimate entity of value."[46] This commitment is reflected in the refusal to engage in the main exercise required by utilitarianism, that is, the summation of effects, like pain and pleasure, across individuals.[47]

Consider the following, rather trivial, example: Should a bus driver on duty be allowed to listen to the radio, even if this is disagreeable to most passengers? A utilitarian would approach the issue by computing the sum total of displeasure caused by the music to the passengers, and comparing this magnitude with the amount of suffering experienced by the driver when the radio is turned off. On the plausible assumption that the driver's ennui without the music is roughly equivalent to a passenger's annoyance at it, it would seem that on such a felicific calculus the driver will lose out to the public: at any given time, a single unit of boredom must compete against a busload of annoyance.

The issue would look quite different from the autonomy perspective. Assume we can plausibly characterize both the driver's interest in music and the passengers' opposite interest in quiet as ARs. Now, the autonomy advocate is not likely to be impressed by the multitude of passengers who assert a right to quiet. For him there is no "public" whose joint interest in quiet prevails over the single driver's desire for music.[48] If we conclude that the ennui suffered by the driver who is captivated in the bus all day long gives his claim to music sufficient weight to prevail over the annoyance caused by the music to a single passenger during a fifteen-minute ride, then it matters not that the passenger is one of many similarly situated individuals. If the driver has a weightier right than each passenger, then she has a weightier right than all the passengers. I will call this way of assessing the relative weights of ARs *the principle of nonaggregation.** It expresses the commitment of the paradigm of autonomy to the "moral importance of the separateness of individuals."[49] According to this principle, an individual's superior claim of right cannot be defeated by other individuals' inferior claims merely because the latter are more numerous.[50]

The relevance of the principle of nonaggregation to the organization's reliance on the violation of individual ARs is straightforward. As long as O_2 wishes to argue its case in terms of the paradigm of autonomy, the most it can do to support its case is to cite the single most severe harm caused to an individual as a result of its injury. This harm will determine the upper limit of the moral weight that can be assigned to O_2's claim. Its case will not be enhanced by showing that many other individuals suffered similar or lesser harm. It follows that when O_2 is involved in a dispute with an individual who can state her case in terms of an AR of hers, then O_2's case, argued in the language of autonomy, is liable to be rather weak. Unable to set against its opponent the sum total of the harm caused to all the individuals affected by the injury, O_2 must rely on a single fragment of that total loss represented by the transgression suffered by a single individual. That may frequently turn out to be trivial compared to the harm impending upon O_2's individual opponent.

The principle of nonaggregation, it should be observed, suggests

---

*The illustration of the driver glosses over a distinction that can be made between situations involving a conflict among different rights of different weights and situations in which the conflict is between different intrusions (that is, intrusions of different magnitude) into the same generic right. The nonaggregation principle would apply, I should think, in both kinds of cases. A single individual's superior right would take precedence over a number of individuals' inferior rights; a greater intrusion into a single individual's right would count for more (would be worse) than a number of lesser intrusions into the same kind of right of several individuals.

It should also be emphasized that the hypothetical of the driver is not meant to assert that the conflicting claims in question indeed rest on autonomy rights. Instead, the point of the hypothetical is to demonstrate one important difference that characterizing the case in utilitarian or autonomy terms would make to its proper analysis.

a moral equivalent to the economists' reliance on "spreading" as a justification for a greater willingness to burden the organization rather than a single individual with a given loss.[51] Spreading stands, roughly, for the proposition that as a result of the diminishing marginal utility of money, the sum total of small losses to many individuals may involve lesser disutility than that resulting from the dislocation to a single individual upon whom a loss of equal monetary magnitude is visited. Consequently, there will be a net gain in utility if a fixed monetary loss is put on an organization, and thus spread over many individuals, rather than imposed on a single individual. Nonaggregation reaches a similar result on moral rather than economic grounds, by pointing out that the overall moral weight of the wrong done to the organization is not equal to, but lesser than, the arithmetic summation of the wrongs to individuals. However, nonaggregation is relatively more restrictive on the organization's claim than is the idea of spreading. Spreading does allow the organization to sum all the individual losses resulting from an injury, though they must be discounted by a factor that represents diminishing marginal utilities. Nonaggregation bars such summation altogether.

Summary

We may summarize our discussion of Case 2 in three points. First, it does not necessarily follow from the fact that the organization was injured that any individual whatsoever was harmed too. Second, even if some individual were harmed, this harm is unlikely to satisfy the requirement of directness and consequently will not qualify as a violation of an individual's AR, nor will it invoke essentially personal sentiments such as love, pity, and compassion. And third, even if the harm to the individuals resulting from the injury to the organization can qualify as a violation of their ARs, the nonaggregation principle greatly weakens the organization's case.

It can accordingly be concluded that it is quite difficult (perhaps impossible) to find a case in which the organization can successfully support a claim to a decision in its favor by relying on the AR of some individual. In order to be able to express its grievances in the language of autonomy, the organization must have rights *of its own*. We have already argued that the organization does not have original autonomy rights. We now turn to an examination of the organization's attempt to rest its claim on a derivative autonomy right of its own.

The Organization's Derivative Autonomy Rights

Derivative autonomy rights (DARs) are claims that are justified in terms of their usefulness for the protection of OARs. In order for an organization to have a DAR, it must have the protection of some OAR as a goal, and the DAR must be thought conducive to the pursuit of that goal. Accordingly, DARs are quite different from the OARs which they serve to protect. OARs are those rights whose violation constitutes a transgression of the individual's "protected moral space,"[52] or, less metaphorically, an interference with the individual's autonomy. A violation of a DAR has quite a different meaning: the DAR only makes the OAR safer, so that a violation of a DAR only increases the risk that an OAR may be violated, or its exercise made in some respect more cumbersome.

This leads to another important difference between OARs and DARs. A central tenet of the paradigm of autonomy is the non-instrumental nature of OARs. DARs, by contrast, are clearly instrumental; they depend for their recognition on the OAR they claim to protect. Saying that DARs are instrumental does not, of course, mean that they belong in the utilitarian camp. They do not engage in the general competition for maximizing social utility. DARs are concerned only with protecting some OAR, and to the extent they do so they enjoy a normative status within the paradigm of autonomy similar to that of the original rights protected by them. They are accordingly likewise partially immune to adverse utilitarian considerations. But they are instrumental nonetheless: they are to be judged and weighed in terms of their efficacy in serving the goal (i.e., the protection of an OAR) on which their normative status depends. They do, therefore, admit of consequentialist considerations and trade-offs as against alternative measures designed to protect OARs.

Case 3 will help us examine more closely the nature of the derivative autonomy rights that organizations may have.

Case 3: O_3, a university, relies on its goal of protecting academic freedom as an argument against a court's reviewing and possibly interfering with a university disciplinary proceeding which resulted in the expulsion of a student who had participated in a demonstration on campus.

Let us assume that academic freedom is an instance of one of the basic individual liberties and is thus recognized as an OAR.[53] By academic freedom I mean, roughly, the freedom to engage in the creation and communication of ideas, scientific knowledge, and the like. It is also plausible to maintain that the promotion and the protection of academic freedom is one of the university's central goals.[54] This is so mainly in the sense that the university provides the needed amenities and the sheltered and congenial environment necessary for a meaningful exercise of that right. The university serves that goal, for example, by instituting a decisionmaking process that allocates resources among its faculty needed for their contemplation and research without at the same time imposing on them restrictions that may interfere with their academic freedom. This decisionmaking process is a valuable asset from the point of view of each professor's academic freedom. A certain degree of autonomy and independence of this decisionmaking process may in turn be necessary for its successful and smooth functioning. To the extent that this is so, the university can now be said to have an autonomy right, which in this case amounts to a right to the independence of its decisionmaking process from intrusive interventions. But this right is obviously of a derivative kind: it is based entirely on the concern for the individual professor's academic freedom. More generally, the university's derivative autonomy rights are rights that are necessary for or conducive to its function in promoting and protecting academic freedom.

The DAR of the university shares to a certain extent the normative status of the OAR from which it is derived. The concern for protecting the professor's right to academic freedom also justifies extending a similar protection to those liberties and immunities of the university which are deemed necessary for assuring researchers such protection. Specifically, if we believe that utilitarian considerations cannot, by and large, override a professor's right to academic freedom, we should also maintain that those rights of the university which are required for the protection of the professor's academic freedom be similarly immune to adverse utilitarian considerations. We may conclude that the university, as such, has a derivative autonomy right to academic freedom, which, like the original autonomy right that underlies it, is also, in Professor Dworkin's terms, a right in the strong anti-utilitarian sense.

However, determining the scope of an organization's DAR is not a simple matter. No great difficulties would arise if the organization were meticulously optimizing the single goal of protecting the relevant OAR. Had this been the case, then the organization's DAR would have been coextensive with its entire activity. Any successful claim to "injury" made by such an organization (i.e., any successful claim that an event constitutes an impediment to the achievement of its goal) would straightforwardly translate into the language of the paradigm of autonomy as a transgression of the organization's DAR. So, to continue our former example, had the university been solely committed to the protection of the academic freedom of its faculty, the university's claim to autonomy would be fully supported by the underlying OAR for the protection of which that autonomy is required. However, as is typical of most large organizations, the university pursues a variety of goals. Some of them are unrelated to the professors' (or anyone else's) OARs.[55] Still, the university, like other organizations, is liable to rely on its DAR in the service of any of those other goals, thereby trying to extend the DAR beyond its legitimate scope as defined by the underlying OAR.

Goal displacement[56] is likely to contribute to the discrepancy between the underlying OAR protected by the organizational DAR and actual organizational claims based on its DAR. For example, sub-units within the organization are apt to engage in activities geared towards the accomplishment of their own sub-goals in a way and to an extent that do not necessarily comport with the achievement of the overall organizational goal. These sub-units are likely to invoke the organization's DAR in protection of their goals, even though the particular activities concerned do not in fact contribute to and may even hinder the OAR from which the organizational right is derived. Our hypothetical is a case in point. The campus police and other disciplinary authorities may pursue their departmental sub-goal of preserving "law and order" zealously and single-mindedly, in ways that are sometimes detrimental rather than conductive to the promotion of academic freedom. The expelled student might have participated, for all we know, in a peaceful demonstration against government intervention in the university's hiring policy. And yet, the university tries to invoke, in this case, its institutional autonomy, expressed in the idiom of academic freedom, as the ground for the immunity of its disciplinary action against the student from the court's intervention.

These observations are simply meant to underline the caution with which organizational DARs must be recognized and applied. The willingness to immunize certain organizational claims to conflicting utilitarian considerations must be coupled with an awareness of the potential for abuse inherent in such immunity. The multiplicity of organizational goals, the phenomenon of goal displacement, as well as organizational tendencies toward self-aggrandizement,[57] all complicate the task of maintaining full correspondence between an organization's DAR and its underlying individual autonomy right.

Conclusion

Our discussion of the normative status of the organization within the paradigm of autonomy may be summarized as follows. Despite the strictly individualistic nature of the paradigm of autonomy, organizations are not entirely excluded from this realm of discourse. But the support rendered to organizational claims by the paradigm of autonomy is limited. Among the four ways in which an organization may try to support its own claims on grounds of autonomy—that is, by either invoking or relying on some individual's AR, or by asserting an OAR or a DAR of its own—the last possibility alone seems to be viable. However, only organizations which have the protection of some OAR as their goal may have a DAR. Furthermore, the scope of their DARs is entirely determined by the extent to which such rights are needed for the effective protection by the organization of the OAR. Accordingly, the organization will have the DAR only with respect to the sub-set of its activities and decisions that are related to the goal of protecting an OAR. In addition, unlike the OAR on which it rests, the organization's DAR can be subjected to consequentialist considerations (though not of a utilitarian nature).

The limited role that considerations of individual autonomy will thus play in broad areas of organizational activity militates against the soundness of attempts, like the ones that have been made with respect to tort law* and contract law,[58] to ground entire legal areas

*Compare Professor Epstein's view, cast in the language of autonomy, that "the first task of the law of torts is to define the boundaries of individual liberty" (Richard A. Epstein, "A Theory of Strict Liability," 2 *J. Leg. Stud.* 151, 203 [1973]); and Professor Calabresi's position that "the principal function of accident law is to reduce the sum of the costs of accidents and the costs of avoiding accidents" (Guido Calabresi, *The Costs of Accidents* [New Haven: Yale University Press, 1970], p. 26).

exclusively in the paradigm of autonomy. Had our tort law, for example, been concerned only with the protection of the "moral hyper-plane"[59] surrounding the individual, many organizational interests would be fair game, to be violated with impunity by anyone. Interpretations of legal structures as founded on the ideal of individual autonomy alone cannot in general adequately account for the legal protection of organizational interests. Such legal theories lead, therefore, to one of two untenable positions. One is the prevailing position that ignores the existence and distinctive nature of organizations, and applies the body of law derived from individual autonomy across the board, to individuals and organizations alike, thus implicitly (and apparently inadvertently) imputing to the latter the same ARs that the former have. The alternative position is to fully recognize the existence and distinctive nature of organizations and draw the normative implications from such a recognition. In doing that, however, we found out that a law built on grounds of autonomy would be applicable to organizational injuries only intermittently and thus would leave organizational interests largely unattended. If we find such an outcome implausible, we should reject the paradigm of autonomy as a sufficient account of the law of torts, or any other legal area, institution, or doctrine that applies to organizations as well as to individuals. To find a firmer ground for the normative status of organizations, we must now turn to the paradigm of utility.

ORGANIZATIONS' RIGHTS WITHIN THE UTILITY PARADIGM

To talk about the paradigm of utility as if it designated a single or uniform theory involves a crude oversimplification matched only by my similar treatment of the paradigm of autonomy. Yet I believe that this approach is necessary for the task at hand, and is warranted by the fact that there is a recognizable core, or common denominator, shared by all utilitarians of whatever more specific persuasion. This core is roughly represented by their debt to Bentham's ideas. At least as a first approximation, the elucidation of the organization's normative status within the paradigm of utility may appeal exclusively to these core ideas, ignoring the important internal divisions within utilitarianism.

Our discussion of the paradigm of utility will be much briefer than the preceding discussion of the competing paradigm. There I spent much time and space describing in some detail the obstacles to the organization's use of the language of autonomy. No similar effort need be expended in the case of utility. My main contention here is precisely the absence of such obstacles that would impede or restrict the ascription to organizations of rights derived from considerations of utility.*

To see this we may resort once again to the analytical framework that we used in the case of autonomy. I will call a legal right justified by considerations of utility a *utility right* (for brevity, UR). We can accordingly distinguish between the organization having an original UR of its own, its invoking or relying on some individual's UR, and its having a derivative UR. Putting aside the case of invoking a right (here, as before, I find little interest in the purely procedural role played by the organization in this case), I will consider first the notion of an original UR. A can be said to have an original UR if the reason for recognizing and protecting his claim to X is the belief that X will make him happier (give him pleasure, increase his utility). By contrast, A has a derivative UR if the reason for satisfying his claim to X is not based on concern for A's own happiness but someone else's, such as when X enables A to contribute to society's welfare and increase its resources, thereby improving the opportunities of people in that society for greater happiness. This distinction between original and derivative utility rights can be illustrated by the different justifications adduced by some utility-minded economists for the right to bodily integrity and the right of private property. The economic justification for the former right rests on the belief that, by and large, individuals value bodily integrity more than those who would violate it value the violation.[60] The second UR, to private property, is primarily justified by economists not in terms of the greater happiness of the

---

*Unlike the paradigm of autonomy, where rights are the essential building blocks of the entire normative structure, the status of rights within the paradigm of utility is quite precarious. One of the main charges against utilitarianism is that it fails to account for individual rights. My argument assumes, however, that, as Professor Lyons argues, "a proponent of the general welfare standard—even a utilitarian—can take rights seriously." David Lyons, "Human Rights and the General Welfare," 6 *Phil. & Pub. Aff.* 113, 125 (1977). The issue can be avoided here by simply interpreting the utility rights to which I refer as legal rights (embedded in some authoritative legal text) which are based on (or are to be understood in terms of) utilitarian considerations.

owner, but by the belief that it is conducive to an efficient resource allocation and thus contributes to overall efficiency and social welfare.[61]

Applying these definitions to the case of the organization, it is clear that as far as derivative rights are concerned the utilitarian is indifferent whether the right bearer is an individual human being or Personless Corporation. The question in both cases is the same, namely, whether the recognition of the right and the satisfaction of the claim are conducive to the right bearer's (whether individual or organization) contribution to social welfare. In analogy to the case of derivative autonomy rights, so also in the case of an organization's derivative utility right (DUR), its claim must be related to (one of) its goals, which in turn must be seen as contributing to social welfare. Once these conditions are satisfied, the organization acquires a DUR that is indistinguishable from such a right acquired in a similar way by an individual.

These definitions may also seem to imply that original URs can be possessed only by individuals (or perhaps other sentient beings): organizations, which themselves experience neither pleasure nor pain, can make no claims that depend on such experiences. In this respect too, then, the organization's utility rights appear to trace the same pattern as its autonomy rights. But this appearance is somewhat misleading. The distinction between original and derivative rights is in fact neither as clear nor as significant within the paradigm of utility as it is within the paradigm of autonomy. A utilitarian is never interested in the claims of a particular individual out of a true concern for that individual's personal welfare. Rather, his concern is always with the general welfare that may be increased by satisfying the particular individual's claim. As put by H. L. A. Hart:

> In the perspective of classical maximizing utilitarianism separate individuals are of no intrinsic importance but only important as the points at which fragments of what *is* important, i.e., the total aggregate of pleasure or happiness, are located. Individual persons for it are therefore merely the channels or locations where what is of value is to be found.[62]

Accordingly, the utility rights we described as original are in an important sense only derivative: A's pleasure derived from X counts in favor of satisfying her claim to X only because of the contribution that A's increased happiness makes to the overall social welfare. If organizations contribute towards the maximization of social utility in some way other than by experiencing pleasure, their status within the paradigm of utility is not essentially different from that of individuals. Furthermore, the point of distinguishing DARs from OARs—namely, to show that the former, unlike the latter, are instrumental rights—is missing in the case of URs. All URs, both those of individuals and those belonging to organizations, are made of the same instrumental stuff.

There is a second important difference between the status of organizations within the paradigm of utility and their status within the paradigm of autonomy. It consists in the relative ease with which organizations can *rely* on a particular individual's utilities. Recall Case 2, in which a plaintiff corporation, whose production of widgets had been interrupted by the defendants, tried to support its claim to damages by pointing to the various individual interests, such as those of shareholders and workers, that were compromised as a result of the interruption and would be restored if damages were paid to the corporation. Of the three arguments I offered against the corporation's reliance within the paradigm of autonomy on the injury sustained by individuals, only the first argument— raising the possibility that no individual had been in fact harmed as a result of the harm to the corporation—is also applicable within the paradigm of utility. However, if the harm to the corporation described in Case 2 did result in a net loss in utility to certain individuals, I can see no analogue to the arguments from direct-ness, love, or nonaggregation that would in principle frustrate or limit the corporation's reliance on those individual losses.

Indeed, as in the case of the organization's DURs, the nature of its claim that relies on the utilities of some individuals is not significantly different from the nature of claims that can be made by the individuals themselves. Once again, the validity of both the individuals' and the organization's claims depends on the con-tribution that satisfying those claims makes toward maximizing social utility. It is only a contingent, empirical factor that the con-tribution to social welfare which validates those claims is via the pleasure and pain experienced by the particular individuals. We may conclude, therefore, that both in having DURs of its own and in relying on URs of particular individuals, the status of the organization's claims within the paradigm of utility does not differ much, in principle, from that of individuals.

This last statement has to be qualified by emphasizing the words *in principle*. Which of an organization's claims do in fact promote social utility is an empirical question. More specifically, to qualify as a UR it must be shown both that an organization's claim is related to one of its goals (which makes it the *organization's* claim) and that the pursuit of that goal is in the social interest (which provides the claim with the necessary normative support). Neither one of these conditions can be taken for granted. Having mentioned in Chapter 2 some of the organization's characteristic dysfunctions, we can easily imagine the organization making claims that are in fact unrelated to any of its goals. Similarly, there is no guarantee that the goal to which a given claim is related does in fact contribute to rather than detract from social utility. Thus, Professor Mishan gives the example of the manufacturing firm that produces negative externalities which outweigh the utility of its products.[63] This is also the case with respect to the organization's reliance on some particular individual's utilities. The description of the organization as *impermeable*[64] expresses the possibility that an injury complained of and sought to be redressed by the organization may not correspond to any harm to particular individuals. Similarly, describing the organization as *opaque*[65] implies that a claim made by it to a particular resource and for a particular decision may not correspond to and reveal the preferences of any particular individuals.

Nonetheless, unlike the case of autonomy, there is nothing in the paradigm of utility that would necessarily, as a matter of principle, limit the range of rights given to organizations and prevent the law from assigning to them utility rights that are coextensive with, or indeed even broader than, those given to individuals.[66]

FROM ENTITIES TO INTERACTIONS

I have so far tried to convince the reader that, in the light of both the distinctiveness and the importance of organizations, it is sensible to view the legal universe as populated by two different kinds of entities: individuals and organizations. But to speak of "entities" does not always correctly represent the basic units that concern the law. Not single entities but the transactions among them are typically at the focus of legal attention and the subject of legal ordering. Accordingly, my initial claim about the law's individualistic view of organizations can be restated as a contention that the law often treats the domain of legal relations as uniform, consisting of one kind of interaction, that is, one that takes place among individuals (I will designate such an interaction an I-I relation). If organizations are to be acknowledged as distinctive legal actors, the domain of legal relations must instead be subdivided into three types of relations: it should be recognized that, in addition to the I-I relation, the law has to deal with interactions among organizations (O-O relations), and with "mixed" interactions, in which individuals interact with organizations (O-I relations).[67]

Each of these three kinds of interaction will be characterized by its distinctive mode of legal argument responsive to the different nature of the participating entities and reflective of the different normative vocabularies employed by them. In light of the preceding arguments, and at the cost of a great oversimplification, we can even venture a rough characterization of the typical normative texture of each interaction. In I-I relations, where both parties are likely to be armed with ARs, the language of rights (in the strong, anti-utilitarian sense), backed up by considerations of individual autonomy, will often seem appropriate. In the O-O context, by contrast, utility considerations are more likely to predominate, occasionally confronted by derivative autonomy rights. Finally, the O-I interaction is often likely to present a clash between utility and autonomy, in which the individual will insist on the supremacy of autonomy rights, whereas the organization will point out the magnitude of the social interest that its claims represent.

This tripartite normative scheme, though crude, suggests nonetheless the potential fruitfulness of mapping entire legal areas onto this three-dimensional picture of the legal universe. Such mapping would in particular draw attention to and facilitate an appraisal of the transformation of certain legal relations that were traditionally of the I-I variety into an O-I or an O-O type of interaction.[68] Several such transformations spring immediately to mind. Industrialization and the rise of large corporations have changed labor relations from I-I to O-I relations; the subsequent rise of trade unions brings them within the O-O class. Appreciating those changes may help, for example, to both understand and advocate the eclipse that we may be witnessing at present of the "termination at will" doctrine that has so far been dominant in labor relations.[69] Some areas within tort law, notably workmen's compensation and product liability, are typically of the O-I variety because of the prevalence in those areas of large corporations. The expansion of insurance companies into many other areas transforms much of the rest of tort law into an O-I or O-O affair. The dramatic rise of strict liability in tort law might be fruitfully examined against this background. The same is true of contract relations. This paradigmatically individualistic legal field also developed special areas that may be characterized by the identity of the parties: "contracts of adhesion"[70] are most frequently of the O-I type, whereas "relational contracts"[71] are often interorganizational and thus are of the O-O kind. Consumer protection, lying on the borderline between contracts and regulatory law, is a legal area dealing predominantly with O-I relations. Landlord and tenant law is undergoing a similar transformation from an area that deals typically with I-I relations to one in which the O-I model prevails.[72]

Subjecting these and other legal areas to a closer critical examination in light of the normative scheme that has been developed in this chapter seems to me a potentially fruitful undertaking. I will not, however, pursue such a "macro" perspective here, but will take a "micro" approach instead. In the following chapter, I will focus more narrowly on the analysis of some particular legal rights, and illustrate thereby in a more specific way how the general normative conclusions we have reached bear on legal argument and make a difference in legal decisions.

Chapter V

The Analysis of Organizations' Legal Rights

Even the modest illustrative venture to be undertaken in this chapter is seriously impeded by the paucity of the available theoretical groundwork. To fully understand the implications of the distinction between the two normative paradigms—autonomy and utility—for the analysis of organizations' legal rights would require, at the least, a worked out substantive theory of autonomy rights, a similarly complete substantive theory of utility rights, and a theory regarding their interrelation. We have in fact none. We must therefore work by the dim light provided by the partial and conflicting theories that there are, supplementing them sometimes by ad hoc arguments, and even more often substituting mere assertion for argument.

STRUCTURE AND APPLICATION OF COMPOUND LEGAL RIGHTS

In relating the preceding theoretical discussion to specific legal issues, my purpose is to show how organizations fit within existing and familiar modes of legal argument. Legal argument typically focuses on or proceeds from the assertion of some *legal right*. By this I understand roughly a generic claim explicitly recognized by authoritative legal materials and conventionally invoked in established modes of legal discourse at the outset of an argument that calls for the satisfaction of a specific claim. I have in mind such things as property, privacy, contract, free speech, and the like, irrespective of their source, be it statutory, common law, constitutional, or otherwise.

To legally vindicate a specific claim, the claim must be articulated in terms of one or another such legal right. Citing the relevant legal right is, however, not the end but only the beginning of legal argument. Unless an identical issue to that raised by the specific claim has already been satisfactorily decided before, the application of the legal right to the particular case will call for the interpretation and elaboration of the right in light of the values and policies that are thought to underlie it. It is at this point that appeal to considerations of utility or autonomy (which in our simplified scheme exhaust the relevant sets of underlying considerations) becomes necessary. The interpretation of legal rights in terms of the underlying values of utility and autonomy leads to a division of legal rights into three kinds. Some legal rights, like the right against self-incrimination, have been traditionally justified, and can only be persuasively argued for, on grounds of autonomy.[1] These legal rights are autonomy rights pure and simple. Other legal rights are, in a similar way, utility rights: a statutory scheme that provides for government subsidies to certain industries may be grounded exclusively in economic efficiency and should thus be interpreted by reference to purely utilitarian considerations.[2] But most of the important legal rights, such as contract, property, and free speech, are neither exclusively ARs nor URs, but both: they have been advocated and are often interpreted both in terms of utility and in terms of autonomy.[3] I will call such legal rights *compound rights*. It is regarding compound rights that the interplay between autonomy and utility in general, and in its application to organizations in particular, promises to be most significant and most interesting.

In tracing the implications of interpreting a legal right in terms of one or the other normative paradigm, I will focus on three aspects, or dimensions, of a right: its *scope*, which denotes the range of issues to which the particular right applies; its *weight*, determined by the range of counterarguments over which the right can prevail; and its *remedy*, the legal measures employed for the protection of the right. To apply a legal right to a particular case, its scope, weight, and remedy must be implicitly or explicitly determined. As I will presently show, each of these dimensions is sensitive to the distinction between arguments of utility and arguments of autonomy, so that the interpretation of the right in terms of the one set of values or the other will often lead to different conclusions along these dimensions.

Now whereas an individual may usually resort to both arguments of utility and autonomy, the organization, as we have seen, must often rest its claims only on the utilitarian leg of the compound legal right. This normative asymmetry between individuals and organizations may be concealed by the fact that both articulate their respective claims by using the same legal label. Yet when the legal right relied upon is a compound one, it may lead to different conclusions regarding its scope, weight, and remedy, depending on the kind of entity that asserts it.

These general observations can be best clarified in the context of a specific right. I will focus for this purpose on private property (property, for short), which is a clear and important example of a compound right: arguments have been commonly deployed in its favor both in terms of autonomy and in terms of utility.[4] The importance ascribed to property by its autonomy advocates is principally based on ideas of personhood and liberty. In the first place, it is argued, property is essentially and intimately linked to personhood: "Property is but the periphery of my person extended to things."[5] It is the shrine within which personhood may flourish and a medium through which a person's will can effectively express itself in the world.[6] Property has also been defended as the bastion of an individual's liberty: property defines and protects the "moral zone"[7] within which an individual may exercise his will with full sovereignty and discretion, unperturbed by the need to account to either government authorities or to other individuals for his wishes, tastes, and choices.[8]

Property is also commonly defended by utilitarians, who portray it as an institution whose justification depends solely upon considerations of social welfare. Some version of this view was held by Aristotle,[9] and it is represented today in an economic garb by the proposition that "the legal protection of property rights has an important economic function: to create incentives to use resources efficiently."[10]

These two sets of justifications, I will now argue, endow property with a different scope and weight and call for different remedial measures for its protection. Consequently, the analysis and the legal ramifications of a property right will often differ, depending on whether the right is asserted by an individual or by an organization.[11]

Scope

If a compound legal right is not to be merely an empty shell, but a meaningful normative concept, the scope of the two rights conjoined in it—the AR and the UR—must include a significant area of overlap. This area provides the compound right with a kind of normative core that makes intelligible the use of a single conventional label to describe the compound right. It is possible, in our example, to speak intelligibly about "property" as a single legal category only insofar as it possesses such a core, that is, insofar as the arguments of autonomy and those of utility that are commonly invoked in support of private property converge in a large number of cases. But while some such convergence is necessary to sustain the coherence of the conventional legal label, it is not required, nor very likely, that the convergence be complete. The more plausible picture of the relation between the scopes of the AR and UR conjoined within a certain compound legal right is that of two partially overlapping circles. The area of overlap describes the compound right's normative core: the applicability of the legal right to cases falling within this area is secured by both considerations of autonomy and utility. In cases falling outside the core, however, the applicability of the right will critically depend on the kinds of arguments that can be marshaled in its support. Accordingly, when asserted by individuals, who as we have seen can typically rest their claims on both "legs" of a compound right, the scope of the right will be coextensive with the area covered by the two circles. However, in the case of organizations, who are restricted in the use of autonomy considerations, the scope of the legal right will often coincide with the area covered by the utility circle only.*

This picture of the scope of compound rights can be illustrated by applying it to the famous "shopping mall" cases, in which the scope of corporate property was at issue.[12] *Lloyd Corp. v. Tanner*[13]

---

*Indeed, the utilitarian considerations that support individual private property may differ from those that apply to organizational property. If that is so, even the contours of the "utilitarian circle" may differ as between individual and organizational property.

provides the typical facts in these cases. Respondents sought to distribute handbills in the interior mall area of a large shopping center owned by the petitioner Lloyd Corporation. Can they do so despite the owner corporation's objection? The special interest for us in these cases resides in the stark way in which they pit the corporation's claim grounded in its property right against individuals' asserted First Amendment rights. By so doing, they help illuminate the nature of the corporation's property rights, which is our present concern.

A possible approach to the issue raised in these cases would be to investigate the scope of the property right relied upon by the corporation,[14] that is, to inquire "whether one of the incidents of petitioner's private ownership of the Lloyd Center is the power to exclude certain forms of speech from its property."[15] Obviously, a determination that the corporation's claim to exclude the handbill distributors from its mall is without the scope of its property right would avoid the clash between property and freedom of speech by eliminating the property right from the competition.

Such a conclusion can indeed be reached if the corporation's ownership of the mall is interpreted as a utility right. Recall that the utilitarian justification of an organization's UR has to do primarily with the social value of the organization's goal-pursuing activity: the UR must be instrumental to the attainment of the organizational goals. To determine the scope of an organization's property right, one must accordingly first examine the relation between the issue with respect to which the property claim is made and the organization's goals. Indeed, in the *Logan Valley* case, which involved picketing on corporate territory, the Court undertook such an examination, concluding that "on the facts of the case" no "significant claim to protection of the normal business operation of the property [can] be raised."[16] Nor, it seems to me, could the corporations' position in the cases under consideration get utilitarian support from an examination of any individual interests that might be indirectly affected by the alleged intrusion on corporate territory: insofar as no diminution in the value of the property as a result of the speech activities complained of (picketing or handbilling) is apparent, no individuals whose interests are linked to those of the corporation (e.g., employees or shareholders) suffered any loss as a result of that intrusion.*

The conclusion to which these considerations lead—namely, that the corporation's property right does not include the power to exclude the "speakers" in these cases—may be objected to on the ground that it derives from an overly narrow focus on the particular case. A legal property right, it might be argued, is a generic right, whose main point is to avoid a costly comprehensive act-utilitarian calculus in each particular case. If the right of exclusion by and large promotes the interests that justify the legal protection of private property (whether corporate or individual), it should not be subjected to the kind of specific utilitarian scrutiny in which we (and the *Logan Valley* Court) have engaged.

There are two answers to this objection. First, notice the limited contours of the investigation we conducted in order to determine the scope of the corporation's property right. Short of an all-out act-utilitarian calculus, the question we asked was only whether the intrusion complained of interfered with any corporate goals at all, or whether it caused indirect loss to any individual whatsoever. In applying this test, we can also be helped by the presence of certain clearly visible indicia (like the fact, emphasized by the Court, that the shopping malls discussed in the present cases were all "open to the public") suggesting that intrusion into a certain corporate territory is unlikely to interfere with any of the corporation's legitimate activities. It would seem that such a minimal test can be easily satisfied, preserving the general presumption in favor of a right of exclusion as incidental to corporate property rights, while allowing for exceptions in cases where the factual premises upholding the general presumption clearly do not apply. It can

---

*Since business corporations do not, by and large, protect individuals against possible violations of their autonomy rights, it is unlikely that corporate property would be successfully cast and protected as a derivative autonomy right. However, even in cases where certain aspects of organizational property rights can be plausibly characterized in this way, the determination of their scope would not differ from the analysis in the text. Like utility rights, derivative autonomy rights, too, are instrumental rights, and their scope should be determined by reference to the relevant organizational goals. The characterization of an organizational property right as a derivative autonomy right would, however, make a difference in respect to its *weight*. See footnote on p. 95 *infra*.

be argued that even a sanguine rule-utilitarian proponent of corporate property rights should ask for no more.

My second rejoinder does not quarrel with the possibility of finding some utilitarian grounds for a broad right to exclusion as incidental to property rights of the corporation. Instead, it seeks to establish the negative claim that there are some arguments in favor of an unqualified right to exclusion which are available to individuals relying on considerations of autonomy, but which are unavailable to defend a similar scope for organizational property. To show this, I will briefly indicate the considerations that determine the scope of property conceived as an autonomy right. Both grounds we have identified as underlying an AR to property—personhood and liberty—suggest such considerations.

Consider personhood first. The idea that property is a medium through which the individual effectuates her will, as well as the related metaphor that property is "an extension of the person," straightforwardly imply a right of exclusion. Unlike an organizational goal, an individual's will is in principle unbounded, and one's property gives one a space, both physical and moral, within which that will is given equally unbounded expression, and from which, therefore, other persons may be precluded merely on the ground that they are unwanted. But even if considerations of personhood would not condone exclusion for reasons that are thought to be arbitrary, capricious, or eccentric, the second autonomy ground for property—the idea of liberty—would still uphold the exclusion by preventing the investigation of those reasons. It is precisely the freedom from having to account for one's wishes and choices, and from subjecting them to public scrutiny, that, according to the argument from liberty, property is meant to secure. In light of these considerations, a broad right to exclusion is firmly grounded within the autonomy paradigm and is an integral part of the AR to property. The fact that these considerations do not by and large apply to organizational property does not, of course, remove the possibility that some other considerations (e.g., of a rule-utilitarian kind) might support a similar right of exclusion for organizations. The present argument establishes a weaker, albeit still an important proposition. Favoring a broad right of exclusion as incidental to individual property while withholding that right from organizational property need not be an arbitrary or an inconsistent position. Consequently, individuals who support their claim by autonomy considerations may enjoy a right to exclusion under circumstances that would not afford a similar right to a corporation.

The importance of this difference in scope between individual and corporate property is well demonstrated by the cases under consideration. By ignoring the difference between individuals and organizations, and by overlooking the different justifications of private property that respectively apply to these entities, the Court finds itself committed to a unitary view of property rights, invariably applicable to corporations and individuals alike. It is understandable, therefore, that the Court should recoil from arguments in favor of the right to exercise free speech on the corporate property in question that "would apply in varying degrees to most retail stores and service establishments across the country."[17] As I have attempted to show, the permission to engage under certain circumstances in picketing or handbilling on corporate territory does not entail any relaxation of the legal protection of individual property rights.[18] The scope of the latter is an independent question, which raises different philosophical issues and which admits a different resolution.*

---

*I am not, however, altogether clear about the proper analysis of these cases had the malls in question been owned by single individuals. Even assuming that such ownership is in principle protected by the autonomy paradigm (which, depending on the specifics of a substantive theory of autonomy rights that one holds, may or may not be the case), I would still be tempted by the view that the malls can nonetheless count as organizational (as opposed to individual) property for the purpose of my analysis. The argument to that effect would be that the imperatives of running a large and complex shopping mall require a correspondingly large and complex organizational structure. If that structure is large and complex enough and assumes the various organizational properties described in Chapter 2, it will become "impermeable" and "opaque." Once such a structure is interposed between the single owner and the property in question, it may be said to drain the proprietary relationship of the immediacy, involvement, and personal control that are the hallmarks of true individual property. The point to be emphasized is that the formal legal structure (individual ownership as against corporate ownership, in this case) is not conclusive as to whether or not the entity in question is properly characterized as an organization for the purpose of the present analysis. See also pp. 113–16 *infra*. Cf. Professor Simitis's description of a shift in German law from a focus on legal form (the company) to the economic reality—the enterprise. Certain duties (e.g., of disclosure) depend on criteria such as number of employees or balance sheet sum, irrespective of the legal form in which the enterprise is conducted. S. Simitis, "Workers' Participation in the Enterprise—Transcending Company Law?" 38 *M.L. Rev.* 1, 16 (1975).

Weight

Some legal disputes may be resolved by considerations of scope alone, when only one of the parties succeeds in demonstrating that his or her claim is protected by a legal right. But suppose that the cases we have considered do not belong in this group—that, contrary to my arguments in the preceding section, it is concluded that the exclusion of intruders in those cases is within the scope of the corporations' property rights. Such a determination does not, of course, conclude the matter. To resolve the dispute, a corporation's property right must now be pitted against the speakers' First Amendment rights. To determine which of the two should prevail, relative weights must be assigned to the competing rights.

Like its scope, so also the weight of a legal right critically depends on its philosophical pedigree. The weight of a compound right will therefore vary, depending on whether it is relied upon in its capacity as an autonomy right or a utility right. Indeed, the special weight claimed for autonomy rights by their proponents is their most important and distinctive feature. This weight consists in the ability of autonomy rights to withstand utilitarian challenges, expressing thereby, as we have seen,[19] the unwillingness to sacrifice vital interests of one individual in order to benefit others. Variably describing ARs as "absolute," "categorical," or "anti-utilitarian," their advocates differ in the precise assignment of weight to them: Are autonomy rights completely immune to all utilitarian considerations, or do they sometimes succumb to social costs but only when they reach "catastrophic" proportions, or would "compelling" utilitarian considerations suffice to defeat them? However, common to all of these positions is the view that the seriousness of a society's commitment to autonomy rights is measured by the amount of social utility it is willing to forego on their behalf. As a result, the characterization of a legal right as an autonomy right gives it a certain advantage in its competition with other rights, an advantage that as a utility right it would not possess.

This conclusion is, of course, far too weak to serve as a formula for the resolution of conflicts among competing rights. We have already observed the lack of consensus among autonomy advocates as to the amount of utilitarian pressure that autonomy rights should be allowed to withstand. This disagreement aside, no theorist has proposed any principled method for establishing the "rate of exchange" between social utility and individual autonomy. Finally, in addition to the respective weights of the relevant generic rights, the resolution of their clash in a particular case must also take into account the extent of their threatened or actual violation: a claim based on a minor infringement of the weightier right may be defeated by a more serious infringement of the lesser generic right.

But whereas the identification of the philosophical pedigree of the opposing legal rights does not in and of itself generate a solution to their conflict, it is an indispensable step in reaching such a solution. This point, too, is clearly illustrated by the "shopping mall" cases under consideration. The Justices divided in these cases in their assignment of relative weights to property and free speech. Compare Justice Marshall's position that "when the competing interests are fairly weighed, the balance ['between the freedom to speak . . . and the freedom of a private property owner to control his property'] can only be struck in favor of speech,"[20] to that of Justice Reed: "The rights of the owner, which the Constitution protects as well as the right of free speech, are not outweighed by the interests of the trespasser, even though he trespasses in behalf of religion or free speech."[21] What both sides overlook is the critical fact that these particular disputes are of the O-I variety. As a result of this oversight, both of the opposing assignments of relative weights to the legal rights at issue are too sweeping, and therefore untenable.

Justice Marshall's unqualified pro-speech position, for example, has some far-reaching implications to which he himself may not want to subscribe. Consider the following hypothetical. P owns a summer house in the country. He finds out that for some years, in his absence from the house during the winter months, a political group used to conduct its meetings in an empty room in the house. Assume that the meetings caused absolutely no damage to the house or to P: on the contrary, the group members cleaned the house after each meeting and occasionally even tended the garden. Furthermore, P's house is the only place in the area where the group could conveniently conduct its meetings. Now P seeks an injunction against any further meetings in his house. Would any justice presently on the Supreme Court refuse such an injunction on the ground that freedom of speech outweighs property? Indeed, the unqualified assertion that as a general matter the right to free speech carries greater weight than the right to private property runs counter to the famous Supreme Court decision in *Rowan v. Post Office Dept.*[22] Upholding unanimously a statute that allows the postmaster, upon notification by a householder, to order a sender of advertising material to refrain from further mailing such material to that householder, the Court said: "In this case the mailer's right to communicate is circumscribed only by an affirmative act of the addressee giving notice that he wishes no further mailing from the mailer. To hold less would tend to license a form of trespass."[23]

However, a pro-speech holding in the shopping mall type of situation can be reconciled with the *Rowan* decision, and Justice Marshall's view can be made less vulnerable to counterexample, once it is realized that neither property nor free speech can be assigned a single weight that would apply invariably to all cases. Instead, the determinative feature that must be taken into account in resolving the disputes under consideration is that these are O-I disputes. The individuals are armed with an autonomy right to free speech, whereas the corporation's ownership is a utility right. One can therefore maintain that the autonomy considerations underlying individual speech outweigh in these cases the utilitarian interests that uphold the corporation's property rights, without thereby committing oneself to a similar protection of free speech when it collides with individual property.*

Indeed, it can be argued that in the *Rowan* case,[24] the relative weights of property and of free speech should be reversed compared to the shopping mall cases. In *Rowan*, a utility right to com-

*The conclusion may, however, differ in the case of an organization that protects individual autonomy rights, specifically in regard to those aspects of its property rights which are necessary for that purpose. As indicated above (see p. 74 *supra*), such derivative autonomy rights also carry the same kind of *extra* weight as the autonomy rights that they protect: that is, they have a similar resistance to conflicting utilitarian considerations. In resolving a conflict between such a derivative autonomy right and other autonomy rights, the relative weights of the competing rights, as well as the magnitude of the likely intrusions into them, should be considered. However, the judge may have a special responsibility to the individual litigants before him, so that their rights will still have a certain advantage over the organization's claim even when the latter is supported by a derivative autonomy right. For a discussion of this special judicial responsibility toward individual litigants, see pp. 145–50 *infra*.

mercial speech is asserted by various firms that are in the mail-order business, and it competes against an autonomy right to property of individual homeowners. Accordingly, the Court's unanimous decision in that case to uphold the property rights as against free speech comports with the present analysis, and would be compatible with a decision favoring speech in the shopping mall situations.

Remedy

Lastly, and from a practical point of view most importantly, the classification of a legal right as either an AR or a UR will significantly influence the choice of remedy. My general claim is that an autonomy right characteristically calls for specific enforcement rather than for a remedy by some substitute, such as monetary compensation. This applies not only to property, on which I will focus first, but also to other legal rights, such as contractual rights, to which I will turn later. The two arguments that support this view parallel the two aspects of autonomy—personhood and liberty—that underlie private property.

The aspect of personhood on which the first argument for specific enforcement draws is the idea of dignity. In a famous passage, Kant makes the following distinction between *dignity* and *price*.

In the kingdom of ends everything has either a *price* or a *dignity*. If it has a price, something else can be put in its place as an *equivalent*; if it is exalted above all price and so admits of no equivalent, then it has a dignity. . . . [M]orality, and humanity so far as it is capable of morality, is the only thing which has dignity. . . . *Autonomy* is . . . the ground of the dignity of human nature and of every rational nature.[25]

The argument from dignity simply points out that, as rights that embody and protect important aspects of personhood, ARs are infused with the special worth associated with the person, which is the unique, nonmarketable worth that is dignity. ARs issue, therefore, in specific claims that, if valid, should be satisfied, as far as possible, in kind, rather than be transmuted into a different medium in which things are fungible and priceable. Even in this abstract form, this argument resonates, I believe, with some widely shared moral intuitions. Most of us would probably feel a certain unease at the spectacle of parents who collect damages for a child killed in an accident. This sentiment may fade in less dramatic situations, but most would still agree, I think, that there is something demeaning in the common practice of assessing, for the purpose of tort damages, the monetary value of an amputated leg or a lost eye, treating in this way our bodily integrity as a marketable commodity. Our body, like our life (or that of our children), partakes of our dignity as persons and therefore resists pricing, which challenges its uniqueness and inviolability.

The view that "property is but the periphery of my person extended to things"[26] endows our property (or in any event, some parts of it) with the special worth that calls for specific enforcement. This, of course, does not deny our right to alienate our property for a price, if we so choose. But as long as we have not freely elected to do so, our property (or whatever part of it that is thought to fit the perspective under consideration) remains infused with our will and bound up, through it, with our moral personality. As such, it should not be forcefully priced away from us.

The traditional libertarian conception of property makes property also a prime example for the second argument for the specific enforcement of ARs: the argument from liberty. This argument draws on the view of autonomy rights as rights that define and protect a sphere in which individuals can exercise full discretion and sovereignty, free from any obligation to explain or justify their choices to other individuals or to the government. It is easy to see that such a conception of the role of autonomy rights is most inhospitable to substitutional remedies. The assessment by a court of the adequate monetary compensation for the violation of an autonomy right must itself involve the kind of intrusion into an individual's protected zone that ARs are meant to avert. In order to enable the court to assess damages, the individual claimant must publicly divulge the reasons for her interest in the object or performance under dispute and objectify its value to her by reference to some external uniform scale that permits monetization. This entire procedure frustrates the purpose of ARs, which is to spare the individual such forced exposure to public scrutiny of her reasons, values, and desires.[27]

Analogous considerations to those that apply to the protection of property in general also argue in favor of specific performance as the presumptive remedy in contracts.[28] Once again, the starting point is an interpretation of contractual rights as autonomy rights. A contemporary version of such a view has been recently elaborated by Charles Fried.[29] He contends that the binding force of contract is to be found in its being a *promise*, and he argues that the obligation to keep promises is, in turn, "grounded not in arguments of utility but in respect for individual autonomy and in trust."[30] Breaching a contract, like breaking a promise, is an expression of disrespect and involves the use (and abuse) of one person by another. According to Fried's view, expectation damages, divorced from considerations of benefit and reliance, "followed as a natural concomitant of the promise principle"[31]: expectation damages are simply meant to give the promisee what was promised him. It should be noted, however, that expectation damages succeed in so doing only when the promise was essentially to pay money or provide monetary gain. When the subject matter of the contract is a specific object or service, expectation damages are no longer equivalent to actual performance. And if such performance is still possible, the considerations previously discussed argue in favor of compelling it through the remedy of specific performance.

According to the suggested view, specific performance should not be considered merely a practical solution to the occasional difficulty of assessing the correct amount of damages, but should be viewed instead as expressing the principled refusal to engage in such assessment whenever the assessment can be avoided. It proceeds from a moral position diametrically opposed to the economist's fundamental assumption (used to buttress damages as the standard contract remedy) that "all goods are ultimately commensurable."[32] The argument from autonomy claims, instead, that once an object (or a service) has been promised, it becomes implicated in an individual's rightful claim to it, and thus ceases, subject only to that individual's will, to be an interchangeable, marketable commodity. Professor Kronman may thus be correct when he contends that "it is likely there are other things that would make [the buyer of a rare manuscript] just as happy as getting the manuscript for the contract price."[33] But according to the argument from autonomy, the point of viewing and honoring the transaction as a promise to be kept is precisely to avoid a coerced exposure of the buyer to an investigation of the constituents of his happiness which would be necessary in order to assess the correct compensatory substitute.

Our discussion of specific enforcement in general, and of specific performance in particular, has been so far entirely one-sided. As my first aim was to make the affirmative case for the specific enforcement of ARs, I have so far ignored the objections from utility that have been made to such remedy. I will take up these objections in a moment. But besides these "external" objections, specific enforcement may also be challenged by considerations internal to the paradigm of autonomy. We have been able to overlook them so far because we focused exclusively on the interests of one side to the legal relation: e.g., the promisee in the case of contract. As soon as we recall the other party, the promisor, the objections to specific performance (and, indeed, sometimes even to the weaker remedy of expectation damages) loom large. They are of two kinds. First, specific performance may in some cases unduly compromise an interest of the promisor, and that interest itself may sometimes be fairly characterized as an autonomy right. This, for example, would seem to be the case with respect to contracts for personal services. The specific performance of such a contract that involves compelling the promisor to work against his will is an unusually intrusive measure that carries the invidious connotations of "forced labor," even if that labor had been initially voluntarily promised.

The other challenge to specific performance may not squarely belong within the autonomy paradigm, but it proceeds on normative grounds which share, and indeed extend, its commitment to the uniqueness and particularity of the individual. I have in mind considerations such as love, pity, and compassion, which I have already associated with the paradigm of autonomy,[34] and which would frequently militate in the present context against extracting from the promisor the promised object, or even its full value. Take the case of the rare manuscript or of a unique painting. You sell me your much beloved Cezanne because you badly need the money. I have now a rightful claim to it. But prior to delivery you come unexpectedly into some money, so now you no longer wish to part with the painting. Shouldn't you be able to frustrate my demand for specific performance by successfully evoking Shylock's brutal imagery against me?

I don't mean this question to be rhetorical in the present context. It does in fact point to a lively controversy, probably even a deep cleavage, in contemporary contract theory. For the purposes of the present essay, I need not enter this fray. Instead, I want only to point out the limited contours of the controversy: the issue can arise only in an I-I relation, when the claim to specific performance rests on autonomy considerations whereas the objection to it is phrased in the language of love, pity, and compassion. The conflict is drained of all such dramatic heat when it occurs within an I-O or an O-O type of relation.[35]

Consider first an I-O relation, in which the painting I have purchased decorates the offices of a large corporation. Surely the corporation cannot evoke love and compassion on its own behalf as a way to avoid delivery of the painting. Nor can it successfully rely in such terms on the attachment that the particular manager who happens to occupy the office with the Cezanne must have to the painting. The manager's attachment is bereft of the proprietary relation to the painting which is an essential constituent of an individual owner's objection to specific performance under similar circumstances. Unlike the individual owner, the manager is not about to be coerced into surrendering the painting, because the painting is not and has never been his to surrender. His affection for the painting is no different in kind from my sentiment towards my favorite Cezannes at the Metropolitan Museum. Though their removal from public display would greatly disappoint me, this would hardly give rise to a legal claim on my part to their continued exhibition.*

The individual promisee's demand for specific performance against an organization is no more vulnerable to the other possible objection to that remedy that I have mentioned. Recall the case of personal services. If I contract with you that I will clean your house

---

*Of course, the manager's disaffection may bear on the decision whether to resort to specific performance, just as my disaffection (and that of the Metropolitan's officials) may bear on the question whether the Metropolitan Museum should be ordered by specific performance to surrender its much treasured Cezannes, had this been the issue. However, these disaffections bear on the respective decisions only as part of the general utilitarian considerations. They lack the preemptive force that an autonomy-based theory of property would assign to the coercive severing of a proprietary relationship between a particular individual and her prized object, a severing of the kind that occurs when specific performance pertains to an individually owned Cezanne. See also my discussion of the significance for the nature of adjudication of the particularity of the individual that is subjected to the court's decision (pp. 145–54 *infra*), and of the element of coercion (pp. 168–73 *infra*).

tomorrow, and tomorrow I regret it, you will be able to obtain a remedy of specific performance against me only on pain of violating my own autonomy claim against forced labor. But no similar obstacle will obstruct your insistence on specific performance if you contracted a company that provides janitorial service and it refuses to send someone over to do the cleaning.[36]

We may conclude that, as against an organization, an individual plaintiff's plea for specific performance is unlikely to encounter objections from competing autonomy considerations or from considerations of love and compassion which might defeat his plea if made against an individual defendant.

Consider now the opposite situation, in which the organization is the let-down promisee. The presumptive remedy here, it would seem, should be damages, not specific performance. The arguments from dignity and autonomy in favor of specific performance do not apply to the organization, while the individual defendant may still defeat the organization's plea for specific performance by relying on her autonomy (as in the case of a contract of employment with the organization) or by evoking the court's compassion for her predicament (having to part with her Cezanne).

Our discussion of specific performance has been confined so far to the paradigm of autonomy. However, the traditional utilitarian view, stated in economic terms, has favored damages over specific performance as the standard contract remedy. Damages are a more efficient remedy than specific performance, it has been argued, for three main reasons: they are easier (and therefore cheaper) to administer; they economize on transaction costs (because in most cases parties would settle on damages anyway); and finally, and most importantly, damages preserve the option, crucial within the economic theory of contract, of breaching the contract when performance would be inefficient. Even though these arguments have not gone unchallenged,[37] I will assume, arguendo, their validity. Still, they do not necessarily undermine the individual's claim to specific performance. The reasons parallel the arguments about the relative *weights* of ARs and URs. If we accept the view that in the case of a broken promise an individual has a valid claim, grounded in autonomy, not only to *some* remedy, but to the particular remedy of specific performance, his claim has a certain resistance to counter arguments from utility. Here as before, we lack a theory that would specify the trade-off rate between autonomy and utility. But given any serious commitment to autonomy, the mere showing (itself speculative and controversial) that *some* utility gains can be expected of a regime of damages compared to a regime of specific performance will not in itself suffice to defeat the autonomy considerations that support an individual's plea for specific performance.

We may also conclude that no similar competition between considerations of autonomy and utility takes place in the O-O context. If the traditional utilitarian position favoring damages as the more efficient remedy is to be believed, the resolution of the issue of remedy in this context is a simple one. This issue may in fact be getting more complicated, but only because of the opposition that the utilitarian supporters of damages have recently encountered within their own camp.

ORGANIZATIONAL FREEDOM OF SPEECH: THE ANATOMY OF A DERIVATIVE RIGHT

One of the most interesting chapters presently being written in American constitutional law is no doubt the one dealing with organizations' First Amendment rights. Few cases within this chapter have drawn so much attention and caused such a controversy as did the Supreme Court's decision in *First National Bank of Boston v. Bellotti.*[38] In a five to four decision, the Court extended to corporate political speech First Amendment protection, and subjected a Massachusetts statute that purported to limit corporate participation in state referenda to "the exacting scrutiny necessitated by a state-imposed restriction of freedom of speech."[39] My excuse for joining the already densely populated debate is that the issue of corporate freedom of speech is a particularly fascinating test case for some of the preceding theoretical points. Specifically, it offers a propitious occasion to watch a derivative autonomy right in actual operation. This excuse also implies a disclaimer. I am presently interested in corporate freedom of speech and in the *Bellotti* decision only insofar as they relate to the main theoretical theme of this chapter. This limited interest naturally narrows the focus of the following discussion and qualifies its conclusions.

An Analysis of Free Speech

As currently understood, freedom of speech is a remarkably complex right.[40] At the cost of some oversimplification, it can be illuminated by mapping it onto the analytical categories we have developed. First, freedom of speech is said to be supported by two sets of interests: those of the speaker, which I will call the "active" aspect of free speech; and those of the listener, to which I will refer as the "passive" aspect. Each of these sets of interests, both the active and the passive, gives rise to a compound right: both arguments of individual autonomy and of social utility have been deployed in support of the speakers' as well as of the listeners' interests, with the emphasis shifting depending on the context and kind of expression involved. Commercial speech comes closest to a pure UR, the arguments on both the active and the passive side mainly focusing on the importance of the free dissemination of commercial information to the effective operation of a free market system. Artistic expression is a stronghold of arguments from speakers' autonomy which underline the crucial importance of that form of expression for personal growth and self-fulfillment.

Arguments based on the listener's autonomy come into the fore in regard to political expression. These arguments emphasize the importance of the free availability and unlimited accessibility of information, ideas, and points of view for one's ability to form independent, informed, and intelligent judgments on public matters. In this respect, speech is singled out as peculiarly bound up with the idea of individual autonomy. Whereas a certain degree of satisfaction of other individual needs and interests can be seen as a necessary precondition of individuals' ability to lead an autonomous life, the continuous flow of uninhibited discursive activity is essential to the ceaseless formation and revision of one's independent judgments which are constitutive of the autonomous life itself. These considerations also suggest a right in the speaker not to be interrupted in her communications which is based on the concern for the potential listener's autonomy interests that I have just described. This speaker right would thus be a derivative autonomy right. A speaker's right may accordingly belong to one of four sub-categories that are summarized in Figure 1.

Each of these four sub-categories of freedom of speech raises

Based on considerations of: Based on concern for:	autonomy	utility
speaker	original autonomy right	original utility right
listener	derivative autonomy right	derivative utility right

Figure 1.   Speaker's Right to Freedom of Speech

different issues and calls for a separate investigation. But for present purposes, we need not concern ourselves with all four. The special weight that is normally assigned to freedom of speech must, within my normative scheme, be carried primarily by its autonomy justifications, both active and passive. Indeed, when a category of speech in which considerations of utility predominate on both the speaker's and the listener's side can be isolated (as in the case of commercial speech), it only qualifies for minimal, if any, consti- tutional protection.[41] We may focus, therefore, with no great loss, on the two autonomy rights speakers have: their own original right to self-expression, and their derivative right, based on the audience's autonomy interests in being able to listen to them. Since organizations are devoid of original autonomy rights in general and of a right to self-expression in particular, only the latter kind of right may apply to them.*

Corporate Free Speech as a Passive DAR

According to the preceding analysis, the main issue of corporate freedom of speech is reduced to the question of whether organizational, specifically corporate speech[†] is protected by a DAR based on the autonomy interests of potential listeners. Insofar as the *Bellotti* majority can be interpreted as posing the main question raised by the case in essentially these terms, and then answering it in the affirmative (and this indeed seems to me their position), their view comports with the present analysis. In this respect, I will argue, the Court's view is sounder than that of its critics. Two main kinds of criticisms have been made against the *Bellotti* decision. One has to do with the nature of corporate speech, and the other focuses on the rights of shareholders. Neither withstands close examination when looked at from the organizational perspective of the present book. However, the support that this perspective provides for the majority's position in *Bellotti* is only partial. As will soon become evident, the same perspective also helps identify an important flaw in the majority's reasoning, thereby undermining the majority's ultimate conclusion.

The first criticism of the Court's position in *Bellotti* is based on the denial that there really is such a thing as "corporate speech":

*In addition, organizations can have speech-related protections that are not in a strict sense speech rights—that is, rights to speak. Certain organizations may have, for example, an important function in protecting or facilitating individual expression; such a function may give rise to various *active* derivative autonomy rights— rights that derive from the (active) speaker right of the protected individuals. I briefly consider this possibility on pp. 112–13 *infra*.

†More precisely, this section deals exclusively with speech by business corporations, as does the *Bellotti* decision under consideration. My conclusions therefore do not necessarily apply to other corporations, notably to the press or other media corporations. The latter obviously raise some distinctive issues not present in the case of business corporations. For one thing, the press (and other media organizations) may be amenable to analysis in terms of *active* derivative autonomy rights of the kind mentioned in the preceding footnote, and discussed on pp. 112–13 *infra*. An examination of speech rights of the press is, however, beyond the scope of this discussion. Similarly, though the present discussion casts doubt on the soundness of the Supreme Court's decisions in *Abood v. Detroit Board of Education*, 431 U.S. 209 (1977), and in *Machinists v. Street*, 367 U.S. 740 (1961) (in which the Court held that the use by a trade union of its members' dues for political purposes violates nonconsenting members' First Amendment rights), the following arguments do not directly apply to that issue.

only individual human beings, this argument points out, can generate and communicate ideas. "Corporate speech" is accordingly seen as just a misleading way of describing the ideas of corporate managers combined with their decision to expend corporate resources for their dissemination.[42] This view considerably weakens, if it does not altogether undermine, the corporation's claim to freedom of speech. Recall that the corporation's claim is derivative from people's interest as the potential listeners to the corporation's communications. If, however, the messages transmitted by the corporation are always attributable to specific individuals, the suppression of the so-called "corporate speech" would result in no loss to the public in communicative content: the same ideas and information would remain in public circulation, with the additional advantage that their individual sources would be exposed rather than hidden behind a corporate veil.

Whereas the withdrawal of constitutional protection from corporate speech would result, according to this argument, in no loss of content, it might still be objected that there will be a considerable loss in amplitude. The communication by individual managers would not be supported and amplified by corporate resources, as it is when corporate speech is recognized and protected. But this objection is a weak one: if corporate speech is conceptualized as essentially reducible to the speech of the individual managers, it is no longer obvious that its amplification by corporate resources should be constitutionally protected.

The formula that, under certain circumstances, equates the expenditure of money to speech would not be of great help in the present case. Even in *Buckley v. Valeo*,[43] the source of that dubious equation, the Supreme Court distinguished limitations imposed on political *expenditures*, which it overruled, from limitations on political *contributions*, which it upheld. By so doing, the Court assigned to the equation of money to speech a rather minimal and essentially negative role. The Court relied on the equation only in order to deny that "the dependence of a communication on the expenditure of money operates itself to introduce a non-speech element or to reduce the exacting scrutiny required by the First Amendment."[44] This reasoning does not apply, according to the Court's opinion, to contributions, because "while contributions may result in political expression if spent by a candidate or an association to present views to the voters, the transformation of contributions into political debate involves speech by someone other than the contributor."[45] If the corporation is inherently incapable of speech, and the only speech emanating from it is that of its individual managers, then the use of corporate resources is rather like a contribution, whose purpose is to amplify someone else's speech and is itself devoid of any communicative element. As such, it does not deserve the kind of protection that the *Bellotti* Court extends to it. I find this argument against freedom of speech by business corporations attractive and its political implications welcome. It must be rejected nonetheless.

The conception of organization that has been presented in Part I supports the Court's repeated assertion that the source of the speech in question is the corporation itself. Speech, no less than cars or widgets, can be a corporate product. Like other organizational activities, speech may also be a global, nondistributive phenomenon, emanating from the corporation without being traceable or reducible to individual utterances. Indeed, given our emphasis in Chapter 2 on decisionmaking as an essential organizational property, speech is particularly likely to be such a nonreducible corporate phenomenon. Recall the centrality to decisionmaking of diverse and varied informational processes. The gathering, filtering, channeling, decoding, and combining of information by different components and actors result in statements with cognitive content (i.e., speech) which are at the same time distinctively and irreducibly organizational. The metaphor of the intelligent machine by which we described organizations is particularly apt at this point. There are many cognitive operations of great social importance that can be in effect carried out only by computers. By performing such operations, computers generate and store knowledge whose suppression may be as harmful to the public's listener interests as would be the suppression of any other form of speech.

The view of corporate speech as a global organizational phenomenon is also supported by the psychological mechanisms of loyalty and identification which we mentioned before. The common expression that someone assumed "the corporate point of view" conveys vividly the primacy of the background of views, values, and tacit understandings that are an essential part of the texture or culture of corporate life, and that individuals pick up and internalize as they enact their corporate role. In this way, even what seems to be the individual utterance of a single corporate manager may in fact be an utterance that was made "from the corporate point of view," embodying or expressing this distinctively corporate background of values and understandings. It is therefore both futile and fallacious to suggest that such speech can be extracted from the corporate context and to recommend that it be viewed instead as uttered by the manager in her "individual" capacity and on her own behalf. She may be neither inclined nor able to perform the same speech acts outside of her office hours (so to speak). Failure to recognize and protect that speech as made in the manager's official capacity, and thus as being irreducibly "corporate" in nature, would result in this particular message being lost to the interested public.

The second criticism of the *Bellotti* decision focuses on the relation between the corporation's speech and the rights of its shareholders. This criticism has a stronger and a weaker version. Neither withstands critical appraisal.

According to the stronger version, the protection of corporate speech (unless the speech is supported by a unanimity of shareholders) violates the dissenting shareholders' First Amendment rights: these shareholders are forced to contribute to the expression of views they do not hold. The argument fails because it greatly exaggerates the link between the shareholders and the large corporation. No one is likely to identify the views of any individual shareholder with the policies pursued by General Motors, whether or not those policies issue in speech. Just like customers, who sometimes express their displeasure at corporate policies by boycotting the corporation's products, shareholders too may wish to publicly express their dissent. But the notion that corporate policies or expressions violate in any way dissenting shareholders' freedom of speech any more than they violate such rights of disgruntled customers or employees completely overlooks the nature of the large modern corporation.

The weaker version of the argument fares no better, and for similar reasons. This version concedes the relative facility with which a minority shareholder can disassociate himself from offensive corporate speech through "exit." But it finds "the necessary compelling state interest" for imposing a requirement of share-holder unanimity as a condition for protecting corporate speech "in the need to protect individual stockholders against being forced to choose between contributing to political or social expressions with which they disagree or foregoing opportunities for profitable investment."[46]

So imagine a wealthy businessman in your small community, who is paying high interest on the money you and other local folks lend him. Unfortunately, he is also a known fascist, and he uses the money he loans (or the profit he makes on it) to publicly express his despicable political views. Does he thereby compromise *your* rights by forcing you "to choose between contributing to political or social expressions with which [you] disagree or foregoing opportunities for profitable investment"? The obvious negative answer applies, it seems to me, with equal force to the case of the shareholder and the large corporation. As soon as the shareholder is conceived as a mere investor, as the weaker version of the argument under consideration correctly portrays him, he is no longer entitled, as a matter of right, to investment opportunities free from any undesirable political ramifications.

These considerations lead to the conclusion that business corporations have a passive derivative autonomy right to speech, that is, a right derived from the autonomy interests of the public to listen to corporate communications, as I interpret the majority in *Bellotti* to hold. However, my analysis does not support the Court's decision to extend in this case full First Amendment protection to the corporate speech in question. The *Bellotti* decision fatally overlooks the important implications of the ground on which it founded the constitutional protection of corporate speech. Describing the corporation's right as a DAR helps identify those implications.

The point at which the present analysis departs from the Court's can be located with great precision. It is where the Court rejects an argument in favor of restricting corporate speech that is based on the concern that because of the wealth and power of corporations, "their views may drown out other points of view,"[47] and will thus undermine the interest "in sustaining the active role of the individual citizen in the electoral process."[48] In reply, the Court invokes the view it adopted in *Buckley v. Valeo*,[49] according to which "the concept that government may restrict the speech of some elements of our society in order to enhance the relative voice of others is wholly foreign to the First Amendment."[50] But notice that what would make this argument cogent is an assumption that those "elements of our society" whose speech may not thus be restricted have themselves an original autonomy right to speak.[51] If they do, then the Court's conclusion is sound: it is one of the central features of autonomy rights that they resist trade-offs. An individual's right to self-expression can no more be suppressed in the name of First Amendment concerns than it can be sacrificed to promote any other interests of other individuals.

This, however, is not the case in the *Bellotti* situation. Since the Court rightly refrained from ascribing to the corporation an active speech right, there is nothing to protect corporate speech against limitations whose purpose is to promote the listeners' First Amendment interests, from which the corporation's rights are themselves derived. We are witnessing here the critical difference, overlooked by the Court, between an original autonomy right to free speech and a derivative right. Both the difference and its legal implications should be spelled out in somewhat greater detail.

The relevant difference between a derivative and an original autonomy right is that the former is instrumental, whereas the latter is not. Within the limits set by its scope and weight, an original AR may not be compromised even for the sake of enhancing the enjoyment of a similar right in others: doing so would be an impermissible act of sacrificing one person to another. By contrast, the whole point of a derivative right is to safeguard or enhance the enjoyment of certain rights by others. A derivative right is therefore measured, as all instruments are, by its effectiveness: it can always be discarded in favor of better ways to attain the same goals.

The legal implications of the proposed characterization of the corporation's right as a DAR can be best stated in terms of the proper standard of review to which the challenged legislation that restricts corporate speech should be subjected. In striking down the statute under attack, the *Bellotti* Court relies on the strictest consti-tutional standard, asking whether the statute "can survive the ex-acting scrutiny necessitated by a state-imposed restriction of free-dom of speech."[52] Insisting that corporate speech is a DAR does not necessarily lead to a general relaxation of this standard and its replacement by a less exacting one. It calls instead for a more complex and discriminating approach that combines two different standards of review. In calibrating the adequate constitutional protection of a DAR, we should sharply distinguish between the "internal" and the "external" enemies of the right in question.

By external enemies I mean reasons provided by the government for restricting the rights that are based on the promotion of some interests and values other than those protected by the derivative right itself. A good example of such an external enemy in the present context is provided by Professor Brudney, when he suggests an economic reason for subjecting corporate political speech to a requirement of unanimous shareholder consent. He argues that "allowing capital to be raised on the condition that its contributors permit management to use it for political purposes may increase the cost of capital."[53] This argument (whether sound or not) clearly proposes to curtail speech on behalf of a different governmental interest, that is, an interest in the cost of capital. It is precisely such threats to the listener's interests that a derivative autonomy right to speech is meant to avert. If the listener's autonomy interests can be compromised by economic considerations at all, it is sensible to at least demand that they be "compelling" considerations, capable of satisfying the most exacting constitutional test.

No similar concerns are raised by a derivative right's "internal" enemies, by which I mean reasons for curtailing the right which appeal to the very same autonomy interests that the derivative right is meant to defend. Such is the aforementioned argument made by the government in *Bellotti*, when it points out the danger that because of the wealth and the size of corporations, "their views may drown out other points of view."[54] Indeed, describing such an argument for limiting corporate speech as an "enemy" may be using an altogether inappropriate metaphor. The proposed policy should better be viewed by the DAR in question as a friendly competitor rather than as a threatening enemy, that is to say, with slight suspicion rather than with outright hostility. After all, both the derivative speech right and its proposed curtailment by the state participate in the same enterprise and draw their normative strength from the same source, which is the individual listener's ability to form independent and informed judgments, based on the free access to an unlimited flow of information and ideas. These considerations suggest that when the government interest that supports the curtailment of a DAR belongs to the camp of internal enemies (or friendly competitors, if you like), it should be subjected to a less exacting standard of review: "intermediate" review or a "rational basis" standard would seem to suffice.

Given the notorious indeterminacy of these various standards of review, it is quite difficult to predict how any given piece of legislation would fare under the different standards. However, in light of the closeness of the vote in *Bellotti* and the majority's emphasis on the exacting standard it employed, relaxing that standard in the way indicated above may be expected to be quite consequential in shaping the constitutional status of corporate political speech.

Organizational Active DARs to Speak

Lest the disclaimer at the beginning of the preceding section be forgotten, let me remind the reader that my discussion of corporate speech does not purport to be an exhaustive treatment of this topic, let alone of the many other issues concerning speech by organizations. Yet there is one additional aspect concerning this broader area which I feel obliged to mention, both because its omission may cause a misunderstanding, and because it exemplifies yet another use that can be made in relation to organizational speech of the idea of derivative autonomy rights. In discussing corporate speech, I have interpreted the *Bellotti* decision as ascribing to the corporation a *passive* derivative right to speak—one based exclusively on the audience's interests. This focus on the passive right, appropriate with regard to business corporations, should not, however, be understood to preclude the possibility that organizations may also have *active* derivative autonomy rights that are based on the right to self-expression of their members or other individuals. An organization will have such an active derivative right insofar as it protects or enhances individuals' self-expression, and to the extent that the satisfaction of certain organizational claims is necessary to the performance of this function.[55]

A case such as *NAACP v. Alabama*[56] is amenable to analysis in these terms. The petitioner organization (The National Association for the Advancement of Colored People) objected to a compelled disclosure to the state of its membership lists. The Court acknowledges that such a compelled disclosure of their affiliation with the

NAACP would violate the members' First Amendment rights. By securing their anonymity, the association protected the members' freedom of expression. "The association," the Court declared, "is but the medium through which its individual members seek to make more effective the expression of their own views."[57] In these circumstances, it seems to me eminently plausible to maintain that the organization in question has a derivative First Amendment right to the secrecy of its relevant records based on the right to self-expression of its members. In addition to implying some general guidelines, which I will not repeat, for determining the scope and weight of the organizational claim, this view of the matter has also the advantage of avoiding problems of standing which arise when the organization is merely seen as *invoking* the rights of its members rather than asserting a derivative right of its own.[58]

THE LEGAL USE OF OCKHAM'S RAZOR

Who's an Organization?

As you may recall, one of H. L. A. Hart's objections (discussed in Chapter 2) to posing questions such as "what is an organization?" to guide normative inquiry was based on his belief that the multiplicity and divergence of conditions under which we apply to collectivities unifying terms are bound to defy any effort to comprehend those conditions within a single definition of "the organization."[59] My attempt to derive from organization theory a unified conception of the organization, described in terms of the organizational parameters discussed in Chapter 2, was meant to demonstrate the feasibility and the fruitfulness of the enterprise that Hart ruled out. But the point that I have thus tried to make should not be overstated. Though the conception of organization proposed here does, I believe, apply to a large and significantly uniform group of entities, it is not to be supposed that the universe, even the legal universe, neatly divides between individuals, on the one side, and organizations that clearly fit my description, on the other. There are obviously many kinds of entities that do not fit into this dichotomy. In focusing on entities such as the family and the community, for example, we are likely to be faced with quite different epistemological and normative issues than those concerning large bureaucratic organizations.[60] Still, the present theory, though by no means applicable for all purposes to all collectivities, can nonetheless contribute to the legal consideration of certain matters pertaining to collectivities that do not have all the organizational characteristics that I have listed.

The picture of the legal universe which permits such an extension of the present theory is unidimensional. It consists of a continuum between two poles—one pole occupied by individuals and the other by organizations that clearly possess the various organizational features that I have listed. The entities that mark the two opposing poles can serve as paradigm cases for the normative analysis of the many other collective entities that lie on the continuum between them. These other collectivities share to a varying degree some or all of the essential features that define the paradigmatic organizations that occupy the organizational pole: they may be more or less formal, or complex, or permanent, etc. Some collectivities will accordingly be sufficiently "transparent" (rather than opaque), "permeable," and otherwise lacking in distinctive organizational features so as to justify extending to them, in a given normative context, the same treatment as befits the individuals of which they are composed. The application of the present theory thus involves an operation that we have so far ignored. It is the determination that must be made with respect to the particular collective entity under consideration whether for the purpose at hand it is closer to the organizational pole or to the individual pole.

This additional operation can be illustrated and clarified by examining the Supreme Court's handling of various organizations' right against self-incrimination. As we shall presently see, in those cases the Court essentially shares the bipolar picture of the legal landscape that I have just described, and it adopts a mode of legal analysis that depends on locating specific entities on a continuum between individuals and formal organizations. However, the Court's use of this method in the context of the privilege against self-incrimination suffers, as the following examination will reveal, from certain ambiguities and inadequacies, which an improved theoretical understanding helps uncover and avert.

The privilege against self-incrimination is commonly seen as rooted in considerations of human dignity and seems to qualify easily as an autonomy right.[61] In its famous decision in *Hale v.*

Henkel,[62] the Supreme Court held that because of its strictly personal nature, the right does not apply to corporations. Later, in *U.S. v. White*,[63] the Court faced the question whether other collective entities, specifically trade unions, are protected by the privilege. In addressing this issue, the Court explicitly adopted an organizational approach. The test that the Court enunciated for determining the applicability of the privilege against self-incrimination is "whether one can fairly say under all the circumstances that a particular type of organization has a character so impersonal in the scope of its membership and activities that it cannot be said to embody or represent the purely private or personal interests of its constituents, but rather to embody their common or group interests only."[64] In deciding that trade unions easily meet this test and are not therefore entitled to the privilege, the Court relies not only on trade unions' separate legal personality but also on organizational variables such as structure, function, permanence, and size.[65]

But whereas *White* dealt with entities firmly located on the organizational pole, in *Bellis v. U.S.*[66] the Court faced an entity that inhabits the continuum. The Court had to decide whether a three-member partnership should be assimilated for the purpose at hand to the entities on the organizational pole, and be deprived of the privilege against self-incrimination (as the majority in fact held), or whether such a partnership should be identified for this purpose with its individual members, recognizing, as did Justice Douglas in dissent, that "this small three-man firm had no real existence apart from the three individual attorneys."[67] A *bona fide* application of the organizational approach to the partnership under consideration must lead, I believe, to Justice Douglas's conclusion. This three-member legal firm ranks so low on organizational dimensions such as complexity, formality, and permanence, and is therefore so permeable and transparent, that only considerable hostility to the privilege against self-incrimination could lead to the assimilation for the purpose at hand of this firm to an organization.[68]

It must also be observed that the initial decision in *Hale* to deny all corporations the privilege against self-incrimination does not withstand criticism either, nor does it comport with the organizational test that has been enunciated in *White* and was misapplied in *Bellis*. "Corporation" is a legal, not a sociological category that ranges over vastly different organizational realities. If the organizational test correctly measures the applicability to an entity of an autonomy right (as I believe it does), then mere legal form cannot be conclusive in the matter.[69] The records of a corporation sole or a closely held corporation may be as "personal" in all relevant respects as are the business records of an individual.[70] Whether or not the privilege against self-incrimination should extend to the latter is not our present concern. But whichever way this question is resolved, the answer must equally apply to the corporation sole or to the small, family owned, incorporated business.

Be this as it may, the Supreme Court's general approach in this area makes self-incrimination decisions into a singularly clear judicial example of the vision of the legal universe as a continuum between individuals and organizations; and of the normative significance of locating specific entities on this continuum. Despite its own inconsistency in the matter, the Court's recognition that movement along this continuum should be propelled by organizational considerations, of which legal form is just one, is particularly noteworthy.

A Typology of Organizations

The self-incrimination cases raise and illustrate some of the problems involved in applying the present theory to specific organizations. The picture of the continuum that I have used was meant to convey some of those difficulties and at the same time to outline a general approach to their resolution. On other occasions, however, the difficulties faced by the law are of an opposite kind: they have to do with the fact that the law must often (as in the case of legislation) address broad categories rather than specific cases. Indeed, even courts that do typically consider specific cases must, for reasons primarily related to the scarcity of judicial resources, resort to rough generalizations and approximations. I will accordingly conclude this section by suggesting a simplifying device, in the form of a normative typology of organizations, that may facilitate the application of the present theory to organizations in situations where a more general approach is called for.

It is clear that some types of organizations are more likely than others to validly support their claims by derivative autonomy rights, depending on whether or not their goals include, as a major component, the protection of individual rights. This suggests a crude and preliminary classification of organizations into *utilitarian organizations,*[71] that is, organizations that do not have the protection of individual autonomy rights as one of their important goals, and *protective organizations* that do have such a goal. Business corporations would seem to provide an example of the former category,* whereas trade unions can be plausibly said to belong to the latter group. The guidance that this typology offers to the law is based on the view that the treatment of protective organizations should reflect the likelihood that their claims may be backed by DARs, whereas the treatment of utilitarian organizations should be typically concerned only with their URs. This simplifying assumption may be particularly helpful for general legal decisions (e.g., statutes), dealing with entire populations of organizations. Thus, for example, whether a statute deals predominantly with a population of utilitarian or protective organizations may determine whether it should be promulgated and interpreted with greater emphasis on utility or autonomy considerations. I will return to this typology in Chapter 9 and suggest its potential usefulness in another context: guiding judicial review of governmental action.

CONCLUSION: THE PARTIAL DISENGAGEMENT OF AUTONOMY AND UTILITY

To conclude this discussion of organizational legal rights, I want to draw attention to a general implication it has for the relationship between the two normative paradigms—autonomy and utility.

That relationship is an inherently unhappy one. The opposition between the two paradigms is manifest in the very description of autonomy rights as anti-utilitarian, and in the concomitant insistence of the proponents of those rights that the point of recognizing them is to preclude at least some utilitarian considerations from certain spheres of life. This conception of autonomy rights, to-

---

*But such classification is only of presumptive value. As the discussion of corporate freedom of speech indicates, the classification of an organization as a utilitarian organization does not altogether preclude the possibility of some derivative autonomy rights.

gether with its underlying ideals of the uniqueness and inviolability of the person, directly lead to the tension that is commonly understood to exist between the two philosophical orientations and their respective legal emanations. As put by Professor Fletcher: "The courts face the choice. Should they surrender the individual to the demands of maximizing utility? Or should they continue to protect individual interests in the face of community needs?"[72] This view of the relationship between the two paradigms is basically that of a zero-sum game: the law is constantly confronted with trade-offs between the welfare of society as a whole and the autonomy of particular individuals. The pursuit of social utility involves the occasional violation of individual autonomy. The protection of individual autonomy takes its toll in terms of a sacrifice of some social welfare. In the absence of a generally acceptable method for reconciling social utility and individual autonomy, every legal resolution of the dilemma is liable to be attacked as either failing to take individuals seriously and to grant them the treatment of respect they deserve, or as being overly deferential to individual interests at an excessive cost to society as a whole.

Attention to the distinctive normative status of organizations carries the promise of some relaxation of this tension. The point is simply that if the preceding arguments that limit the applicability of autonomy concerns to organizations are sound, broad areas of organizational activity are of only marginal interest to the advocate of individual autonomy. In these areas, the legal treatment of organizations may be determined by considerations of utility, uninhibited by the moral constraints imposed by the ideal of individual autonomy. While it offers no lasting peace between utility and autonomy, the organizational perspective does suggest in this way the possibility of partial disengagement between them, for their mutual benefit.

The advantage gained in this way by the utilitarian is obvious. He is given in certain areas nearly exclusive authority over the legal treatment of organizations, immune to the usual challenges from the advocates of individual autonomy. The autonomy advocate benefits from the partial disengagement too. Pointing out the limited reach of some of her claims is likely to increase their appeal. The force of the utilitarian's charge that autonomy-inspired moral self-indulgence involves exorbitant social costs bears an inverse relation to the size of the domain within which autonomy claims are made. Extracting from that domain certain areas of organizational activity is bound, therefore, to measurably weaken the opposition to the protection of autonomy rights, especially given the centrality of organizations in many spheres of social life. So whereas greater vigilance in the protection of individual rights may be called for in the organizational society, the preceding considerations suggest that the protection may be attained at a somewhat lesser toll in terms of aggregate social welfare than may be commonly expected.

Part III

Organizations and the Theory of Adjudication

Chapter VI

The Expanding Reach of Judicial Decisions

The general conclusion concerning substantive legal rights which we reached and illustrated in Part II also applies to the law's institutional arrangements. In both cases, the presence of organizations splits what has hitherto been considered a normatively uniform state of affairs. Legal institutions cannot remain impervious to organizational realities any more than legal rights and doctrines can, and they too must accommodate the different entities, and hence varied kinds of interactions to which they apply. In this part of the book, I demonstrate this general claim by discussing what is commonly considered the central legal institution—that is, adjudication. As it is routinely faced with large-scale organizations, adjudication undergoes fundamental changes. An examination of those changes from the organizational perspective that has been developed in the preceding chapters will cast, I hope, some new light on a number of important controversies in the theory of adjudication.

TWO MODELS OF ADJUDICATION

Our discussion of adjudication is greatly facilitated by a relatively recent development in the theoretical treatment of this institution—namely, the construction by several writers of two opposing models of litigation.[1] The articulation of two models both clarifies and challenges the previous, largely tacit and seemingly nonproblematic conception of that institution.[2] It clarifies that conception by forcing into the open its particular assumptions and its specific features; it challenges it to the extent that each of the two models succeeds in presenting a plausible conception composed of different assumptions and features. Although the various pairs of models that have been proposed do not wholly coincide, they evince sufficient uniformity to warrant a view of them as representing a single dichotomy between two general visions of the nature of adjudication. I will call these two visions the *arbitration model*[3] and the *regulation model*,[4] and treat them as abstractions from, or summations of, a number of such dichotomies.

The various features of the two models are all related to a radical difference in the main function they respectively assign to the judicial process. According to the arbitration model, "the lawsuit is a vehicle for settling disputes between private parties about private rights"[5]; whereas, according to the regulation model, "not the resolution of the immediate dispute but its impact on the future conduct of others is the heart of the matter."[6] These opposing assignments of function directly imply some contrasting properties of adjudication which it will be helpful to spell out.

To do so, let me first distinguish two dimensions along which judicial decisions as respectively depicted in the two models can be differentiated: a dimension of *time* and a dimension of *persons*. Along the "time" axis, the arbitration model describes adjudication as backward looking: it focuses on a transaction between the parties which has already taken place. The point of the process is to remedy something that went wrong in that transaction. In this sense, it can be said that adjudication has to do with the past.[7] By contrast, the regulation model describes adjudication as forward looking: its main point is to shape the form of future transactions and interactions.[8]

Along the "persons" axis, proponents of the arbitration model emphasize the exclusive focus of adjudication on the parties to the litigation.[9] The regulation model, by contrast, admits of no such predominance of the particular litigants: other people are likely to be affected by the decision as well, and their interests (welfare, etc.) are the judge's legitimate concern as much as those of the litigants.[10] The arbitration model may accordingly be characterized as a conception of adjudication which focuses on the past and on the parties, whereas the regulation model focuses on the future and on everyone affected.

This mapping of the two models along the two dimensions yields an immediate return: it readily discloses, as Figure 2 helps to

persons dimension		
time dimension	parties	everyone affected
past	arbitration model (1)	(2)
future	(3)	regulation model (4)

Figure 2.   Models of Adjudication

demonstrate, that the two models of adjudication current in the literature are not exhaustive.

This figure draws attention to the possible significance of the empty boxes. Box 2 raises the problem of adjudication which is committed to the settlement of a particular dispute, but which inescapably implicates the interests of nonparties as well as those of the parties; box 3 indicates a form of adjudication whose main point is to shape the future conduct of the particular parties. I will later show that these two intermediate states are of special interest in the context of organizational litigation.[11]

Another distinction I want to draw is between the *effects* of a judicial decision and its *concerns*. The term *effects* is self-explanatory. By *concerns* I mean the likely effects that are taken into consideration by the judge and thus serve as grounds for the decision.

The arbitration model can accordingly be understood to claim that the judge's concerns primarily comprise the effects of the decision on the parties before him. The regulation model implies no such limitation, suggesting instead that judges concern themselves with all the significant effects that their decision is likely to have.

THE RELATIONSHIP BETWEEN THE MODELS

In talking about the two models, I have so far maintained a certain ambiguity, common in legal theory, between their descriptive and normative claims. Indeed, the models are variably used both as descriptions of adjudication and as recommendations of what it should be like.[12] They give rise, therefore, to disputes concerning both their respective descriptive adequacy and the soundness of their normative recommendations. On the descriptive side, one finds the claim that both the arbitration model and the regulation model are correct, insofar as they describe two historical stages in the evolution of the central role of adjudication: we are witnessing, it is sometimes suggested (more or less explicitly), an historical transition from a judicial preoccupation with the resolution of the particular dispute, adequately depicted by the arbitration model, to a concern with setting social policy, and with shaping future patterns of conduct aimed at some social goals, as described by the regulation model.[13] Others deny that any such transformation is taking place. This denial, however, rests on two conflicting grounds. Some maintain that adjudication is now, as always, primarily committed to the just resolution of particular disputes.[14] Others, on the contrary, claim that the arbitration model was never true to the real mission of the courts, and that something or other like the regulation model can better capture the historical as well as the contemporary truth about adjudication.[15]

The agreement on the normative front is not greater. Some writers insist that the arbitration model contains features intrinsic to the judicial process[16] and argue that this model should serve to guide judges in the execution of their role.[17] The regulation model commands no less ardent normative support from other writers.[18] Some of them view the arbitration model as a mere pretence, hiding by misleading rhetoric the social policymaking in fact engaged in by judges. If nothing else, adopting the regulation model will cure the hypocrisy that the arbitration model nurtures.[19] Others view the arbitration model as a set of theoretical shackles unduly inhibiting judges from engaging in the important tasks of "social engineer- ing"[20] or "the articulation of our public values"[21] that lie ahead.

Finally, there is a view of the relationship between the two models which merges the descriptive and the normative. This view does not conceive of the models as trying to depict different histor- ical realities, nor does it consider them to posit competing, mutu- ally exclusive ideals. Rather, this latter view amounts to the propo- sition that the two models are, both in theory and in fact, inexorably linked in every institutionalized mode of adjudication. Far from being descriptive or normative alternatives, the two mod- els are to be understood as complementary, representing adjudi- cation as a Janus-faced institution. In conjunction, the two models reflect a view of the judicial process as ridden with tension.[22] A clear exponent of this last perspective on the relationship between the two models is Professor Martin Shapiro, who maintains that "judging inevitably involves lawmaking and social control as well as conflict resolution,"[23] and that "judicial lawmaking necessarily creates a fundamental tension between courts and their basic social logic."[24]

All these conceptions of the relationship between the two mod- els, whether that of succession, competition, or tension, have one feature in common. They all conceive of adjudication as essentially a single, uniform institution, amenable to adequate portrayal or guidance by means of a single (albeit sometimes a compound) model. In contrast to all these conceptions, I will advocate a view of adjudication as a more heterogeneous institution, assuming dif- ferent forms and discharging different functions in various con- texts. Instead of succession, competition, or tension, this view de- picts the relationship between the two models as one of division of labor. While some elements of both models can probably always be discerned in all forms of adjudication (a fact emphasized and pos- sibly exaggerated by the "inherent tension" view), we can also expect, according to this alternative position, that under different conditions one model or the other will predominate. Adjudication can contemporaneously both resemble the arbitration model when dealing with some issues, and assume a more regulatory mode when dealing with others.

My argument is that such division of labor does indeed make good sense in the organizational society.[25] The rise and increasing prominence of the regulatory model is in part related, I want to suggest, to the organizational transformation of society. The view of litigation conveyed by the arbitration model as essentially a self-contained private matter, involving exclusively the rights and interests of the contending parties, loses in plausibility the more legal transactions, and hence litigation, involve large organizations.[26] Seen in this way, the regulation model does not replace the arbitration model, nor is it locked with it in deadly competition. Instead, the regulation model offers a perception of the judicial role and a description of judicial decisionmaking which are peculiarly suited to organizational adjudication, whereas the arbitration model can more successfully describe and commend a style of decisionmaking befitting litigation among individuals.[27]

The argument that links the regulation model to organizational litigants and the arbitration model to individuals has two parts. In the remainder of this chapter, I will examine a number of ways in which organizations enhance the effects of judicial decisions both along the time dimension and along the persons dimension. These enhanced effects do not, strictly speaking, contradict occasional proclamations of judges that their concerns are predominantly limited to the fair resolution of the particular dispute.[28] Yet it seems sensible to expect that unless there are some very good reasons to the contrary, concerns and effects should by and large coincide: that a decisionmaker should strive to take account of at least the major likely effects of the decision. The more judicial decisions tend to have effects beyond the resolution of the particular dispute, the more wary one is likely to be of believing or recommending that judges systematically ignore or downplay those other effects.[29] If this hypothesis is correct, then a belief in the descriptive or normative adequacy of the arbitration model betrays a tacit assumption that the effects of adjudication do not, in fact, extend much beyond the particular dispute and the particular parties.[30] By contrast, the further the effects of a decision extend beyond the particular dispute, the more likely they are to force themselves on the judge as (tacit or explicit) concerns—that is, as grounds for the decision. Since organizations augment the social ramifications of judicial decisions, they incline the judge toward the regulatory mode.

However, this part of my argument creates only a *prima facie* case in support of the proposed link between organizational litigants and the regulation model. This is so because the hypothesis about the desirable overlap between effects and concerns on which this argument rests has been qualified by the absence of strong reasons to the contrary. But arguments made in favor of the arbitration style in adjudication do suggest such reasons that should move the judge to adopt a relatively narrow perspective, focusing predominantly on the past transaction and the particular parties. In the next chapter, I examine some such arguments and attempt to demonstrate that their force depends on an individualistic conception of adjudication, that is, on a view of litigation as involving individuals only. The strictures on judicial decisionmaking advocated by the arbitration model, I will argue, do not apply with similar force to organizational litigants. In conjunction, the two parts of my argument suggest some good reasons for the judge to lean toward the regulation model in the case of organizational litigants, even as he adheres to the arbitration model when adjudicating individual disputes.[31]

ORGANIZATIONS AND THE EFFECTS
OF JUDICIAL DECISIONS

It is quite obvious that even if the judicial decision is oriented solely to the particular parties and their dispute, its effects are bound to extend in both directions indicated by the dimensions of time and persons explained above. First, the particular decision reached is likely to affect parties other than the litigants. The imprisonment of the accused in a criminal trial may have a grave significance for his family but cheer up his deadly enemies. A decision awarding an exorbitant sum of damages in a tort case will often impoverish not only the defendant but her creditors too, and send both the successful plaintiff and her spouse on a round-the-world tour.

Other consequences that normally flow from a judicial decision have to do with the decision's impact on future behavior. In general, given that any judicial decision is some indication of the way courts are going to decide in similar situations in the future, the particular decision becomes part of the predictive data on which people are going to rely in shaping their transactions so as to avoid or bring about similar decisions. Two kinds of such future effects can be distinguished: the decision's effects on the future conduct of the parties themselves, and its effects on the conduct of other people who come to know of it. Since all three kinds of effects that we have listed are, from the point of view of the arbitration model, unintended side effects, I will call them, following the analogous economic usage, judicial externalities. Notice that the three kinds of externalities which I have distinguished correspond to boxes 2–4 in Figure 2: the direct effects that the resolution of the dispute has on nonparties correspond to box 2; future effects of the judicial decision on the parties themselves correspond to box 3; whereas the future effects on nonparties (in addition to the parties) belong in box 4. I will now try to show that each of these externalities is likely to increase in the organizational society and in relation to organizational litigants.

Box 2: Effects on Nonparties

Beginning with box 2, it is hard in general to think of any judicial decisions that would have absolutely no indirect effects on nonparties. Only if the litigants live on separate, otherwise uninhabited islands, and thus carry the fortune or misfortune inflicted upon them by the judicial decision to their respective isolated places of abode, will the effects of the judicial decision go no further than the immediate parties involved. However, the more our conception of society resembles this picture of individual isolation, the fewer judicial externalities we would expect. Conversely, the farther away from the archipelago of isolated islands we travel, and the more interdependent society as we conceive it becomes, the more judicial externalities we would expect. However, the picture of a society composed of isolated individuals, each one inhabiting his or her own island, recalls the familiar atomistic imagery characteristic of the liberal philosophical and legal tradition. By contrast, a high degree of interdependence is a salient feature in descriptions of the organizational society, particularly those descriptions that invoke the systems imagery to describe the interconnections among organizations. A decision concerning an organization is accordingly more likely than one pertaining to an individual to reverberate through the system, affecting in various ways other organizations and, through them, multitudes of individuals.

A second factor in the dramatic increase in judicial externalities caused by organizational litigants is simply the result of the large scale of the organization's operations and transactions, and hence the likely large magnitude of the subject matter of litigation. It is very much the point of many organizations' existence that they can bring to bear large, combined resources (not usually available to single individuals) on large-scale and widely coordinated projects (not feasible for individuals). The sheer magnitude of the resources sometimes at stake in organizational litigation ensures that the judicial decision will have allocational and distributive ramifications ranging over many individuals not present or represented in court.

Finally, and most importantly, the very admission into court of organizations seen as legal entities creates a rift between the nominal parties to litigation and the individuals whose interests ultimately underlie in one way or another the organization's claim and justify its legal recognition. Viewed as a coalition, the organization represents the diverse interests of different groups of individuals. These interests will often (though not always) be significantly affected in various ways by the judicial decision aimed at the organization. Even a judge who habitually purports to focus only on the parties before her must realize that when those parties are organizations her decision will affect many individuals who populate the area behind the "corporate veil" but do not participate in the proceedings, and that the soundness of the decision must ultimately be measured by those effects.

As a result of these three factors, litigation involving large organizations will often fit the model depicted in box 2: the resolution of the particular dispute will have relatively far-reaching consequences for many individuals (possibly for society as a whole) who are not litigants. To focus in such cases on the "parties," as the arbitration model requires, may sometimes prove impossible. But more frequently, it will just seem foolish. The question of how to resolve fairly a dispute between two parties arising out of a past transaction can easily be transformed in this way into a complex computation of the likely effects of different possible resolutions on the conflicting interests of numerous individuals not present in court.

Box 3: Future Effects and the Structural Injunction

Other factors push organizational litigation toward the model described in box 3, which emphasizes the impact of the judicial decision on the future conduct of the particular parties. The first factor that has this effect is the routine and recurrent nature of organizational operations. Like the machine to which it has been likened, the organization performs a recurrent set of operations in the execution of a function or the pursuit of a goal. Consequently, a particular transaction that leads to litigation is often one of a series of similar transactions in which the organization will be involved in the future. Thus, the seemingly backward-looking resolution of the particular dispute is likely to shape those future transactions, more so than in the standard case of the individual litigant.

The likelihood that the judicial decision will indeed be brought to bear in the future on similar transactions is increased by another organizational property, that is, *planning*. Naturally, if behavior (either individual or organizational) were always spontaneous, without any prior consideration or deliberation, consequences, including legal consequences, would not be taken into consideration as determinants of action. It is only to the extent that conduct contains an element of planning that the judicial externalities we are now considering may occur. While one could easily overstate the matter, planning is, generally speaking, both a virtue and a standard of organizational activity, whereas spontaneity is praised and practiced more often where individual humans are concerned. Organizations, which typically engage in relatively thorough formal and long-range planning, are more likely to be guided by the prospect of future judicial decisions than are individuals, whose calculating rationality may more often give way to spontaneity and caprice as important and acceptable predicates of action.

Permanence is another organizational property we have mentioned which increases the future effects on the litigating parties which a judicial decision is likely to have. An organization's existence is indefinite in time, and so the organization may carry the marks of a judicial decision indefinitely into the future.

The final, and in a way the most important, organizational feature responsible for increased future judicial externalities is what I referred to in Chapter 2 as the manipulable structure of organizations. The term conveys the idea that organizations are deliberately structured entities, and that this structure is always amenable to deliberate modification. Forming an organization, just like signing a contract or constructing a machine, comprises an element of "presentation"[32]: it is the creation in the present of a structure that will work itself out in the future in a more or less predictable and specified manner. As a result, a decision concerning the organization which brings about (whether intentionally or not) a change in its internal structure is very likely to have lasting effects on the organization's future performance.

These factors, especially the one last mentioned, create for the judge a powerful opportunity (and temptation) to form his present decision in a way that will in fact have lasting and hopefully desirable effects on the future conduct of the organization. The *structural injunction* is the form in which the judiciary has responded to this opportunity (or succumbed to this temptation). It is a relatively new and highly controversial form of remedy, in which the judge fashions, by means of an injunction (or decree), some changes in the internal structure of an organization, changes that are meant to avert in the future the kind of grievances that the organization has allegedly brought about and that led to the litigation. Since the structural injunction is the most typical and salient feature of organizational adjudication that exemplifies the model described in box 3, a further comment on it is in place here.

Commentators tend to present the structural injunction as a departure from the traditional judicial role of providing a present remedy to a past grievance. Instead, the structural injunction is said to involve the court necessarily in a prolonged and constant involvement wih a process of shaping the future.[33] However, this need not be the case. The main attraction of the structural injunction, at least in the strict sense of this term, resides precisely in the fact that the judge does not have to be involved in a constant process of reshaping the future when she issues such an injunction. Instead, her activity (decision) can be limited to the present: it can be an essentially onetime operation, which brings about a present change in the structure of the organization. It is, however, of the essence of structure that it works itself out by shaping future events. Not the judge, nor the decree, both of which operate in the present, but the structural change in the organization brought about by the decree carries the effects of the judicial decision a long way into the future.

Of course, this description of the nature of the structural injunction is an idealization. The "present" is a dubious concept of indefinite duration, and thus it sometimes may take a longer "present" to tinker with the structure of the organization than that associated with more traditional forms of legal remedy. Nevertheless, the realization that in the case of the structural injunction the judge can bring about a particular change, here and now, is essential to its proper understanding. It is by means of the organization's manipulable structure as well as the other organizational properties that I have listed that the effects of this decision are carried into the future.[34]

Box 4: The Regulation Model

Moving finally to box 4, which describes the effects of the judicial decision on the future conduct of nonparties as well as the parties, we will add only one factor to those already enumerated. It is quite simply the knowledge by nonparties of the judicial decision. Obviously, if the decision is unknown to anyone but the parties involved, it will not have the further consequence of influencing nonparties' future behavior. It is equally clear that judicial decisions are seldom if ever secret, and thus are virtually always bound to have *some* future impact on nonparties. Still, for two reasons, it seems reasonable to believe that the dissemination of knowledge of judicial decisions is positively correlated with the rise of large organizations.

The first reason has to do with the different picture of a society composed of individuals compared with a society composed of large organizations. The large number and relative isolation of the individuals in the individualistic society seem to require a very elaborate communications system to inform each individual about court decisions.[35] In the organizational society, by contrast, there is a relatively small number of large interdependent units, which makes the dissemination of information in general, and of court decisions in particular, easier, and therefore more likely.

The second reason has to do with a difference between the entities themselves. Organizations are much more likely than individuals to command the time and resources needed in order to learn in advance of their actions about potentially relevant judicial decisions. Unlike individuals, organizations are often equipped with specialized "sensory mechanisms" in the form of permanent legal staffs, whose role is to gather pertinent legal information and bring it to bear on the organization's activity. The point is not only that legal advice will be relatively less costly for most organizations than for most individuals (though that may also be true) but, more importantly, that in the case of many organizations legal advice is institutionalized. Thus, the legal point of view is likely to be represented with greater regularity and permanence in the organization's decisionmaking process than it is in the case of most individual actors.*

CONCLUSION

The relationship between organizations and the nature of adjudication can be summarized as follows. We have characterized modes of adjudication in terms of two dimensions along which they can be distinguished: a dimension of *persons* (litigants and nonlitigants) and a dimension of *time* (past and future). The organization is a peculiar entity as far as these two dimensions are concerned. As far as the dimension of persons is concerned, the organization is a mode of *unification*. It presents to the court the semblance of unity, of a single litigant, while at the same time it consists of a plurality of individuals and interests, not nominally present in court. As far as the dimension of time is concerned, the organization is a mode of *presentation*: it compresses a diachronic sequence of events into a synchronic structure. On account of both these features, a decision that is directed to the organization and in the present is likely to affect many individuals and shape the future. In terms of Figure 2, it can therefore be concluded that the very nature of organizations as litigants transforms the judicial process, forcing it to move from box 1, describing the arbitration model, into boxes 2 and 3, toward the form of adjudication described in box 4 as the regulation model. This movement, I will now argue, is not seriously inhibited by the normative considerations that underlie and support the strictures imposed by the arbitration model on judicial decisionmaking. Consequently, in the organizational setting the judicial decision may be informed by concerns that are (roughly speaking) coextensive with the decision's expanded effects.

*It should be emphasized that the arguments in this section do not imply that organizations are in general more amenable to legal control than are individuals. Whether or not this is the case depends on many factors not examined here. That organizations augment the effects of judicial decisions does not mean that those effects would be necessarily the ones desired by the legal decisionmaker.

Chapter VII

The Form of Organizational
Adjudication

INTRODUCTION

The very presence of organizations in court as litigants generates, we have seen, pressures on the judicial process which cause it to drift from the mode of *arbitration* toward the mode of *regulation*. In this chapter, I will suggest some arguments why these pressures should not be resisted. More precisely, my argument is that *regulation* is a more suitable (or less objectionable) form of adjudication in dealing with organizations than with individuals, in that some of the main arguments in support of various features of the arbitration model presuppose individual litigants, and do not apply to organizations. My strategy will consist, in the main, in linking the two models of adjudication respectively to the two philosophical orientations that were discussed in Chapter 4: the paradigm of autonomy and the paradigm of utility. Roughly, my claim is that various characteristics of the arbitration model make sense within the paradigm of autonomy, but make less sense within a utilitarian regime.[1] To the extent that individual autonomy is the ideal that animates the arbitration model, this model becomes less relevant to organizational litigation.

To show this, we must first spell out, in somewhat greater detail than we have done so far, the difference between the two models of adjudication. Generally speaking, the most distinctive mark of the arbitration model is the sharp distinction it draws between the mode of decisionmaking appropriate for a legislature and that appropriate for a judge.[2] The regulation model, by contrast, tends to blur that difference in some important respects. Subject to the obvious limitations on judicial decisionmaking imposed by relevant statutory provisions, the discharge of the judicial task as depicted by the regulation model resembles good legislative practices much more than it does under the arbitration model. I will focus on four features of adjudication as described by the arbitration model, all of which sharply distinguish the judicial style of decisionmaking from the legislative style. Two of these features are already familiar to us from the discussion of the two models in the preceding chapter. There I described the two models along two dimensions: *time* and *persons*. Along the time dimension, the arbitration model was characterized by a concern with the past: the judge focuses on the details of a past transaction and decides in accordance with the preexisting rights that were implicated in it. This clearly distinguishes him from the legislator, whose task includes the regulation of future transactions on the basis of policies that have the welfare of society in mind. The second familiar feature of adjudication as seen from the *arbitration* perspective is related to the persons dimension: I mean the judge's special concern for the litigants, the actual parties before him. It is the just resolution of *their* dispute which is his prime objective, whereas the general social ramifications of the decision, which are all-important for the legislator, are for the judge only of secondary significance.

The third feature that distinguishes judicial decisionmaking from legislation is the former's, but not the latter's, strong commitment to consistency in decisionmaking, reflected in the method of precedent.[3] Fourthly, judges as described by the arbitration model are distinguished from legislators by their passivity: judges are expected to rely exclusively on the litigants' conception of the issues, the facts, the interests, and the remedies involved in the controversy.[4]

As a general matter of sound decisionmaking, these four features of adjudication are quite problematic: they impose on the judge fairly drastic constraints, dramatically inhibiting thereby her ability to search for a socially optimal decision. The judge is constrained from taking full account of the effects of her decision on society's welfare; she is bound to follow previous decisions even though she may be thereby perpetuating the folly of her predecessors; and she must passively accept the positions and facts as presented by the litigants though she may find them lacking or misconceived. It is doubtful that a utilitarian, mindful of society's

welfare, would impose or accept such handicaps.[5] These constraints on the judge can be more plausibly seen to rest on a non-
utilitarian normative foundation that is sufficiently powerful to
override the utilitarian's misgivings about them. Such a normative
foundation can be found, I will show, within the paradigm of
autonomy. It is from this perspective that the insistence on a sharp
difference between the modes of decisionmaking applicable in adjudication and in legislation, and the imposition on the former (but
not on the latter) of such seemingly counterproductive constraints,
can make better sense. However, the support given by the paradigm of autonomy to the difference between legislation and adjudication in decisionmaking strategies depends on a particular conception of the difference between the types of decisions that these
two institutions characteristically make.

The distinction most commonly drawn between legislative (or
regulatory) and judicial decisions points out that the former are
typically general decisions whereas the latter are particular decisions. For our present purposes it is important, however, to separate two different senses of the general-particular distinction. First,
a decision can be particular or general in reference to the transaction to which it pertains. Judicial decisions are typically
transaction-specific—they deal with a particular transaction—as
opposed to legislation that is normally transaction-general, pertaining to a generically described, indeterminate series of future
transactions. Secondly, a decision can be person-specific or person-
general: judicial decisions are commonly thought of as addressing
a specific individual, identifying him or her by a proper name;
legislation uses no proper names but deals instead with (more or
less) broad categories of individuals. The common failure to distinguish these two aspects of the general-particular distinction
probably results from the fact that they appear as the two insepara-
ble sides of the same coin: by dealing with a particular transaction,
the court's decision must also, it may seem, deal with the particular, identifiable parties to that transaction.[6]

However, the view that transaction-specificity (or generality)
and person-specificity (or generality) are coextensive overlooks the
phenomenon of organizational litigants. For the purpose of the
present arguments, the most important change in the nature of
adjudication wrought by organizational litigants has to do precisely
with the fact that they split apart the two aspects of the general-

particular distinction. When the litigants are organizations, the judicial decision no longer uses proper names nor does it address particular individuals. Thus, the judicial decision becomes person-general even as it remains transaction-specific.

Now, as it happens, and as I shall soon indicate in greater detail, it is the person-specificity aspect of the supposed particularity of judicial decisions which counts most. This aspect underlies the various justifications suggested by the autonomy paradigm for the special constraints that the arbitration model imposes on judicial decisionmaking. But if this is true, then the support provided by the autonomy paradigm for the arbitration model is no longer available when organizations rather than individuals are the litigants. In that case, judicial decisions, much like legislative decisions, are person-general, and they can be reached, therefore, through the more legislative style of decisionmaking recommended by the regulation model.

We shall now turn to a more detailed elaboration of this general argument by discussing, in succession, the four constraints on judicial decisionmaking which we have listed.

PAST ORIENTEDNESS

The judicial decision is inevitably torn between its role in settling the particular dispute between the specific parties and its effects in shaping the law that will govern future transactions and other parties. Roscoe Pound called these two functions of the judicial decision the "deciding" and the "declaring" functions, and long ago noted the tension and the trade-off involved in carrying both of them out: "In the meantime there has been sacrifice of particular litigants and sacrifice of certainty and order in the law, as decision has fluctuated between regard to the one or the other of the two sides of the judge's duty."[7] While the tension is perennial, there are different ways to strike the balance. One way, advocated by Professor Wasserstrom, is to have the judge come up with the best general rule that will subsume the case under consideration, and then decide the case in accordance with that rule.[8]

The balance suggested by the arbitration model is quite different: it puts much more emphasis on the priority of the particular transaction between the parties, and attempts to reduce the intrusion of the future effects of the decision on the decisionmaking process. One famous and highly influential version of such an attempt on which I shall focus is Ronald Dworkin's *rights thesis*.[9] According to this thesis, judges should not base their decisions on grounds of policy, that is, on the likely effects of the decision on the welfare of society as a whole, but rather on principles—on arguments having to do with the preexisting legal and moral rights of individuals.[10] How can a judge be required to disregard, in good conscience, the effects of his decision on the social welfare? Dworkin's answer is that when a judge decides a case on grounds of policy (rather than as a matter of a party's right) his decision amounts to "tak[ing] property from one individual and hand[ing] it to another in order just to improve overall economic efficiency."[11] This, argues Dworkin, would be wrong, since "we all agree that it would be wrong to sacrifice the rights of an innocent man in the name of some new duty created after the event." A judicial decision is, however, free of such wrongdoing if it is based on an argument of principle, because "if the plaintiff has a right against the defendant, then the defendant has a corresponding duty, and it is that duty, not some new duty created in court, that justifies the award against him."[12]

It should be first noted that this argument has a distinctively individualistic flavor. The intended rhetorical force of invoking "the rights of an innocent man," and likening the reliance on policies to their "sacrifice," clearly depends on a strictly individualistic imagery. Replacing the "innocent man" in the above statement by the "innocent corporation" turns it from the intended conclusive rhetorical argument into an invitation to investigate the problematic and uneasy relations between individual rights, the public interest, and corporations.

In accepting that invitation, we must turn to the substantive (as opposed to the rhetorical) aspect of Dworkin's argument. We will then discover that this argument is a reflection of Dworkin's explicitly Kantian view of the relationship between individuals' rights and social welfare. Dworkin holds, you may recall, "the antiutilitarian concept of a right." The distinguishing feature of a right so understood is that "if someone has a right to something, then it is wrong for the government to deny it to him even though it will be in the general interest to do so."[13]

In justifying the power of such rights to overrule considerations of social welfare, Dworkin invokes the Kantian idea of human dignity. "This idea," writes Dworkin, "associated with Kant, but defended by philosophers of different schools, supposes that there are ways of treating a man that are inconsistent with recognizing him as a full member of the human community, and holds that such treatment is profoundly unjust."[14] Hence, "the invasion of a relatively important right must be a very serious matter. It means treating a man as less than a man, or as less worthy of concern than other men. The institution of rights rests on the conviction that this is a grave injustice, and that it is worth paying the incremental cost in social policy or efficiency that is necessary to prevent it."[15]

So understood, Dworkin's injunction that judges should only enforce preexisting rights rather than promote social policies is the institutional reflection of the philosophical belief in the priority of individual rights over considerations of social utility which we have associated with the paradigm of autonomy. The rights thesis, accordingly, may be seen as a reiteration, in the formal language of the judicial role, of the substantive idea of autonomy rights and their relation to utility considerations discussed in Part II of this study. If individuals have rights that should preempt considerations of social utility, it follows straightforwardly that a judge, confronted with such rights, should enforce them irrespective of the utilitarian implications of such enforcement.* This reading of the rights thesis permits us, therefore, to delineate its limits in terms of our prior conclusions regarding autonomy rights. Organizations, we have argued, do not have autonomy rights of their own, and subject to the qualifications based on the existence of organizational derivative autonomy rights, the rights thesis should not apply to organizational litigants.

Dworkin's argument for the rights thesis must, however, be understood to go beyond the mere reiteration in the context of litigation of the position that individuals have rights which preempt utilitarian considerations. This more expansive interpretation of Dworkin's argument for the rights thesis rests primarily on his

---

*That is, up to the point where the utilitarian costs become heavy enough (e.g., by assuming "catastrophic" magnitude) that they should be taken into account. I have already noted the absence of a theory that spells out the proper "rate of exchange" between autonomy and utility.

statement that "the rights thesis supposes that the right to win a law suit is a genuine political right."[16] If our prior interpretation of the justification for the rights thesis were complete, then "the right to win a law suit" would be redundant. If all the rights thesis does is to protect what we called autonomy rights, that is, individual rights which preempt utilitarian considerations, then there is no need for an additional, independent right to win a lawsuit. The substantive rights on which individuals rely suffice to bring them within the rights thesis, directly implying that the court should enforce them in derogation of conflicting utilitarian considerations, without a need for the mediation of another right, namely, "to win a law suit."

The status of the right to win a lawsuit can, however, be elucidated by attending to another notion that figures in Dworkin's argument, namely, that of *unjust* or *unfair surprise*. A party can defeat the court's reliance on a policy consideration to overrule his claim by pointing out "that it is unjust to take him by surprise."[17] The party's reliance on the injustice of the surprise is puzzling: if the claim is itself a claim of right, then it is that right, rather than the element of surprise, which requires a decision in that party's favor. If, for example, a court reaches a decision that violates a litigant's right to free speech, the decision is wrong because it violates that right, not because the litigant did not expect the violation. The reliance on the injustice of the surprise makes sense only when the substantive claim does *not* rest on a right which deserves judicial protection in derogation of utilitarian considerations. We may apply this conclusion to the right to win a lawsuit as well: this right is no longer redundant when the substantive claim itself does not entitle the party to a judicial decision in disregard of the implications of upholding that claim for the welfare of society as a whole.

We may conclude, therefore, that the rights thesis is broader than the range of individual rights that justify, in and of themselves, the sacrifice of social utility. Rather, Dworkin's theory can be understood to assign a distinctive value to the protection of well-founded expectations. When an individual acts under the justified impression (generated by previous judicial pronouncements, accepted social practices, etc.) that that action entitles her to a judicial decision in her favor, the individual has thereby acquired "a right to win a law suit," which immunizes her from a later "unfair surprise" inflicted on her in the name of forward-looking considerations of social policy.

The injunction against "unjust surprise," protected by "the right to win a law suit," must accordingly itself be of an order of importance sufficient to justify the sacrifice of possible utilitarian gains. In other words, according to the broader reading of the rights thesis, it supposes that upholding well-founded expectations is supported by considerations of individual autonomy. The argument to that effect is a familiar one. Without a certain degree of predictability, one's exercise of one's freedom of will becomes pointless. It is for this reason that once an individual's interest or plan has attained a certain degree of crystallization and definitiveness, it is no longer to be frustrated even for worthy reasons of social policy. The very fact that an individual relied for good reasons on a certain state of affairs may invest that state of affairs with a moral significance which it otherwise lacks.[18] In this way, the existence of a well-founded expectation, and its converse—the unjust surprise—"upgrade" a claim, which is not itself an autonomy right, into such a right, justifying a judicial decision to uphold the expectation in the face of contrary policies.

As should be plain, this additional protection extended by the rights thesis to individual interests does not apply to organizations. The very fact of frustrating organizational "expectations" (plans) does not in itself implicate individual autonomy. Of course, the frustrated plan may impinge upon an organizational DAR. But then it is this right, rather than the surprise involved in its violation, that argues for a decision in favor of the organization. The surprise *as such* does not add to the normative status of the organization's substantive claim. Accordingly, there is no point in speaking with respect to an organization of an independent "right to win a law suit." This is, of course, not to deny that organizational "expectations" need protection, and that uncertainty is a serious problem for organizations. Increasing uncertainty by reducing the security of expectations typically involves a loss in utility terms and should accordingly be taken into account among the various policy considerations that apply to the case. My point, however, is that there is no independent moral reason to *exclude* utilitarian considerations merely to avoid taking an organization by surprise;

whereas such reasons may well exist, according to my interpretation of Dworkin's view, with respect to individual litigants.
Unprotected by an independent (autonomy) right to win a lawsuit,
organizations can do no better than rely on the merits of their
claims, which, unless they invoke a derivative autonomy right,
means relying on the utilitarian merits of those claims.[19]

But even as they do so, organizations' own interests may often
turn out to comport, rather than collide, with a future-oriented
approach by the court. The main reason for this lies in an important
difference that often exists between individuals and organizations
in regard to their respective stakes in the judicial decision. The
individual litigant's encounter with the law is typically a unique
occasion in which he has relatively high stakes. There is little attraction for him, therefore, in the judicial strategy recommended by
Wasserstrom, according to which the judge must first formulate the
socially most desirable general rule that pertains to the case under
consideration, and then decide the case according to that rule. If the
individual litigant loses in the particular controversy, he can take
little comfort in the thought that the rule under which he lost will,
in the longer run, yield the right decisions most of the time. As far
as he is concerned, the rule misfired, and the unfairness of the loss
to the particular individual is not mitigated by the overall gains, *to
others*, that the rule has in store.

All this, however, is much less true when organizations, not
individuals, are the litigants. Marc Galanter characterized organizational litigants as "repeat players," as distinguished from
litigants who are "one shotters." Repeat players, Galanter observed
"can . . . play for rules in litigation . . . whereas a one shotter is
unlikely to."[20] The organization's stake in the single, particular
lawsuit will often be negligible compared to the volume of future
similar transactions that it will conduct, and that will be influenced
by the rule enunciated by the court. The backward-looking model
of litigation and the exclusive concern with who would receive the
actual "purse" is therefore often inadequate as a description of the
interests of the parties themselves as far as organizations are concerned. For the organization, unlike the individual, a rule that
works well most of the time is a good rule: in the longer run, the
organization is likely to reap the benefits of the rule which will
offset its occasional misfires.[21]

There are two other aspects of organizations which point to the possibility that an organization may engage in litigation though it is quite indifferent as to its outcome. First is the organization's interest in certainty and predictability. Two characteristics of organizational operations make organizations particularly interested in the certainty of the law pertaining to their future transactions: organizations typically engage in relatively long-term planning and operate by establishing "standard operating procedures." On both accounts, organizations have a high stake in clarifying the law, and they will therefore be inclined to enter a "test case" type of litigation, the main point of which is to clearly determine the relevant legal rules.[22] The organization is not interested, in such cases, in the resolution of the particular dispute, nor even in the content of the rule adopted by the court, but only in the clarity and certainty of such rule.

Organizations may also sometimes engage in litigation solely because of an institutional need to externalize decisions that are difficult to reach within the organization.[23] An insurance company may, for example, litigate a large claim that, in terms of its own interests, it should have decided to settle instead, just because its internal structure does not allow for such a decision, or because such a decision creates overly large career risks for the relevant decisionmakers. What prompts the organization to litigate in such circumstances is the need for some authoritative resolution of the case rather than a genuine interest in a particular outcome.[24]

As these arguments suggest, when organizations are concerned the arbitration model may not give an adequate account of the purpose of adjudication even from the litigants' own point of view. An alternative procedure—for example, the one that recommends that the court focus its attention on the merits of the general rule under which the particular case is to be decided—may often better respond to the peculiar organizational interests in the judicial process.

PARTIES ORIENTEDNESS

The second limitation on the scope of judicial considerations suggested by the arbitration model is the idea that the judge should consider only (or predominantly) the effects of the decision on the actual parties before her. The judge's primary responsibility is to the litigants, and her main task is to settle their dispute equitably *as far as they are concerned*.* This special attention to the parties raises a question about the moral ground for discriminating between the interests of the litigants and those of any other individuals (who might sometimes be described abstractly as "society as a whole") who are likely to be affected by the decision. Why should the judge give any primacy at all to the parties before her over those not present in court, be they few or many? A possible answer to this query is: precisely because they are before her.

It should be first noted that any attempt to single out some effects on some persons as intrinsically more significant to a decision must be repugnant to the utilitarian creed. As pointed out by Bernard Williams, the utilitarian is committed to the notion of *negative responsibility*, that is, to the view that individuals bear equal responsibility for all the foreseen consequences of their decisions, irrespective of how these consequences come to pass.[25] Utilitarianism is accordingly inhospitable to a theory of adjudication which discriminates between persons and kinds of interests. It can, perhaps, accommodate the special concern with the parties and their claims on prudential grounds, based, for example, on an empirical guess that the parties are likely to be most severely affected by the decision. However, such a rule of decision does not amount to anything more than a rule of thumb, a presumption to be rebutted by the actual facts and likely effects of each particular decision.

The paradigm of autonomy, by contrast, suggests three related arguments for the special attention paid by the judge to the parties

*This constraint on judicial decisionmaking is different from that based upon Dworkin's distinction between principles and policies, discussed in the previous subsection—since the latter is compatible with a position that allows the consideration of rights of parties other than the litigants, if such other persons' rights might be implicated by the decision. Dr. Raz raises the possibility that "Dworkin really has in mind not that judicial decisions should be based on rights rather than goals, but that they should be based on the interests of the litigants (or on the morality of their conduct in the events which are the subject of the litigation) excluding the interests of others as well as wider moral considerations." Joseph Raz, "Professor Dworkin's Theory of Rights," 26 *Political Studies* 123, 133 n. 2 (1978). Professor Greenawalt considers at length the same hypothesis about Dworkin's position, but provides textual evidence to support an opposite conclusion, namely that Dworkin does admit the rights of nonparties as relevant to the judicial decision. See Kent Greenawalt, "Policy, Rights, and Judicial Decision," 11 *Ga. L. Rev.* 991, 1016–26 (1977).

before her. The first argument is based on the rejection by the autonomy advocate of the utilitarian idea of negative responsibility, and its replacement by the notion of integrity. As stated by Professor Williams, it is "the idea . . . that each of us is specially responsible for what *he* does, rather than for what other people do."[26] It involves "tak[ing] seriously the distinction between my killing someone, and its coming about because of what I do that someone else kills them: a distinction based, not so much on the distinction between action and inaction, as on the distinction between my projects and someone else's projects."[27]

To illustrate the application of this line of reasoning to the judicial role, take a dramatic example: the death penalty. Jerry is charged with murder, and Judge Janice is asked by the prosecutor to impose the death penalty. The prosecutor argues that, according to the most updated research on the matter, failure to do so will reduce deterrence and result, within the next year, in three more killings than if Jerry is executed. Now assume that the statistics offered by the prosecutor are reliable, and that the judge accepts this piece of information as true. Is it dispositive of her moral responsibility in the matter? Should she now proceed to pronounce Jerry's death sentence with a clear conscience, without any further moral qualms? The argument from integrity suggested above gives a negative answer to these questions. There is, as far as the judge's moral responsibility is concerned, a significant difference between the three lives that might be lost unless Jerry is hanged and Jerry's life. The difference lies in that Judge Janice is called upon to kill Jerry. It is Janice killing Jerry—pure and simple. Judge Janice may, of course, think it a good thing that she should kill Jerry. And she might think it a good thing precisely because she thereby saves three lives. But she kills Jerry nonetheless. That's what is at stake. If she refrains from killing Jerry, she does not thereby decide to kill three other persons. She does not kill them. Others will. The argument from integrity suggests that this makes an important difference.

This analysis does not ignore, but rejects, a possible counter-argument based on the notion of the judicial *role*. The view that in issuing a death sentence the judge kills the defendant is wrong, one could object, because it ignores the fact that the judge acts in her judicial, not in her personal capacity. I find such objection misplaced. The notion of *role* helps define Janice's moral responsibility; it does not replace it. The fact that in considering whether Jerry should die Janice acts in her judicial capacity is of course highly relevant to the determination of her moral responsibility in the matter. There are things a person is morally entitled (or even obliged) to do only in carrying out a certain role. But it is still the person who does those things, and it is still his or her moral responsiblity for them that is at stake. In spelling out the requirements of the judicial role, the paradigm of autonomy is, therefore, delineating the moral responsibility of an individual (that is, the judge) under certain conditions. In so doing, the paradigm of autonomy must of course comport with its own principles of moral responsibility, of which the idea of integrity is one. It must therefore recognize the difference between the judge's moral position vis-à-vis the litigants with whom she directly interacts and other individuals, though of course the difference may be sometimes overriden by other considerations.[28]

The second argument that can justify a discriminating approach to the various persons affected by the judicial decision, paying special attention to the litigants, is the argument from *directness* elaborated at some length in Chapter 4.[29] I will not repeat but only briefly remind the reader of that argument and point out its relevance to our present concern. Roughly, the notion of directness involves drawing a line between those persons who are the intended objects of one's deliberate action and other persons on whom the impact of that action is only by way of an unintended side effect. The agent has a special responsibility with respect to the former category of people, not present in the case of the latter category. Consider the judge who is faced with the decision whether to foreclose the mortgage of the proverbial impoverished widow who has defaulted on her monthly payments.[30] After long deliberations, the judge decides that as far as the parties are concerned, justice (fairness, equity, respective rights, balance of interests, or what have you) requires a decision for the widow. It is then pointed out to the judge that her decision for the widow is likely to harm other widows in the future, who will find it more difficult to obtain loans. To that argument the judge may reply, in the idiom of directness, that her decision directly affects only the widow and the particular lender-plaintiff, and thus her primary responsibility is to them. This special responsibility is not canceled by the unintended side effects that the decision is likely to have on other people in the future.

The third argument for the primacy of the litigants has also already been mentioned in the course of our general discussion of the status of organizations within the paradigm of autonomy. It is what Charles Fried calls the *personalist argument*.[31] As you may recall, it has to do with the special duties of love and friendship born of personal acquaintance which exist with respect to particular individuals but are absent in the case of "abstract persons having only such characteristics as make them the appropriate objects of duties of justice and fairness."[32] The personalist argument offers another straightforward reason for a special concern that the judge should have for the lives and interests of the particular individuals with whom she is engaged in a personal relation in court.

The three arguments that I have outlined above—the argument from integrity, the argument from directness, and the personalist argument—are closely related. They all share a belief in the moral significance of the uniqueness of the individual and of the moral importance of the interpersonal relation. What is distinctive about the trial as a forum for decisionmaking is, according to these arguments, the fact that it consists in a personal interaction between three particular individuals: the two parties and the judge. Therein lies the great moral drama of the trial. The nature of adjudication must reflect this drama. The special concern for the parties, emphasized by the arbitration model, is accordingly born of the special moral considerations that attach to the *treatment* of one individual human being by another.

The characterization of the judicial decision which underlies this entire line of argument is that it is a *personal* decision, issuing from and pertaining to particular, identified individuals. But obviously this characterization of the trial no longer holds true when organizations, not individuals, are the litigants. The "presence" of an organization in court deprives the process of its essentially personal character and renders judicial decisionmaking impersonal. The judge is no longer interacting with any particular individual whose fate is directly determined by the judicial decision. The fact that she deals with an organization should not, of course, obscure for the judge the plain truth that her decision will ultimately affect in various ways different people. What the argument, however, does establish is the proposition that unlike individual litigants, none of the individuals indirectly affected by the decision in the case of organizational litigants should be singled out for *special* concern. Rather, the judge is both free and obliged to give equal weight to all persons who are likely to be significantly affected by the decision concerning the organization. None of them stands to the judge in this special relationship that entitles one to the protection of those values involved in the treatment of one individual by another.

THE METHOD OF PRECEDENT

A similar analysis leads to a parallel conclusion with respect to the third feature that, according to the arbitration model, must distinguish adjudication from legislation. This feature is the great importance that precedents have in adjudication: courts seem to be exceedingly anxious to demonstrate a consistent approach to similar situations, and go to great lengths to justify new decisions in terms of older ones. The need to justify new decisions by demonstrating their consistency with old ones is a peculiarly judicial strategy. No legislator is similarly bound or expected to make new decisions by reference to and in the light of old ones. Nor is this decisional strategy free from puzzlement. It has the effect of forcing a judge to perpetuate the folly of his predecessors, since in case he finds the prior decision a good one, there is no need to bind him to it by the doctrine of *stare decisis*.[33]

Granted that there is an element of stability and predictability preserved by the method of precedent. But this alone does not supply a sufficient account of the insistent judicial preoccupation with precedent. First, the reverse side of stability and predictability is conservatism and rigidity. The perpetuation of prior decisions may be harmful even if those decisions were correct when made, just because they may have become outdated. Secondly, if the value of stability and predictability were both so overwhelming and successfully served by the method of precedent,[34] there would be no reason to free legislation from that blessing completely. If, on the other hand, the contribution of precedents to stability is not of such preemptive importance, then all that the argument based on it suggests is that in deciding a case this particular value should be considered among other values.[35] It seems unlikely that when so considered precedent would win much of the time on the sheer weight of its contribution to stability and predictability.[36]

Considerations such as these,[37] I believe, have led Professor Dworkin to conclude that the special role played by precedent in adjudication must be explained "by appeal . . . to the fairness of treating like cases alike."[38] Now, this phrase, as it stands, is quite obscure. Why is it fair to treat like cases alike? We surely are not committed to such a principle in our daily lives. On the contrary, we often treat "like cases" differently merely for the sake of variety, diversification, or experimentation. There is no abstract general duty to treat like cases alike. If you service one of your cars every 6,000 miles, you face no charges of unfairness if you fail to do the same to your other car. Those who recurrently and persistently do the same things on similar occasions are more likely to be scorned as compulsive neurotics than praised for exemplary fairness. The phrase remains obscure until we realize that it does not refer to "treating cases" but rather to "treating people." Properly understood, the principle is plainly about the fairness of treating people in like cases alike. A possible reason why this corrected principle is indeed a principle of fairness has to do with the postulated moral equality of all people. If the cases (that is, the surrounding circumstances) are equal, and yet the treatment awarded to the individuals involved is different, that difference may be accounted for in terms of a difference between the individuals themselves (or, which is the same thing, a different attitude of the decisionmaker toward the individuals involved). Treating individuals differently in the same circumstances might therefore be viewed as an indication of an invidious violation of the postulate of individuals' moral equality. The principle of treating like cases alike is therefore a principle of fairness, since it guards against such a violation of individuals' moral equality and against the arbitrary and prejudicial treatment of some individuals by authority.

The insistent resort by courts to precedent as a means to ensure that "like cases be treated alike" can now be understood in the light of the special circumstances that distinguish judicial from legislative decisions. It is again the personal nature of the judicial decision which more dramatically challenges the ideal of equal treatment and makes the moral equality of individuals highly vulnerable. The occasion that calls for tailoring an individualized norm also permits the incorporation in that decision of considerations that single out the particular individual concerned for preferential or detrimental treatment. The elaborate intellectual mechanism by which courts demonstrate that like cases are treated alike can be accordingly understood as a demonstration that all individuals are treated alike, that is, in Dworkin's happy phrase, with equal concern and respect.[39] In this way, the individual who is otherwise completely exposed to the state's authority is shielded by the court's strong commitment to treat him as a member of a larger and more anonymous group, composed of those similarly situated individuals whose cases had been decided in the past.*

Once again, this argument for the method of precedent depends on the assumption that the judge addresses a particular individual. It does not hold when the court's decision pertains only to large, anonymous, impersonal groups of people, as is the case when the litigants are large organizations. In these cases, the distinctive nature of adjudication which justifies the insistent resort to precedent is strongly attenuated. The court need no longer artificially "generalize" its decision. It may instead be allowed to face the issues head-on, much as a legislature would do, without excessive engagement in strategies whose main justification is no longer present.

---

*It should be pointed out that this argument is different from the familiar argument that precedent contributes to "the prevention of partiality or prejudice" (Arthur Goodhart, "Precedent in English and Continental Law," 50 *L.Q. Rev.* 40, 56 [1934]). As Professor Wasserstrom points out in criticizing the latter argument, the doctrine of precedent can just as much perpetuate the initial biases of the precedent-making judge, and thus increase, rather than decrease, the overall amount of prejudice in the system. Richard Wasserstrom, *The Judicial Decision* (Stanford: Stanford University Press, 1961), p. 79. My point is that the doctrine of precedent helps eliminate a special kind of bias or prejudice: the one invoked by and directed toward the particular individual. It thus helps to eliminate the special offense to the person involved in singling out the particular individual for mistreatment, and it mitigates the domination of litigant by judge. Unlike the more general point made by Goodhart, mine is not, therefore, open to Wasserstrom's objection.

Before concluding this section, it should be noted that the method of precedent as here analyzed exposes a fundamental tension within the arbitration model. In the preceding section we emphasized the special significance that the particularity of the individual litigants has within this model. The personalist argument, for example, draws upon the particularity of the parties to the litigation and elaborates the implications of the personal relations that characterize it. The judge, we have argued, is called upon to respond to the uniqueness and the humanity of the parties, and thus give preeminence to their claims over those of other interests that may be implicated in his decision. The method of precedent bespeaks a different spirit. It is, I have argued, a strategy to neutralize the personal aspect of adjudication. It forces the judge to assume a detached position that ignores the particular individuality of the litigants by assimilating them into the impersonal group of prior litigants whose cases were previously decided.

These conflicting tendencies within the arbitration model are not surprising. Both can be explained in terms of the individualism of this model. This individualism tries to respond to both the moral equality and the empirical, concrete uniqueness of individuals. Love and friendship, invoked in the personalist argument, respond primarily to the latter. Justice and fairness, on which the method of precedent rests, respond to the former. Ideally, there is no real contradiction between these two sets of values and sentiments. To see that this is so, we may resort to Dworkin's helpful distinction between "treatment as an equal" and "equal treatment."[40] The moral equality of all persons requires that each individual should be awarded "treatment as an equal," that is, be treated with "equal concern and respect." This, however, does not necessarily redound to an actual "equal treatment" of all individuals. Equal concern and respect for each individual is compatible with a treatment that responds to the individual's full and unique humanity, taking into account the particular circumstances of his or her life. Ideally, one can treat people with equal concern and respect, in accordance with their moral equality, doing, at the same time, full justice to their particularity and uniqueness.

But this is true only ideally. The various strictures imposed by the arbitration model on judicial decisionmaking contemplate human weaknesses and imperfections that dominate the second-best world in which adjudication actually takes place. The response to human particularity may, in fact, not be in terms of love and friendship, but rather in terms of bias, prejudice, and hatred, which will deny to the litigants not only an equal treatment, but also treatment as equals. In trying to diminish these dangers, the method of precedent, with its attempt to infuse the treatment of particular individuals with a certain degree of abstraction and generality, also diminishes the ability of the judge to respond positively to the full and unique humanity of the litigants.

To sum up, the ideal of impersonal justice is compatible with love and compassion for the individual in his uniqueness and particularity. Nevertheless, when these two strands are combined in a real-world institution, they are likely to generate conflicting strategies meant to guard against the corrupting effects of human weaknesses on these two ideals. Accordingly, adjudication is torn between an emphasis on the preeminence of the litigants, calling for a full recognition of their uniqueness and particularity, and an emphasis on abstraction and generality needed to safeguard fairness against the dangers of bias and prejudice. My point is that this tension prevails in adjudication only so long as it deals with individual litigants. The twin ideals that generate this tension are no longer operative when the litigants are large, impersonal organizations. In this case, the judge need neither give priority to the plight of particular individuals present in court nor resort to precedent as a means to ensure fairness to those individuals.

JUDICIAL PASSIVITY

Judicial passivity designates the exclusive reliance by judges on the positions taken by the parties; these positions are assumed to exhaust the range of facts, issues, and remedies to be considered by the judge. Looked at from a utilitarian perspective, this too is a puzzling feature. As a social decisionmaker, the judge should be expected to generate the best possible decision. What is the best possible decision will sometimes be influenced by what the parties to the litigation think is the range of good decisions. But while the fact that they so believe should, in such cases, be given appropriate weight in reaching the decision, there seems to be no *prima facie* reason to maintain that this factor should be dispositive of the case. It seems odd to systematically cripple a sound utilitarian calculus by excluding relevant options and perspectives merely because the parties did not happen to endorse or present them. Here again, a possible account of judicial passivity is linked to an individualistic view of adjudication, that is, the assumption that the judge deals with particular individuals whose interests are at stake.

This account is based on two attributes of individuals—moral and psychological. On the moral side, judicial passivity can be understood as a reflection of individuals' autonomy, whereas on the psychological side it is a response to their subjectivity. Judicial passivity expresses the belief in the ultimate right of every individual to shape his or her own life, to choose one's goals and define one's interests. No one else can intervene in this process without violating the individual's freedom of will, and thereby his moral autonomy.[41] Thus, because of the ideal of individual autonomy, no one is entitled to substitute one's own opinion for the individual's regarding his or her wants and interests. Because of individuals' subjectivity—that is, because of the ultimate inscrutability of their minds—no one is capable of confidently doing so either. The common expression that the individual is the best judge of his or her interests reflects this elementary piece of psychological wisdom that we cannot ultimately penetrate other people's minds and that we always remain in this sense in an inferior position to assess their preferences and decisions. Respectful of their autonomy and baffled by the inscrutability of their minds, the judge, faced with individual litigants, remains passive: it is entirely up to them to present him with their respective visions of their lives, their interests, and their claims.

But insofar as judicial passivity is indeed based on individual autonomy and subjectivity, it has no place with respect to organizational litigants. As I have argued, individual autonomy should not be confused with organizational autonomy. In fact, given the oligarchical and oppressive propensities of organizations, the two are frequently antagonistic to each other. Consequently, the claim made on behalf of the organization is not immunized from active judicial scrutiny by any individual's moral autonomy. Nor does subjectivity bar judicial activism with respect to organizations. Organizational claims are the products of inter-personal processes, in which positions must be articulated and justifications given. Furthermore, conceived as an instrument for the achievement of some goals, organizations must support their claims by a means-ends rationality that is capable of objective state-ment and is accessible to other minds just as to the decisionmakers themselves. We may conclude that the moral and psychological attributes that advise judicial passivity with regard to individual litigants are absent when organizations are concerned. The judge may therefore exercise greater freedom and initiative when dealing with organizational litigants than he is used to doing in the case of individuals.[42]

CONCLUSION

In the previous chapter, we saw that the participation of or-ganizations in litigation is likely to increase considerably the effects of judicial decisions and carry them far beyond the particular liti-gants and the resolution of the particular dispute. This creates a pressure, and a *prima facie* reason, to take these effects into consid-eration in reaching the judicial decision, thus shifting from an arbi-tration model of adjudication toward a regulation model. However, the arbitration model, seen as a normative model, insists on some restrictions on judicial decisionmaking which distinguish it from legislation and inhibit its drift toward the mode of regulation. We have focused on four such restrictions: first, that the judge should be concerned with existing rights to the exclusion of the general future effects of his decisions; second, that the judge should be predominantly concerned with the parties rather than with the effects of his decision on others; third, that the judge should decide the particular case in the light of precedents; finally, that the judge be passive, relying exclusively on the presentations of the parties. The insistence on these restrictions can be best understood, I have argued, in terms of arguments from autonomy which presuppose a conception of adjudication as a personal interaction among partic-ular individuals, which stands in sharp contrast to the imper-sonality of legislation. However, these arguments are inapplicable to a major segment of contemporary litigation in which organizations rather than individuals take part, thereby removing the personal element from the judicial process. In this way, organizations obliterate an important difference between the nature of the judicial and the legislative decision, and undercut the arguments made within the arbitration model for the various restrictions on judicial decisionmaking. Free of these restrictions, judges may adopt, in the case of organizational litigants, a more regulatory, legislation-like, mode of decisionmaking. More specifically, they may give equal weight to the various interests affected by their decision, take into account arguments based on desirable policies as well as arguments framed in terms of existing rights, play down the importance of justifying their decisions by precedents, and perform a more active role in determining the interests, shaping the issues, and designing the remedies involved in litigation.

The result we have reached replicates in the context of adjudication the general conclusion we reached in Chapter 5 regarding the partial accommodation between autonomy and utility which the proposed organizational perspective allows. By adjusting her style of decisionmaking to the nature of the litigants (that is, to whether they are individuals or organizations), the judge may be able to escape to a certain degree the dilemma between the opposing pressures and attractions of arbitration and regulation, a dilemma that a more unitary view of adjudication presents in full force.

This happy conclusion must, however, be qualified in four ways. First, it ought to be read only as a matter of the different relative emphasis that should be given by the judge to the various conflicting decisional strategies that compose the two models. An attempt to practice any of the aspects of either of the models in its purity is likely to lead to a caricature of the judicial process.[43] Secondly, my argument has been in the main a negative one. It only shows that some important arguments in favor of the restrictions imposed on adjudication by the arbitration model do not apply to organizations. It does not follow, however, that sufficient support for the same restrictions cannot be found in the case of organizations elsewhere, notably in some utilitarian considerations. So though I do in fact believe that withdrawing from these restrictions the support of arguments based on individual autonomy does considerably weaken them, I have not, strictly speaking, affirmatively established that a change in judicial strategy of the kind I have described is indeed warranted.

Third, in dealing with adjudication, I have distinguished organizational from individual litigation. This plainly overlooks the important group of O-I cases, in which the litigation takes place between an individual on the one side and an organization on the other. The oversight is not, however, as dramatic as the importance of this category of cases may make it seem. Though these "mixed" cases obviously introduce additional complexities into the judicial role, the implications of my arguments for the judicial treatment of such cases are, it seems to me, fairly straightforward. To explore these implications in any detail at this point is likely to be more tedious than fruitful, but their general direction can be briefly indicated. The "mixed" cases, pitting an individual litigant against an organization, call for a correspondingly mixed judicial strategy, one that draws selectively on both models of adjudication and that treats the parties, in terms of the preferred style of decisionmaking, asymmetrically. Here, too, the theory of adjudication traces the substantive theory of organizations' rights developed in Part II. So, for example, the court may rely on certain considerations of social policy to defeat the organizational litigant's prior "expectations" (if on balance such a decision is socially desirable), though similar considerations would not be permitted to ground a decision against the individual litigant in a way that would take him or her by unfair surprise. Similarly, to give just one more illustration, the judge may feel free to scrutinize more thoroughly and actively the organization's statement of its claim than he is permitted to do with regard to the individual party's presentation of his or her case.

Finally, my discussion has emphasized the pitfalls of an overly unitary conception of adjudication. However, it is equally important to realize that the willingness to subdivide adjudication into categories marked by fundamental differences in decisionmaking processes must also have its limits. The concept and the institution of adjudication, like other concepts and institutions, can bear only so much internal strain. At a certain point, the use of the same concept to designate what have become its radically dissimilar sub-categories may be confusing, just as the use of the same institutional structure for serving essentially different social functions may be inefficient. My conclusions regarding the radical differences in the nature of adjudication occasioned by large organizations therefore raise the question whether the same institutions and the same officials who settle individual disputes should also be charged with overseeing interorganizational conflict and cooperation.

Part IV

Law, Organizations, and the State

Chapter VIII

Individual Rights and the Political Structure of Society

INTRODUCTION

The topic of this part is at once too central to the subject of the present study to be entirely left out, and too momentous to be adequately considered in the space that can be here allocated to it. That no general account of basic legal relations and fundamental legal entities can be complete without an examination of the role and status of the state can hardly be disputed. The state is omnipresent in legal relations both as the promulgator of the law that shapes them and also very frequently as a party directly involved in legal transactions and disputes. Obviously, one's conception of the state, its proper role and normative status, must importantly influence one's legal thinking. It is equally clear, however, that we cannot hope to do justice within the confines of this study to the complexity and variety of legal issues associated with our conception of the state.

But let me immediately confess a degree of disingenuousness in these protestations of misery. Being forced by considerations such as these into an avowedly truncated treatment of an otherwise intractable subject is not, as many writers would testify, an altogether unhappy predicament. It affords quite an attractive opportunity to discuss the subject while being sheltered at the same time by a convenient excuse from at least some criticisms that a less constrained forum might call forth. Both the need and the ability to discuss the state at this point as a legally significant entity are enhanced by the nature of my central contention on this issue, which is that the normative framework that has been suggested here for dealing with organizations in general is in fact spacious enough to accommodate for certain purposes the state as well. This framework, I will argue, can illuminate some of the normative features that are commonly associated with the state and some of the problems having to do with the normative status of the state relative to other social actors. To appreciate the contribution of the proposed organizational perspective to the legal conception of the state, it must be contrasted with the prevailing legal conception. The latter suffers from weaknesses that an organizational perspective helps to expose and remedy.

When speaking of the prevailing legal conception of the state, I do not mean to imply that legal thinking regarding the nature of the state is any more autonomous than it is in other matters. Quite the contrary. I take the legal treatment of the state to be a product of certain views in political philosophy and political theory which are merely reflected in the law. A discussion of the legal conception of the state is therefore necessarily at the same time a comment on political theory and philosophy. My point, accordingly, is that contemporary political philosophy that informs legal discourse about the state is essentially still wedded to an individualistic picture of society. By this I mean an image of the political structure of society as consisting in the juxtaposition of two kinds of entities: the state on the one hand, and the multitude of isolated, atomistically conceived individuals on the other. I will call this basic image *political individualism*. Its main feature for my present argument can be stated perhaps more accurately in the negative. It is the failure to address seriously the political implications of the organizational nature of modern society.[1] This is a negative that should not be difficult to prove. It is enough to read through the works of such prominent contemporary exponents of the liberal tradition as Ackerman,[2] Dworkin,[3] Nozick,[4] and Rawls[5] and to discover that nowhere does any one of them seriously consider the significance to his political philosophy of the social and political role of organizations. If the existence of organizations is mentioned at all, it is in a perfunctory manner, typically by subsuming organizations under the generic term *individuals*, to which the state (or government) is juxtaposed.[6]

This individualistic frame of mind, which tends to ignore organizations as distinctive entities, has a concomitant tendency to exaggerate the uniqueness of the state as a political and legal entity.

In a political universe inhabited only by atomistically conceived individuals, the state naturally looms large as an institution unique in its power, size, and complexity. An organizational conception of society, by contrast, diminishes the gap between the state and other entities comprised within political society and reduces the sense of the state's uniqueness. The exaggeration of the state's uniqueness induced by political individualism is two-faced. On the one hand, it breeds great apprehension of the state, conceived as a locus of coercive and potentially repressive force. On the other hand, the state (or at any rate, a democratic state) tends to be seen as expressive of the popular will and as a guardian of the public interest. It is thus endowed with special legitimacy not to be found elsewhere in political society.

This is, of course, an extremely rough and vastly oversimplified picture, but it is sufficient in order to point out some of the main weaknesses that mark the conventional legal approach to the protection of what are commonly referred to as fundamental individual rights.* First, as indicated by the orthodoxy that constitutional rights are rights against the state only, political individualism singles out the state as a potential menace to individual liberties, and insists on the unique importance of protecting individual rights against it. But as some commentators have observed, such insistence can easily become single-mindedness, and thus be self-defeating. Inasmuch as legal thinking is still influenced by political individualism, it is likely to be relatively oblivious to the need to protect individual rights and liberties against encroaching and powerful bureaucracies other than the state. Secondly, and somewhat paradoxically, political individualism tends at the same time to underestimate the importance of some intermediate organizations that protect individual liberties against the state as well as against other organizations. Finally, by underlining the state's special legitimacy as a true representative of the political community and a devoted servant of the public interest, political individualism inspires an excessive degree of ambivalence toward individual rights. Even ardent advocates of those rights tend to conceive them both as imposing severe constraints on the state's ability to pro-

*There are certain ambiguities in this expression which, however, need not be removed for the purpose of my present arguments. Suffice it to indicate that I have in mind roughly the kinds of individual rights which are listed in the Bill of Rights.

mote the public interest and as standing in permanent opposition to the majoritarian political process.

These common perceptions that are induced by political individualism all tend to weaken and constrict the legal protection that is given to individual rights in the organizational society.

The unsuitability to present social and political realities of the dominant view regarding the protection of individual rights which we have just outlined becomes clearer as soon as we depart from political individualism and replace it with a background of political theory that fully recognizes the distinctiveness and importance of large organizations. I will call such political theory (deviating somewhat from common usage) by the generic name *political pluralism.*[7] Political pluralism is a generic name because, as used here, it does not stand for a single, unified, political theory. Instead, it comprehends a variety of views and ideas scattered among many and quite divergent writers. I will introduce the more specific views comprised within the general theme of political pluralism in the form of five "models." Four of these models—*the organizational society, private governments, neo-feudalism,* and *the corporate state*—are discussed in the present chapter. Each of them helps to diagnose and to suggest a remedy for one or another of the inadequacies to which I have just alluded in the dominant conception of individual rights induced by political individualism. The fifth model—*the organizational state*—will be discussed in the next chapter. By applying to the state the same normative framework that has been developed in this study to deal with large organizations in general, this model unifies and accentuates the expanded vision regarding the protection of fundamental individual rights suggested by the other models.

THE ORGANIZATIONAL SOCIETY MODEL: BEYOND THE MINIMAL STATE

The General Argument

The natural place to begin the critique of the view inspired by political individualism of the relation between individual rights and the state is where the opposition between them is thought to be greatest. This opposition is nowhere more pronounced than it is in the libertarian tradition, which maintains that little if any of the state's activities can be justified in view of the extensiveness of individual rights and liberties. In what follows, I will focus on the well-known and highly original philosophical exposition of the libertarian position in Robert Nozick's *Anarchy, State, and Utopia*.[8] My aim is not to take issue with libertarianism as such. Rather, the purpose of the following discussion is only to demonstrate the extent to which Nozick's conclusions regarding the narrow scope of the legitimate state depend on an individualistic conception of society, oblivious to the presence and distinctiveness of organizations.

In the opening statement of his book, Nozick defines the problem of the state as follows: "Individuals have rights, and there are things no person or group may do to them (without violating their rights). So strong and far-reaching are these rights that they raise the question of what, if anything, the state and its officials may do. How much room do individual rights leave for the state?"[9] Not much, concludes Nozick. The only legitimate state is the minimal state, "the night-watchman state of classical liberal theory, limited to the functions of protecting all its citizens against violence, theft, and fraud, and to the enforcement of contracts, and so on."[10] "The minimal state is the most extensive state that can be justified. Any state more extensive violates people's rights."[11]

The dependence of this extreme view on political individualism is straightforward. Only if the sole entities with which the state must deal are individuals armed with the kinds of autonomy rights ascribed to them by Nozick does each and every action of the state raise the possibility of violating such rights. The more extensive the rights individuals have (and Nozick believes they are extensive indeed), the more restricted is the state in its legitimate activities. This conclusion does not, however, follow if the premise of the argument is discarded, that is, if we view society as consisting of entities other than individual human beings. The organizational society model simply draws attention to this point—namely, that the state is faced not only with individuals among whom it need tread with great care so as not to overstep their "moral boundaries" defined by their autonomy rights; it is also faced with an array of formal organizations, which, as we argued, are distinct from individuals and are not possessed of the same autonomy rights that individuals have. As a result, the moral constraints that inhibit the state in its dealings with individuals to the extreme extent described by Nozick are not equally operative when the state deals with organizations. The state may therefore undertake tasks that go beyond the functions of the night-watchman, provided it carries out those additional functions in the domain of organizational activity, where the autonomy rights of individuals are not at stake. The state may, for example, engage in economic regulation for the purpose of increasing overall utility (social welfare, efficiency), provided the regulated actors are, as indeed they are most likely to be, large business corporations. This can be accomplished, as the arguments in Chapter 4 attempted to establish, without transgressing the "line (or hyperplane) [that] circumscribes an area in moral space around an individual."[12]

Individual and Corporate Tax

This general point can be illustrated and further elaborated by examining in some detail one of the main handicaps that individual rights impose, according to Nozick, on the state, namely, that the state may not collect taxes. "Taxation of earnings from labor," argues Nozick, "is on a par with forced labor."[13] "Seizing the results of someone's labor is equivalent to seizing hours from him and directing him to carry on various activities. If people force you to do certain work, or unrewarded work, for a certain period of time, they decide what you are to do and what purposes your work is to serve apart from your decisions. This process whereby they take this decision from you makes them a *part-owner* of you; it gives them a property right in you. Just as having such partial control and power of decision, by right, over an animal or inanimate object would be to have a property right in it."[14] The same argument, Nozick claims, is true with respect to taxation not only of income from labor, but also of "interest, entrepreneurial profits, and so on."[15]

This account of what taxation necessarily amounts to is exhaustive of the options open to the state only because of Nozick's conception of the modes of property ownership to which taxation can apply. A property right, Nozick maintains, "may be held by an *individual* or by a *group* with some procedure for reaching a joint decision."[16] However, according to my preceding arguments, property can be held and accumulated by an entity such as Personless Corporation, which is neither an individual nor simply a group of individuals. As indicated by our analysis of organizational rights in Chapter 4, taxing the profits of Personless Corporation, and corporate taxation in general, can provide the state with a source of income which does not involve the violation of any individual's autonomy rights.

Indeed, Nozick's own view concerning the nature of rights violation comports with my analysis and leads to the same conclusion. Nozick insists on the distinction, critical to my argument about organizational autonomy rights, between just making someone worse off and violating one's right. He rejects, accordingly, the view that "people are forced to do something *whenever* the alternatives they face are considerably worse."[17] Rather, Nozick argues, "the fact that others intentionally intervene, in violation of a side constraint against aggression, to threaten force to limit the alternatives, in this case to paying taxes or (presumably the worse alternative) bare subsistence, makes the taxation system one of forced labor and distinguishes it from other cases of limited choices which are not forcings."[18] Imposing a tax on a corporation does not involve the threat of force against any individual in violation of the side constraint against aggression. The worsening of the economic alternatives faced by individuals as a result of the tax assessed against corporations is not, therefore, the product of an intentional intervention "in violation of a side constraint against aggression, to threaten force to limit the alternatives." Instead, it is more like the innocuous governmental action described in the following hypothetical.

Imagine that the protective agency that is Nozick's minimal state comes into some money: it gets, let us say, a large donation from a citizen overcome by misplaced patriotism. The state, aware of the skyrocketing prices of dental medicine, decides to provide with this money cheap dental services to its citizens. It opens a subsidized clinic just across the street from Dr. Drill. Dr. Drill resents the competition, and for good reason. Losing his erstwhile local monopoly, he is presented now with less desirable options than before. He cannot, for one thing, go on charging his usual exorbitant rates and stay in business. Nevertheless, it seems to me, on the basis of the above-quoted passage, that Nozick would want to argue that there is nothing wrong with the state's conduct in this case. No coercion, no forcing, were applied to Dr. Drill. At no time did the state threaten to use force against him in violation of the side constraint against aggression. The bare fact that Dr. Drill is worse off as a consequence of the state's activity does not in itself condemn that activity. My argument is that the effects of corporate tax on individuals are of a similar kind. If the tax itself is not levied from individuals, and is not backed by threats of aggression against them, then the tax is not disqualified by the fact that ultimately some individuals (such as consumers or shareholders) will be worse off. Their predicament will be like Dr. Drill's. In neither case did the state transgress the moral side constraints that strictly confine it to its "minimal" role.

Assume now that Nozick, contrary to what seems to be required by the above-quoted passage, wants to deny this conclusion. He does, after all, find the state's opening of the dental clinic objectionable just because it results in making Dr. Drill worse off. We would have, in this case, to ascribe to Nozick two conceptions of coercion: coercion in a strong sense, which involves the limitation of the alternatives available to a person through threats of force in violation of the side constraint against aggression; and coercion in a weak sense, which merely involves the limitation of the alternatives available to a person—just making him worse off.[19] Corporate taxation, unlike personal taxation, does not involve "strong" coercion. But, according to the present argument, it is still disqualified by coercion in the weak sense, that is, by the very fact that it makes some individuals worse off. It must first be conceded, I think, that whatever the force of Nozick's analogy between income tax and forced labor, it is greatly attenuated when the complaint against the tax rests on the weak conception of coercion. It may, however, be interesting to note that, even in its attenuated form, Nozick's analogy between taxation and slavery as applied to corporate taxation fails.

For a tax to count as "forced labor," even by the stretch of imagination needed when the tax is directly imposed only on corporate profits, it must be assumed that at least indirectly the tax is paid by some individuals. Some individuals must be worse off on account of the tax in order for there to be someone to complain that he or she was unduly subjected to coercion in the weak sense.

This may seem a very weak condition that must be satisfied as a matter of course: surely, if the government levies a tax, any tax at all, the burden must ultimately fall on some individuals.[20] The obviousness of this proposition is, however, diminished by the argument I have made in Chapter 4 to the effect that a harm to the organization need not always affect any individuals at all.[21] That argument, you may recall, relied primarily on the idea of organizational slack, and it applies to corporate taxation as much as to other forms of deprivation. I will now suggest two additional arguments to the same effect which apply more specifically to the issue at hand.

The first argument proceeds from the economic theory of incidence, which explores who ultimately bears the burden of the tax.[22] The one definite property of this theory is its notorious inconclusiveness.[23] Any argument based on it can be finally resolved only on grounds of "burden of proof." Accordingly, Nozick would be hard put to persuade anyone that the corporate tax is ultimately paid out of the pockets of workers or consumers.[24] The most one can confidently do is plead ignorance on the matter. Shareholders, too, do not necessarily bear the burden of the tax in any meaningful sense. As a result of capitalization, the existence of the tax on corporate profits is likely to be reflected in the prices of shares. These prices will adjust themselves to the present value of the anticipated reduction in the yield of the investment in stock due to the tax.[25] Consequently, a person buying stock under a regime of corporate taxation pays less for the stock, in proportion to the expected decrease in dividends attributable to the tax. He, too, cannot complain, therefore, of any loss occasioned to him by the tax.[26]

The second argument is that even if a regime of corporate taxation does have some negative effect on the income of the various individuals related to the corporation, this fact would not in itself provide a foothold for Nozick's objection. We may begin with the observation that one thing that the state is likely to do with the money it collects through the corporate tax is to build and maintain the enormous infrastructure that supports and enables the corporate economy. Obvious examples include public education that trains workers and broadens the market, public health that is essential to the health and thus the efficiency of the working population, and roads and railways for necessary transportation.[27] Now, all these are public goods, and having them provided by the corporations themselves, within a free market, would involve considerable transaction costs, resulting especially from the problem of the free-rider.[28] It is precisely the state's unique position as ultimate coercive power which allows it to provide cheaply those public goods needed for the operation of corporations, saving the transaction costs that would otherwise be incurred. Consequently, the overall effects of the state's activity, including both the taxation and its partial use for the cheap provision of public goods for the corporate economy, may be for the overall benefit of all the individuals related to the corporations. Since, in that case, there would be no individual who is, all things considered, worse off as a result of the tax, the state may impose corporate tax without thereby violating any individual's rights, even in the weak sense contemplated by the notion of "weak coercion."

This argument must be protected against a possible misunderstanding. It may seem that I have tried to reintroduce the active state through a back door that was in fact deliberately locked by Nozick. Nozick is of course familiar with the arguments for the more-than-minimal state based on the notion of public goods and the problem of the free-rider. His denial of the legitimacy of the active state must rest not on ignorance of these arguments but on their rejection. His position must be that the state has no business violating the free-riders' individual rights by coercing them to contribute toward a public good that they profess not to desire.[29] Doesn't my argument merely fly in the face of Nozick's position without advancing the debate? To see that this is not the case, we must invoke again the distinction between strong and weak coercion. Nozick's position must be that the state is not justified in exercising strong coercion against the free-rider (e.g., by taking some of his property) even if in the long run doing so would benefit him or her, as well as others. At the time of the intended violation, there is a right at work which protects the individual and serves as an absolute side constraint on the state. Such a constraint does not admit of trade-offs in terms of future benefits that might accrue from a present violation. Corporate taxation, however, involves, as we have seen, no such strong coercion. We thus invoked the notion of public goods and the problem of the free-rider not in order to offset a violation of an individual right (which would be impermissible) but rather in order to determine whether such a violation, in the form of coercion in the weak sense, takes place at all. Coercion in the weak sense would take place if, and only if, corporate taxation made some individuals worse off. By invoking the problem of the free-rider and the effectiveness of the state in providing public goods, I have tried to deny that that is the case: if the state's effectiveness is great enough, then no individual is, as a matter of fact, ever worse off as a result of corporate tax, and therefore no individual rights are ever violated by its continued levy.

Conclusion

This journey beyond Nozick's minimal state has been somewhat prolonged and arduous, so its payoff must be underscored. First, my arguments, if correct, suggest that by paying fuller attention to the organizational nature of modern societies, the seeds of an activist state may be found even in the midst of a strictly libertarian theory such as Nozick's. The conversion in this way of a staunch libertarian into a supporter of the activist state is no trivial matter.

Secondly, even those who, like myself, do not share the starting point of the journey—Nozick's equation of income tax to forced labor[30]—may still find interest in its destination. Nozick's view is, I think, an exaggeration of a stark fact that few are likely to dispute—namely, that the internal revenue system has become (in democracies such as this country) perhaps the single most pervasively oppressive and intrusive governmental instrument. One may resent this state of affairs and yet acknowledge the overriding social benefits secured by taxation. For those who hold this (probably common) position, the preceding discussion, if sound, should be quite consequential. It offers a powerful consideration not only for the retention of corporate tax (which is periodically challenged as unnecessary or redundant),[31] but indeed for viewing it, other things being equal, as the preferred form of taxation that should be allowed to replace, whenever feasible, individual income tax.

Unhappily, as is so often the case, other things are unlikely to be equal. The present discussion does not therefore purport to resolve the dispute regarding individual and corporate taxes, though it does, it is hoped, highlight an important dimension of that debate.

THE PRIVATE GOVERNMENTS MODEL AND THE PROTECTION OF INDIVIDUAL RIGHTS

The insight contained in the organizational society model—that society is made up of organizations as well as of individuals—relieves the state from some inhibitions that commitment to individual rights may be otherwise thought to impose on it. We are taken a step further by the bolder claim that is conveyed by the private governments model.[32] This is the claim that many large organizations possess some features (functions, powers) that have been traditionally associated exclusively with the state. According to this model, political power is not concentrated in a single body, namely government. Rather, the various large organizations that inhabit society also constitute, in Philip Selznick's apt expression, systems of governance.[33] In the eyes of the proponents of the private governments model, these organizations "could be even more oppressive than the state."[34] Furthermore, not only do such organizations resemble government in their oppressive potential, but membership in many of them is in fact as coerced and inevitable as is membership in a state. In the organizational society, writes one proponent of this model, "man, to satisfy his wants, has no alternative but to join up or go under."[35]

Seen in the light of the private governments model, constraints imposed on the state out of concern for individual rights may not only sometimes be unnecessary (as was argued in the preceding section), but they may also turn out to be inimical to the protection of those rights. A discussion of individual rights within the framework of political individualism invariably casts the state in the role of the archvillain. As a unique repository of coercive political power, the state is seen as posing a constant threat to individual rights: the greater the power wielded by the government, the greater the threat to those rights. Consequently, various devices, institutional and normative, are required to curb the power of the state and check its oppressive potential. However, in a society dominated by large organizations, the democratic state may assume the role of a countervailing power, which can protect individual rights and liberties from the increasing encroachment by expanding bureaucracies.[36] In the oppressive environment of private governments, Henry Kariel points out, the power wielded by the state may be the individual's only resort.[37] An activist stance by the state vis-à-vis other organizations may therefore not only be tolerable from the point of view of protecting individual rights, but it may indeed be affirmatively required from that perspective. A clear and well-known example of government assuming such an active role occurs in labor law. There, by means of a network of legislative provisions and institutional arrangements, government is expected to protect individual employees from certain forms of abuse, not only by their employers,[38] but even more importantly for our purposes, by their own unions.[39]

The private governments model helps to identify and avert two additional dangers to the protection of individual rights implicit in political individualism. One is the exclusive preoccupation with the protection of fundamental rights against the state, at the price of not paying sufficient attention to similar dangers that other organizations may pose to the exercise of those rights. The prevailing view that fundamental human rights are rights against the government is the natural outgrowth of an image of society in which the state, or the government, is seen as the sole center of organized political power, and consequently as posing a unique threat to the basic liberties of individuals. This view is manifest, as I have already mentioned, in the orthodoxy that the Constitution defines and protects rights as against government only. However, this orthodoxy, as well as the vision of the political order which underlies it, has often come under attack from the perspective of the private governments model. The view of many large organizations as governments carries with it the implication that the single-minded focus on protecting individual basic liberties against the government is misguided.[40] Individual rights and liberties, it has been argued, such as freedom of speech or due process of law, can be meaningfully and fully enjoyed only if guaranteed within the various systems of governance which actually dominate individuals' lives.[41] The notoriously strained application of the *state action* doctrine, anxious to find traces (no matter how attenuated) of governmental involvement in the affairs of a particular organization as an excuse for applying to the organization constitutional standards, should be seen as a symptom of the problem pointed out by the private governments model, rather than as an adequate solution to it.[42]

Finally, the equation between state and organizations suggested by the private governments model draws attention to the dangers to individual rights which inhere in the opposite equation, implicit in political individualism, that is, the equation of organizations to individuals. The tendency to assimilate organizations to individuals which we have associated with political individualism may naturally lead to the assignment to organizations of the kind of fundamental rights that properly belong to individuals only. The costs that such a move might have in social utility have already been mentioned in the previous chapters. The private governments model alerts us to the possibility that such an ascription of rights to organizations may have an additional cost, in terms of the protection of individual rights as well. The reason is straightforward: if organizations are seen as potentially repressive systems of governance, treating them as individuals and granting them the protections, immunities, and liberties of individuals will just enhance their repressive power. Take, for example, the right to private property which we have previously discussed. Hobhouse's famous characterization of organizational property as "property for power" (as opposed to "property for use")[43] intimates the potential threat to the rights and liberties of individuals which is posed by excessive protection of organizational property.[44]

The possibility of ascribing to organizations fundamental individual rights might seem a fanciful idea, were it not for the fact that an entire chapter in American constitutional history was shaped by the courts' adoption of such a position. The Supreme Court's wholesale application to corporations of various constitutional rights, particularly those guaranteed by the Fourteenth Amendment[45] (most dramatically in evidence during the *Lochner* era),[46] has quite definitely increased the power of corporations over individuals and resulted in the constriction of individual rights. The striking point is that by implicitly relying on the assumptions of political individualism, the Court attempted to justify such decisions by using a rhetoric of individual rights.[47]

The ascription of autonomy rights to organizations can thus be interpreted and criticized, from the perspective of the private governments model, as a reflection of political individualism which is oblivious to the distinctiveness of organizations. However, as our next model will suggest, support for certain rights of organizations can also be found within the pluralist vision itself.

THE NEO-FEUDALISM MODEL AND THE AUTONOMY OF ORGANIZATIONS

The neo-feudalism model[48] shares with the private governments model the division of the political universe into three kinds of distinctive entities: individuals, organizations, and the state. However, it reverses the respective roles assigned by the private governments model to the two latter entities—organizations and the state—in their relation to individuals. Rather as in political individualism, so in the version of pluralism which I call neo-feudalism, the state is singled out as the greatest potential menace to individuals and their rights. Intermediate organizations—trade unions, churches, political parties, and other voluntary associations—serve as buffers between individuals and the otherwise omnipotent state, shielding individuals against its potentially oppressive power, and affording them a congenial environment within which their rights and liberties can be enjoyed with relative security. Thus, only through their membership in various organizations is individuals' normative status assured, and their share in the values distributed by the political process safeguarded.[49]

I have already indicated the similarity in the normative implications of neo-feudalism and political individualism: both lead to the ascription to organizations of rights against the state. But this similarity should not be overstated. The solicitude for organizational rights which is common to both perspectives does not necessarily pertain to the same organizations or to the same rights. In the preceding section, I pointed out how by using individualistic rhetoric the Supreme Court extended constitutional protections to corporate property. This is hardly the kind of organizational right that a neo-feudalist is likely to advocate. Not corporate property but the autonomy of voluntary associations and their relative immunity from state interference in their internal affairs are his prime concern. It is perhaps a measure of the Supreme Court's attachment to political individualism that insofar as it has recognized organizational rights, these have tended to be of the kind compatible with the individualistic conception of organizations (pertaining in most cases to corporations), whereas "recognition of the principle that associations have rights different from those of the persons constituting them has been somewhat grudging in American constitutional law."[50]

It should be emphasized, however, that while the marks of neo-feudalism in constitutional law are few, they are not absent altogether. The main example of the neo-feudalist influence on constitutional thinking would seem to be the Supreme Court's deferential attitude to the autonomy of religious organizations, which has been interpreted by some commentators as evincing the neo-feudalist strain in pluralist thinking.[51]

It follows from these observations that failure to address the concerns raised by neo-feudalism can be as detrimental to the protection of individual rights as is the oversight of the normative implications of the private goverments model discussed in the preceding section. Political individualism may thus lead to the overprotection of some organizational interests just as it can induce the underprotection of others.

It is also important to note in this context that the juxtaposition of the private governments model and the neo-feudalism model discloses a familiar and perennial tension within political pluralism. This consists in a radical difference in the two models' respective conceptions of the nature of organizations and in a corresponding difference in their conception of the state and its proper role. Proponents of neo-feudalism view organizations as essentially benign groupings, within which the individual can find true expression for his or her interests and aspirations. At the same time, they tend to paint the state in dark colors, emphasizing the dangers that lie in the coercive power wielded and monopolized by it. Proponents of the private governments model, on the other hand, emphasize the bureaucratic, oligarchical nature that organizations tend to assume. They focus, consequently, on the oppressive power accumulated within organizations and on the need to protect individuals against the various bureaucracies that govern their lives. This picture of organizations is typically accompanied by a benign conception of the state, which emphasizes its greater legitimacy, acquired through the democratic political process, and the availability of better means of control over the use of its power compared to those available with respect to other organizations.[52] The tension within pluralism expressed by these two models is reflected, as we have seen, in their conflicting normative implications. Neo-feudalism gives normative support to claims of autonomy made by organizations, thereby strengthening them as against the state. The private governments model, in contrast, is suspicious of any autonomy claims by organizations. It is their oppressive power that must be curbed, and the only one to do so is a robust, interventionist, democratic state.[53]

The incompatibility between the normative implications of these two strands of pluralism is, however, more apparent than real. Just as "there is no logical inconsistency in a group's being at the same time a shield against and a source of coercion,"[54] so there is no inconsistency in the state being at the same time a major protector of and a major threat to individual liberties. While the neo-feudalism and private governments models do in fact represent diametrically opposed political orientations of their respective pro-ponents, the two perspectives can be reconciled to a considerable extent. A normative order committed to the protection of individ-ual rights must decide between the claims to autonomy, advanced by both individuals and organizations, on the one side, and the state's justifications for infringing such autonomy, on the other, in a way that is least injurious to individual rights. In the simple political universe depicted by political individualism, this task is an easy one: the more confined the state is in terms of the justifications available to it for overriding claims of autonomy, the better for individual rights. No such straightforward, clear-cut position is, however, available within political pluralism that takes notice of the messages conveyed by both the neo-feudalism and the private governments models. A normative order that tries to respond to both types of messages cannot be all "pro-state" or all "pro-organization." To reconcile and integrate both visions of a pluralist political reality, a normative order must be more refined and discriminating than that, willing to differentiate between dif-ferent organizations and different kinds of claims advanced by the three kinds of entities. The *organizational state* model that will be discussed in the next chapter offers, I believe, such a unified and versatile approach. But before introducing it, let me examine by means of the next model yet another important aspect of the plu-ralist view.

THE CORPORATE STATE MODEL AND THE
COUNTERMAJORITARIAN PROBLEM

The pride that Americans take in the institution of individual rights against the state is often mixed with a certain embarrassment regarding that institution's countermajoritarian nature. This pride and embarrassment are inextricably bound together: it is widely believed that the extent and the seriousness of the commitment to individual rights are measured by the ability of these rights to override the majority's will as expressed through the political pro-cess. The problem of individual rights in a polity that adheres to an ideal of majority rule is further compounded by the avowedly non-majoritarian nature of the judiciary—the institution charged with the elaboration of those rights and their enforcement.

These remarks are not meant to deny that compelling arguments have been made for the compatibility between individual rights and democratic values as well as for the legitimacy of protecting such rights through judicial review. Nonetheless, the very characterization of the institution in question as countermajoritarian is likely to breed in the democrat's heart a certain disquiet about it and have a chilling effect on the zeal with which a court would strike down, in derogation of what is deemed to be the popular will, a state's action or decision.

This ambivalence toward rights against the state rests, however, on the belief that the governmental decisions and operations challenged by those rights are themselves a true expression of the majority's preferences. In other words, the countermajoritarian conception of rights depends on a view of the political process as an essentially successful method for aggregating and effectuating individual preferences. Though there is no logical necessity in the matter, it seems easiest to sustain a belief in the workings of majoritarian politics within the framework of political individualism. The simple picture of the political structure of society painted by that model, in which individuals are the only actors, is likely to induce a conception of the political process in the image of the ballot or the referendum. Though probably no one any longer actually holds such a view of the political process (any more than one is likely to admit to being a political individualist in the sense in which that expression is used here), some belief that governmental action results from a significant, albeit rough, approximation of such a process[55] seems to be implicit in the persistent concern in constitutional law with the countermajoritarian problem.[56]

The problematic and complex relationship between the end products of the political process as they issue in various governmental actions and decisions and the actual preferences of a majority of the population becomes much more visible as soon as the political role played by various groups and organizations, outside of the governmental structure as well as inside it, is fully recognized. By the *corporate state* model,[57] I mean to draw attention to one aspect of the predominance of organizations as political actors. The message conveyed by the corporate state model is a moderate version of broader and more extreme claims once advanced under the title of "interest group pluralism." Interest group pluralism amounted to an attempt to reduce the entire political process to the interaction among various interest groups and organizations, demoting individual majoritarianism to a secondary position, or completely discarding it as a mere facade.[58] The pendulum of political theory seems to be swinging now in the opposite direction, re-emphasizing the role of the individual and the importance of majoritarian politics within the political process. This, however, does not obliterate the true insight contained in interest group pluralism, which is the importance of supplementing, though not replacing, the description of the political process in terms of majoritarianism with a reference to the political role of various organizations. One important way in which this core insight is currently seen to exert influence on political theory is in the considerable attention given to the political participation and influence of large corporations. While preserving democratic majoritarianism as a central element in politics, the corporate state model insists on the need to supplement this description by focusing on the various ways in which large organizations, particularly business corporations, impinge on the political process.[59]

Figure 3 is a schematic representation of the corporate state model's main claims. The upper part of the scheme describes the flow of political influence in a pure majoritarian system: the only kind of input into the state's decisionmaking mechanism are individual preferences. Those preferences are computed by that mechanism and generate political decisions. The figure also describes the three channels through which corporations are said to influence political decisions.[60]

Channel number 1 describes political decisions directly made by corporations. Thus, for example, corporate economic decisions (e.g., about investment, location, and innovation) influence the

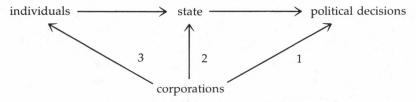

Figure 3.   The Political Process

economy; their environmental policy (or the lack thereof) shapes the environment; and by giving (or withholding) donations, corporations determine the scope of a whole range of social (cultural, scientific) activities.

Channel number 2 refers to the influence corporations exert upon the government (federal, state, and local), and thus to their direct impact on the political decisions made by the state. This influence is exerted in a variety of ways, ranging from formal lobbying on the federal level (conducted either by individual corporations or through associations such as the Chamber of Commerce), through personal connections, monetary support to politicians, the co-optation of regulatory and other administrative agencies, and setting the tone of mass media, down to the occasional near-domination of local politics.

Channel number 3 stands for the indirect participation of corporations in majoritarian politics via their influence on individuals' choices. This is the most controversial, but arguably also the most important of the kinds of impact that corporations have on the political process. Through their direct easy access to masses of employees, and through their use of the mass media, corporations occupy a strategic position to generate public support for favorable political decisions. Beyond such direct influence geared at particular decisions, it is argued that the entire culture is permeated with corporate ideology and values,[61] giving birth to the "organization man,"[62] whose preferences, values, tastes, and ideals are significantly shaped by corporate propaganda.[63]

These three channels of corporate influence introduce three respective types of distortion into the political process in terms of the adequate reflection of individual preferences. Through channel number 1, the majoritarian decisionmaking process is completely bypassed, and consequently the corporate state gives rise to a host of decisions of great public importance which do not even purport to be a product of the democratic process or to reflect individual preferences. We are thus faced with a problem of *exclusion*, in that on matters decided through channel 1, most individuals' preferences are completely excluded from the decisionmaking process.

Channel 2 introduces a distortion that may be called *double counting*.[64] The positions held by corporations and directly infused into the decisiomaking process through this channel are often also the preferences of individuals—e.g., managers or stockholders—and are therefore counted as individual preferences within the majoritarian political process. These ·preferences are, so to speak, "counted twice." Furthermore, due to the strategic advantages of corporations, those same preferences, when presented as corporate interests and introduced through the second channel, gain in weight and impact with no necessary relation to the number of individuals subscribing to these preferences or to the intensity with which they so subscribe.[65] The distortion introduced through Channel 3 is a form of *falsification*: the individual preferences injected into the political process are no longer authentic and free individual choices, but rather distorted and manipulated versions thereof.[66]

So far, I have assumed that the preferences of corporations correspond to the preferences of some individuals—be they the managers or the shareholders, or possibly some other group. This, however, is not necessarily the case. Our description of organizations as *opaque*[67] implies that a position taken by the corporation can be sometimes meaningfully attributed only to *it*, in that no individual can be found whose personal preferences inform or coincide with the corporate position. We may call such corporate preferences *artificial preferences*. The intrusion of artificial preferences into the political process constitutes a fourth way of corrupting its ability to register individual preferences.

The conclusion that through exclusion, double counting, and falsification, and by generating artificial preferences, corporations (and, to a varying degree, other organizations) distort the process of majoritarian politics has a direct bearing on the issue of individual rights and on the role of courts in resolving individuals' claims against the state. The farther political reality departs from the simplified image (or the ideal) of pure majoritarianism, the stronger becomes the case for judicial activism in the face of governmental action. The case is strengthened in two ways. First, discarding with respect to a particular state action the premise that it reflects the majority's choice removes one possibly potent objection to a court's intervention in that area. Secondly, the identification of specific imperfections in the operation of the majoritarian political process gives rise to an affirmative argument, based on majoritarian concerns, for judicial activism. Such activism may sometimes be positively required precisely in order to correct such imperfections and reaffirm the majority's preferences that have been muted or distorted in governmental operations.[68]

What all this comes down to is a counsel of suspicion: governmental positions cannot always be assumed to enjoy the backing of a majoritarian political process. This suspicion, however, does not have to be a general one, but can be selective. Courts should scrutinize governmental claims with special care whenever they deal with areas—such as, for example, environmental policy—in which corporations (or other powerful organizations) seem to have high stakes. In such areas, courts must look suspiciously at the rhetoric used by the state to justify its position and must maintain a heightened awareness of the possibility that not the public interest or popular will, but rather corporate or other special interests, inform the government's position.

CONCLUSION

The individualistic legal conception of organizations, described and criticized in Chapter 1, has as its corollary an individualistic conception of the state, which I call political individualism. Political individualism overlooks the significance of organizations as distinctive components in the political structure of society, and hence as essential in any adequate account of the state and its role. I have contrasted political individualism with four different models of what I call political pluralism. While they all recognize the significance of organizations to our conception of the state, each of them brings out a different aspect of that recognition. In this way, each of the models contributes a different dimension to the critique of the myopic view of the issue of individual rights induced by political individualism. In the next chapter, I will introduce another pluralist view of the state, the *organizational state* model, which, while preserving the main insights contained in the various models discussed so far, makes the state amenable to normative analysis in terms of the organizational perspective that has been developed in this study.

Chapter IX

The Organizational Conception
of the State

THE ORGANIZATIONAL STATE MODEL

The common denominator of the four pluralist models discussed in Chapter 8 is their tripartite vision of political society, in which individuals, organizations, and the state are recognized as significantly distinctive entities. In this respect, the fifth model, to be presented now, involves a more far-reaching use of an organizational perspective. By portraying the state itself in organizational terms, the *organizational state* model challenges both the state's uniqueness as an entity, with significantly distinctive features of its own, and its unity, that is, the conception of it as a single entity.

The challenge to the state's normative uniqueness posed by applying to it an organizational conception is not new. The French jurist Léon Duguit, for example, described the state as a "complex public service corporation,"[1] whose acts have to be justified by, and whose decisions draw their authority and legitimacy from, the pubic services which it is the duty of this particular corporation to provide.

More recent developments not only buttress the amenability of the state to analysis in organizational terms but also suggest that it may be more fruitful and accurate to view the state (or government) not as a single organization but rather as a loose coalition of more or less independent organizations.[2] Such a conception of the state is primarily a product of the enormous expansion in the size of government and the scope of its operations. The large size and complexity of modern government call for and bring about a relatively high degree of decentralization. The decentralized units undergo a process of bureaucratization in which they define their own institutional sub-goals, develop their peculiar operating procedures, carve out an area of special expertise, and become attached to their own constituencies. They thus grow farther apart, attaining an increasing degree of functional independence that makes their subsumption under a single unifying category such as "government" decreasingly plausible or informative.

Furthermore, the dividing line between the set of organizations that are conventionally called government and other, "private" organizations is progressively blurred.[3] Quasi-governmental units are established in which governmental and private resources are meshed in some new organization, which can be described as being on the (vanishing) borderline between the public and the private spheres.[4] By "contracting out," traditionally governmental functions are undertaken by "private" enterprises, but within the framework of an ongoing contractual and supervisory relationship with governmental agencies.[5] Other "private" sectors are regulated by law to an extent that allows them a degree of independence no greater than that afforded to some agencies that are tied more closely and formally into the governmental structure.[6]

The twin tendencies of government toward decentralization and bureaucratization thus suggest an essential similarity and continuity between governmental and nongovernmental organizations. We are accordingly likely to find in many governmental bureaucracies the same organizational features that were listed in Chapter 2, and, consequently, we can apply to these governmental organizations the normative analysis pertaining to organizations in general which was proposed in Chapter 4.

This reductionist exercise, which resolves the issue of the state's legal status by in effect eliminating the state as a distinctive entity from the tripartite structure maintained by the other pluralist models, has both formal and substantive advantages. On the formal side, the advantages are those of economy and uniformity. We abide by Ockham's dictum when we cut down the number of basic entities used for the purpose of normative analysis, and we attain a degree of theoretically welcome uniformity by comprehending the state and other organizations within a single normative framework.

The substantive advantages of the proposed approach depend on the soundness of the general normative conclusions regarding organizations which have been reached in this study. If the claim that the state resembles other organizations in some important respects is correct, then the application to the state of our general normative framework will be as fruitful (or as fruitless) as this framework is when applied to other organizations. At any rate, the very attempt to derive normative implications from a vision of the state as a loose coalition of semi-independent bureaucratic organizations is, I believe, a useful exercise in demystification.

However, whatever the benefits, both formal and substantive, of the present exercise, they are likely to be purchased at a prohibitively high cost unless prefaced with an emphatic caveat— namely, that the reductionism in which we will now engage, taken by itself, is no sounder than is its counterpart in political individualism which was denounced in the preceding chapter. Perhaps more than elsewhere in this study, it is important now to remember that what is presented here does not purport to be a comprehensive and exhaustive theory, but a single, partial perspective, to be qualified and supplemented by other points of view.

NORMATIVE IMPLICATIONS

Conceived in organizational terms, the state neither inspires particularly great awe nor does it arouse special deference. Like other organizations, so also governmental bureaucracies are seen under the present model as instrumentalities whose legitimacy and normative status depend on their ability to discharge certain functions and to promote certain goals.

In the simplified normative universe presupposed in this study, these goals and functions must ultimately serve one of two sets of values: they must either promote social welfare or contribute to the protection of some individual rights. In fact, both sets of concerns are commonly imputed to the state. As a result, the state's normative vocabulary straightforwardly follows that which we have devised for use by other organizations. The state's legal claims may accordingly rest either on utility rights, based on its goal of promoting social welfare, or on derivative autonomy rights, based on its goal of protecting individual rights.

By referring to the state in the singular, this last statement ignores, however, the other aspect of the organizational state model, that is, the disassembling of the state into its manifold constituent organizations. The tasks of particular governmental departments, agencies, and other bureaus are likely to be differently related to the twin goals of social utility and individual rights. This difference will be reflected in the normative character of legal claims made by the various governmental organizations.

In order to deal with this variety, it may be helpful to employ with respect to the state the same rough typology of organizations which was proposed in Chapter 5.[7] As the reader may recall, I introduced there a distinction between *utilitarian organizations*, whose goals are predominantly linked to the promotion of society's general welfare, and *protective organizations*, whose goals explicitly comprise the protection of some individual rights. As a crude approximation, it should be possible to classify some governmental bureaus—those whose tasks are defined in terms of some aspect of social welfare—as utilitarian organizations, and treat their legal claims (at least presumptively) in a way that befits utility rights. Similarly, we should be able to characterize other governmental bureaus—those charged primarily with the protection of individual rights—as protective organizations, and presumptively expect their legal claims to be supportable by derivative autonomy rights.

The immediate advantage of such an approach is that it dispels the inclination, encouraged by a rhetoric that refers to the state (or to government) as a single unified entity, to adopt a pro-government or anti-government attitude in relation to the issue of individual rights. This inclination is manifest in the tension that we have observed within political pluralism between the private governments model, whose proponents tend to be suspicious of "private" organizations and relative supporters of "the state," and neo-feudalism, the sympathies of whose advocates are reversed. By "splitting government apart," and by underscoring the essential similarity between its constituent bureaucracies and non-governmental organizations, the organizational state model leads to a certain accommodation between the seemingly conflicting insights contained in these other two models. It suggests that, at least in some cases, it makes better sense to consider the relevant claims advanced on the side of "government" as made on behalf of the particular governmental bureaucracy—the agency, the department, etc.—which is directly involved in the matter under consideration. Such a pluralistic view of the government itself may allow us to adopt a more discriminating normative position with respect to it. We may be willing to acknowledge wide-ranging derivative autonomy rights in some governmental organizations, and at the same time we may want to restrict other governmental organizations and limit their rights, prompted by specific considerations having to do with the functions of those organizations and the threat they pose to individual liberties. This suggested accommodation marks the intricacy of the enterprise of protecting individual rights in the organizational society. This enterprise often requires the pitting of one organization against another, irrespective of their governmental or nongovernmental affiliation, and the delicate balancing by courts of their respective claims to power and autonomy.

To be sure, organizations hardly ever state their legal claims in the abstract language of power or autonomy. In the legal field, they guard their autonomy and try to increase their power by making concrete claims cast in the vocabulary of specific legal rights and duties. Some implications for the substantive analysis of those legal claims that follow from their characterization as either utility rights or derivative autonomy rights were discussed in Part II and need not be rehearsed here. All I want to point out in this respect is the essential similarity between the analysis of substantive legal claims made on behalf of "government" and those made by other organizations. I will now indicate another, though related, implication of the present perspective, which has to do with the desirable degree of a court's activism (or restraint) when reviewing governmental action.

ACTIVISM OR RESTRAINT
IN JUDICIAL REVIEW

The application to governmental bureaucracies of the distinction between protective and utilitarian organizations, with its correlative assignment of DARs and URs to those bureaucracies, provides a clue (though by no means the only clue) to the stance courts should adopt when engaged in judicial review (whether of a constitutional kind or not). By the courts' stance, I mean the extent of their intervention or abstention, activism or restraint, in relation to various governmental actions and decisions that are subject to judicial review.[8] A court's stance, whether active or passive, does not accordingly refer to the substantive standards by which the court assesses the propriety of government action but only to the degree of the court's willingness to probe into a particular transaction and subject it to a thorough examination in the light of such standards, whatever they may be. The court's stance is made operational by means of a variety of institutional and doctrinal devices such as the initial considerations as to whether to issue a certiorari, principles of ripeness and standing, and principles defining the "scope" of review which guide the court in its decisions. These devices allow the court to economize on its limited resources by abstaining in a great many cases from a full substantive assessment of government action.

Though a court's activist or deferential stance is in this way distinct from its substantive position, there is an obviously close relationship between the two. This relationship is comprised of two elements. The first has to do with the relative importance, from the court's perspective, of the values implicated in the case under consideration. The second has to do with the likelihood that those values would in fact be advanced by the governmental action, even if that action is unchecked or unimpeded by the court's intervention. One would expect the court's relative activism to be correlated with the former factor and inversely related to the latter.

To see how the assignment to various government bureaucracies of URs and DARs may influence the courts' stance in reviewing government actions, we must recall the relationship that we have assumed to exist between those two kinds of rights. A commitment to individual autonomy rights requires a special solicitude with respect to their protection (and hence the protection of DARs necessary for that purpose) in the face of conflicting claims made on behalf of society's general welfare.[9] Insofar as courts share (and indeed, as many believe, embody) such a commitment, the degree of their activism or deference regarding governmental action should vary depending on their estimation of the likelihood that individual rights thought by the court to be important would be violated in a certain sphere of governmental action. This estimation is somewhat facilitated by the organizational perspective that is proposed here. The point can be best made by focusing on the role of courts in supervising the relationship between governmental and "private" organizations. Though the fact is somewhat obscured by the habit of referring to government (or the state) as a unified, homogeneous entity, commentators have pointed out that the courts' stance in reviewing governmental action varies in relation to different government agencies and other bureaus.[10] The organizational approach offers both support and guidance for such a selective attitude.

The first thing to notice is that from our present perspective there is nothing distinctive about the relationship between a governmental and a private organization. Instead, it is just an instance of the general category of interorganizational relations, that is, an O-O relationship. The depiction of the state-organization interaction as an O-O relation suggests an important corrective to the above-mentioned view according to which courts' stance in judicial review varies in relation to the different governmental bureaus that are under review. The degree of a court's activism or passivity cannot be determined solely by its conception of the particular government agency (or other bureau) whose actions are challenged. Instead, the court must consider the nature of the interaction in which it is invited to intervene, meaning that it should take account of the relevant properties of both organizations—the governmental and the nongovernmental—that are parties to the dispute. The same governmental bureau may accordingly be subjected to a different degree of judicial supervision, depending on who is its counterpart in the particular transaction.

As I will now show, the characterization of both governmental and nongovernmental organizations as either protective or utilitarian can help us to formulate, albeit only in a rough and schematic way, some propositions regarding the appropriate degree of judicial activism in reviewing various governmental actions.

We can begin with the relation that, from the perspective of individual rights (here assumed to be the courts' paramount concern), should concern the courts least, and with respect to which they should therefore adopt a relatively restrained stance. It is a relationship that involves a protective government organization on the one side and a utilitarian nongovernmental organization on the other. The reason for a court's relative passivity regarding such a relationship is quite plain. A protective governmental organization can deviate from its legal mandate in one of two ways: it can either exceed it, evincing greater zeal than it should in the protection of rights, or it can be overly inhibited in its activities and underprotect those rights. The latter possibility should be, of course, a cause of concern for a court mindful of the adequate protection of rights, but it is unlikely to be the subject matter of the utilitarian organization's complaint: by definition, such an organization is not institutionally concerned to vindicate the individual rights that are under-protected by the delinquent government agency.

The other possibility, that of overprotection of individual rights by the governmental bureaucracy, can have two kinds of ramifications. One is to unduly compromise the complaining organization's utilitarian interests. But though this should be deemed undesirable (*ex hypothesi*, from the point of view of the relevant legislative scheme), such effect is not terribly distressing for the courts: as guardians of individual rights who are in general willing to pay a price in social welfare for the protection of those rights, courts will not be overly alarmed by the general suspicion that the price paid in a certain area is somewhat excessive. It is the constriction, not the expansion, of an individual right which concerns them most and calls for their active intervention.[11]

The other possible ramification of a protective governmental organization's overzealousness does, however, threaten the violation of individual rights: in protecting the rights of some individuals with exaggerated vigor, the organization may trample the rights of other individuals.

This possibility needs special emphasizing because it can easily be overlooked. Once we classify an organization (whether governmental or not) as protective, we may be tempted to impute to it a generally favorable attitude to individual rights. To resist such a temptation, we must be alert to the radical difference between the nature of the typical case of an individual's commitment to rights (or, for that matter, to other goals and values) and an organization's commitment. In the case of the individual, it is customary and appropriate to interpret the commitment to a particular right in terms of a more or less coherent emotional and intellectual scheme, which permits sound extrapolation from the person's stand regarding some individual rights to his or her stand regarding other rights. But an organization's goals (unlike the values of particular individuals within it) are devoid of the affective and cognitive qualities with which individual normative positions are typically suffused. To describe an organization as protective only indicates the existence within it of certain standard operating procedures and decisionmaking mechanisms whose operation is interpretable in terms of their contribution to the protection of some specific rights. Such description does not therefore connote a particularly benign picture of the organization as necessarily more solicitous or less detrimental to individual rights in general than are utilitarian organizations. Indeed, like all other organizations, protective organizations, too, are subject to the syndrome of goal-displacement (described in Chapter 2).[12] They are likely to pay exclusive attention to the specific rights to whose protection they are institutionally committed, while disregarding and occasionally violating other, and possibly more important rights.

The possibility that a protective governmental organization would be guilty of violating individual rights is therefore a serious one, and one that should concern the courts. However, like the underprotection of rights by the governmental bureau, so also their violation by it is not likely to be the subject matter of the utilitarian organization's complaint in the kind of interaction presently under discussion. The possibility of rights violation by a protective governmental organization does not therefore add to the courts' interest in the interaction between such an organization and a utilitarian organization, and should not spur the courts into a more activist stance with respect to that interaction.

As an illustration of the interaction presently under discussion, consider the Equal Employment Opportunity Board and its relation to a large business corporation suspected of a Title VII violation.[13] If courts must economize on their resources, they should be thoroughly deferential to that agency's position when it takes action against the delinquent corporation. As the preceding analysis pointed out, the corporation's resistance to the EEOB's proposed action is likely to hinder, not promote, the cause of individual rights. And though, like other organizations, EEOB may be guilty of overzealousness, seeking to impose on the corporation an excessively costly degree of compliance, the result, though suboptimal, will be biased in a relatively welcome direction that should not particularly concern the court.

Contrast this case with one in which the same government agency, the EEOB, confronts not a corporation (which I take to be a utilitarian organization) but a university. As you may recall, I have already suggested[14] that one of the university's main functions is the promotion and protection of academic freedom, which can be viewed as an individual autonomy right. The interaction between the EEOB and the university exemplifies, accordingly, an interaction between two protective organizations. Here courts can no longer treat the risk of the governmental agency's overzealousness with relative equanimity. Excessive measures in protection of equal employment opportunity may here encroach upon the university's derivative autonomy rights, whose protection is necessary in order to safeguard academic freedom from unwarranted governmental intrusions. Furthermore, unlike the case of the business corporation, it is both likely and appropriate that the university should resist the agency's excessive measures on grounds that have to do with the protection of the right to academic freedom.[15]

Similar to the example of the EEOB is that of the National Labor Relations Board. Here, too, courts may be relatively less concerned, and therefore relatively deferential to the Board when it deals with business corporations, whereas they should more carefully scrutinize the Board's decisions that negatively affect a trade union. Insofar as unions exist in order to protect the rights of individual employees, their governmental regulation should be reviewed with a certain degree of heightened awareness.

Notice, however, a difference between the case of the *EEOB v. The University* and the case of the *NLRB v. The Trade Union* which allows us to rank them differently in terms of the appropriate intensity of judicial review. In the latter case, both of the organizations, the governmental and the private, are protecting essentially the same kinds of individual rights. Their mutual accommodation, even with little judicial intervention, is therefore likely to redound to an acceptable (even if not optimal) level of protection of those underlying employee rights. The former case, by contrast, pits against each other two protective organizations that are concerned with a different set of substantive values. The EEOB is likely to focus exclusively on the protection of equal employment rights, whereas the university is likely to be primarily mindful of the importance of academic freedom. An active umpire, who will bring to bear on the transaction a less parochial view than that of either of the two organizational contenders, may therefore be needed in order to make sure that one set of values does not unduly eclipse the other.

I have so far discussed relations involving governmental protective organizations. I will now mention some considerations relevant to the courts' attitude in reviewing the actions of utilitarian governmental organizations. Consider first the interaction between such a government agency and a private utilitarian organization. The regulation of airlines by the Civil Aeronautics Board, antitrust actions taken by the Federal Trade Commission, and rulings by the Federal Power Commission regarding oil and gas companies can all be classified as belonging to this broad category of governmental activities. Government policies in this area, as well as the corporate interests directly affected by them, are likely to be predominantly of a utilitarian kind. Conflicts between the governmental and the private utilitarian organizations are thus unlikely to give rise to issues of individual rights. From the perspective of protecting individual rights, this entire area is accordingly of relatively limited judicial interest. Courts may therefore soundly adopt a deferential, restrained stance in this area.

It should, however, be observed that this recommendation for judicial passivity is somewhat less compelling than was the similar recommendation I made regarding the case of a protective government organization that deals with a utilitarian private organization (such as in the case of the EEOB versus a business corporation). In the latter case, we have seen, the most likely distortion that may result from the courts' failure to intervene is an overprotection of certain individual rights, purchased at an excessive cost in utility terms; whereas in the kind of case presently under consideration (involving utilitarian organizations on both sides), the allegedly inadequate governmental action, which the court is asked to rectify, will most likely only lead to utility losses without a corresponding increase in the protection of rights. Insofar as the currency of individual rights is intrinsically more valuable to courts than are utilitarian values, the bias in favor of rights created by the courts' passivity in reviewing the actions of a protective government agency should be of least concern to courts. Courts may, however, be somewhat less indifferent to the allegation that certain government actions systematically reduce social utility, when they can find no comfort in the thought that some extra protection of individual rights is attained thereby.

Finally, we reach the relation that ranks highest in our scheme in terms of the appropriate degree of judicial activism. It is that between a utilitarian government agency and a private protective organization. Here the private organization's derivative autonomy rights may be at stake, and they may be unduly compromised by the government agency's single-mindedness in promoting its utility goals. Consequently, the courts' protection of the derivative autonomy rights, and hence indirectly of the individual autonomy rights, threatened by governmental policies may be called for in these cases with special urgency.

I have already mentioned the actions taken by the FTC in the antitrust area as examples of a relation that involves utilitarian organizations on both sides of the interaction and is typically informed by purely utilitarian considerations. As such, I suggested, it is not the kind of relation that should concern courts most. The operation of trade unions may sometimes interfere with certain aspects of the free market economy no less than do some corporate practices forbidden for that very reason by antitrust laws. It is clear, however, that imposing on trade unions analogous constraints to those that apply to business corporations would give rise to radically different concerns that have ultimately to do with the unions' ability to effectively defend employees' rights. The fact that trade unions are precluded, by and large, from the strictures of antitrust laws reflects in part the recognition by Congress of this crucial difference.[16] Elsewhere, when the legislative mandate of a governmental utilitarian agency does not distinguish between its relation to utilitarian and to protective private organizations, that line must be drawn by the courts. It will be manifested in a more active stance adopted by the court when the utilitarian agency's actions are directed toward a protective organization than when the same agency deals with a utilitarian organization.

These observations are summarized in Figure 4, which ranks the various governmental operations we have discussed in terms of the intensity of judicial review they call for.

This ranking is, of course, just as crude as the typology that underlies it is coarse-grained. Furthermore, this ranking and the

the appropriate judicial stance	type of governmental organization involved	type of private organization involved	comments
1. active	utilitarian	protective	
2.	protective	protective	the two organizations protect different rights
3.	protective	protective	the two organizations protect the same rights
4.	utilitarian	utilitarian	
5. passive	protective	utilitarian	

Figure 4. Stances of Judicial Review

preceding discussion are one-dimensional: they measure degrees of judicial activism exclusively in terms of a single factor, which is the potential threat that certain government actions pose to individual rights. The exercise of deriving this ranking has been, I hope, nonetheless worthwhile. First, especially when it comes to devising their general strategy and to planning their economy of energies and resources, courts must rely on some crude approximations that will be mainly of presumptive value in their actual decisionmaking. Secondly, and for my present purposes more importantly, the ranking of the judicial stance that the organizational state model helped us derive provides a vivid demonstration of the more abstract dual point that this model is supposed to convey. It is the importance of taking into account in legal decisionmaking the organizational properties, both descriptive and normative, of government, and of bearing in mind that those properties differ with respect to different governmental agencies and other bureaus in ways that are legally consequential.

Conclusion: Organizations, Position-Holders, Communities, and Oversize Bees

The main purpose of these concluding remarks is to place the present study in somewhat broader context. I shall do so by first relating the present theory to some other views of organization, particularly to the radical critique of bureaucracy; and then by considering some further matters that a complete legal theory for a bureaucratic society might have to explore. I will try, however, to keep these comments very brief, so as to succumb only sparingly to the temptation—which a conclusion commonly presents to an author—to reach beyond the bounds of one's theoretical structure.

To begin with, I should like to observe that in contrast to the heated polemic tone—conveying either a general pro- or anti-organizational attitude—which often marks discussions concerning organizations, the instrumental view of organization espoused in this book conceives organizations in rather neutral terms. Instruments are of contingent, derivative value, but they are of value nonetheless. However, like other instrumentalities—knives, for example—organizations, too, have dangerous propensities. The attitude to organizations thus fostered by their instrumental conception is one of circumspection. The aim is to use the tool to good effect, while reducing the risk of doing unnecessary damage. This, at any rate, has been the goal of the theory of organizational rights which has been the centerpiece of this essay. I have presented this theory in emphatic contradistinction to the tendency, encouraged by the models of personification and aggregation, to ascribe to organizations the same rights as those that belong to individuals. The conception of the organization as an "intelligent machine" leads instead to a sharp distinction between rights that apply to

individuals and those that apply to organizations, significantly constricting the latter. This is particularly evident in regard to those
organizations—such as business corporations—whose claims by
and large rest on utilitarian considerations bereft of concern for
individual autonomy. In this respect, then, the present theory is
less generous toward organizations in general, and business corporations in particular, than some of those organizations' more
ardent apologists may wish it to be.

It should also be emphasized, however, that the present theory
is equally opposed to a view of organizational legal rights which is
held by some of the organization's detractors and which has also
exerted a measure of influence on the legal treatment of organizations. I have in mind the so-called "concession theory" of
corporate legal personality, according to which corporations (and
other organizations) owe their existence to the state. Consequently,
this theory claims, organizations can have no other rights than
those explicitly granted to them by their creator, and they can be
rightfully subjected to whatever constraints the state wishes to
impose on them. As should be clear, the theory of organizational
rights proposed here rejects both the premise and the conclusion of
the "concession theory" in its various manifestations. Far from
being the state's creation, organizations are portrayed here as a
primary generic category of social entities, a category under which
the state's own bureaucracies are also subsumed. Furthermore, the
respective normative status of these entities (the governmental
ones included) is firmly grounded in sound considerations of political morality, of the same kind (though with different substantive
consequences) as the considerations that ground and determine the
legal rights of individual human beings.[1]

My refusal to indiscriminately espouse a condemnatory or lau-
datory view of organizations is also expressed in a central thesis of
this essay, namely, that in the organizational society the pursuit of
social utility need not conflict with the protection of individual
rights as frequently as is commonly believed. By recognizing that
organizations often serve as "moral buffers" that bring about a
qualitative change in the moral texture of social relationships, and
by differentiating between individuals and organizations both in
terms of the applicable substantive principles and the appropriate
institutional structures, the law can attain a higher level of social

utility, coupled with a greater degree of respect for individual autonomy, than may otherwise be thought possible.

It may seem, however, that this attempt to link the instrumental view of organization with a claim to increased room for individual autonomy makes sense only so long as we ignore (as I largely did in this study) the individual constituents of the organization—whom I shall call the position-holders. My rejection of simple-minded reductionism in dealing with organizational realities does not, however, imply a denial of the obvious truth that organizations are constituted, at least in part, by individuals and their actions. While it may often be fully intelligible, adequate, and sufficient to focus exclusively on the O-O aspect of a relationship, the same transaction obviously involves numerous individuals, in their capacity as position-holders within the organization. It is plain, moreover, that a theory of law in the organizational society must come to terms not only with the organizational phenomenon but also with "organization man."

Once our attention is drawn to the position-holder, to the organization man and woman, a potentially more sinister side of the organization, on which the organization's critics predominantly focus, comes immediately to light. This sinister side is conveyed most vividly by the very metaphor—that of an intelligent machine—which has been proposed here as adequately capturing the normatively essential attributes of the organization. The mechanical metaphor directly induces the familar and ominous imagery of the individual position-holders as the "cogs" of that machine, an imagery that naturally fuels much of the anti-organization sentiment. Indeed, insofar as this image is valid, this essay's attitude of relative neutrality toward organizations can no longer be plausibly maintained. Rather than offering the opportunity for a benign accommodation between the claims of individual autonomy and social utility, organizations may themselves be the main battleground in the struggle between these clusters of values: whatever contributions organizations make to society's welfare (or even to the protection of individual rights) is necessarily purchased at the price of depriving the "organization man" of his (or the organization woman of her) individual autonomy. In this view, the massive suppression of individual autonomy is the very essence of bureaucratic organization; liberation may require nothing short of dismantling or radically transforming these social entities, thus raising the specter of staggering costs in social utility which such a program will arguably entail.[2]

Nothing I have said in this book refutes this familiar radical critique of the bureaucratic organization, and it is not my aim to attempt such a refutation at this point. For one thing, even accepting the critique would not undermine the present theory, though it would render it transitory: a temporary recipe for dealing with organizations on the (apparently long) march to the ultimate doomsday or utopia held up by the critique. It may nonetheless be worthwhile to point up a weak link in the radical position, one that is directly related to my theory. It has to do with a certain complexity in the relationship between individual autonomy and the instrumental view of bureaucratic organizations, a complexity that is commonly overlooked by the critique. My point is that the insistence on the instrumental conception of organizations may itself be an important antidote to the coglike status of organizational position-holders. To conceive of the organization as a sheer instrumentality is *pro tanto* to begin to wriggle out of its oppressive grip and to assert one's individuality and supremacy over it even while discharging one's tasks within it.

To see this more clearly, let us take a closer look at what the cog metaphor might signify. Two different claims can be discerned here. One is that organizations often treat individual position-holders as dispensable and fungible resources—as mere means to the organization's ends. A normative theory of organizations which is predicated on their instrumental view (such as is the present one) plainly tends to ameliorate these dangers. It is precisely by insisting on the sheer instrumentality of the organization and by asserting the priority of individual autonomy over considerations of social utility that individuals can protect their rights and freedoms within and against the organization.[3]

The cog metaphor implies, however, a second, deeper, and potentially more devastating critique of the organization. It is that organizational position-holders are not only treated as cogs but are actually becoming ones: by fully internalizing the organizational point of view, individuals are espousing an instrumental self-definition that pervades their entire being, shaping their social interactions and molding their world view. But notice an element of paradox in this familiar charge. If the Organization Man does indeed lose his soul to the corporation, as the critics argue, then he at any rate is unlikely to share the instrumental view of organizations which fuels the critics' attack on them: no one is likely to construct and maintain a self that is subservient to and derivative from what one takes to be a mere machine. If we now read this paradox in reverse, we can get a clue to a possible answer to the critical attack. By adopting and assimilating the instrumental conception of organization emphasized in this study, individuals may gain a certain immunity from having their souls overtaken by bureaucracy. The concept that is best suited, I think, to describe this immunity and the accommodation between individual and organization which it implies is that of role-distance.[4] As I use it here, this concept stands for the idea that certain social roles, notably those defined by and discharged within formal organizations, can be acquired and carried out without being fully internalized, that is, without being fully integrated into the self. The self can thus be distinguished from such social roles, and individuals can engage in these roles while preserving a certain psychological distance between their selves and their role behavior. The instrumental conception of the organization can thus be refracted and experienced on the individual level in terms of the phenomenon of role-distance. The continuum that I have previously described between the individual actor and the full-fledged formal organization[5] can be roughly recapitulated in the case of the individual position-holder in terms of the role-distance that he appropriately maintains: the more a collectivity assumes the bureaucratic features of the formal organization, and thus the closer it resembles the "intelligent machine," the greater the role-distance that might be appropriately maintained by position-holders in that organization.[6] I can here do no more than simply state the view, which I share, that it is in the space created by role-distance—between the self and the role—that some reprieve from the repressive potentialities of the organization is afforded and an opportunity for the exercise of autonomy and the expression of personhood is provided.[7]

There are three obvious dangers associated with the notion of role-distance: they are those of destruction, manipulation, and alienation. None seems inevitable, however. The destructive potential of role-distance is plain: the manifestations of role-distance can range from failure to fully carry out one's task to active attempts at organizational sabotage.[8] But role-distance need not take the form of role-rejection. There can be more positive forms of distancing, in which one maintains a certain remove even as one carries out one's tasks meticulously and zestfully.

Role-distance also opens up opportunities for manipulation. One can take advantage of the perquisites and powers of one's office while using one's role to deliberately and self-consciously hide from the appeals of one's fellow human beings.[9] However, the opportunity for manipulation is reduced, if not altogether eliminated, if role-distance is the shared norm. Here the position-holder's interaction with others is always mediated, as it were, by a *wink*: by a tacit reference to the shared understanding that one is "merely" acting out one's role in a way that does not fully implicate and engage one's self. By means of this "wink," the position-holder hints to her counterpart at the ever-present space of individuality and autonomy opened up by role-distance while at the same time discharging her official duties. The interaction is thus not completely drained of its human dimension and warmth. These qualities are instead only provisionally and partially suspended by tacit mutual agreement based on the mutually perceived desirability of the organizational role and its adequate performance.

Finally, role-distance may, but need not, signify alienation from one's role. As Erving Goffman points out, "although the person who manifests much role distance may, in fact, be alienated from his role, still, the opposite can well be true: in some cases only those who feel secure in their attachment may be able to chance the expression of distance."[10] Perhaps even more importantly, we should not confuse one's organizational role with the work one does in discharging that role. (That the two are distinct is evidenced, for example, by the obvious possibility that a single role may call for the execution of different kinds of work on different occasions.) Thus the role-distance of which I am talking describes one's attitude only to the particular organizational setting in which one carries out one's work, not to the work itself. The latter may be fully engaging and fulfilling, or monotonous and alienating, irrespective of the social setting in which it is carried out.

Keeping firmly in mind the instrumental conception of the organization helps to foster a capacity and propensity for role-distance. Widely spread, such a conception can provide the necessary background for a shared norm of role-distance; it would at the same time diminish the occasion for the manipulative handling of roles, by making apparent to all parties involved the essentially contrived or playful attitude to organizational roles. It can now be seen that insofar as the law participates in the formation of basic social attitudes of the kind discussed here, its consistent adoption of an approach to organizations which is predicated on the machine metaphor along the lines elaborated in this study may help induce the instrumental conception of organization and hence encourage role-distance as the appropriate stance toward one's organizational position. By a reversal of the paradox that marks the radical critique, the law's very adoption of a strictly instrumental view of organizations may help in this way to counter the oppressive tendencies that inhere in this instrumental mode of social organization, and thus indirectly augment the zone of individuality and autonomy.

Unhappily, however, even this modestly optimistic conclusion cannot be left unqualified. By reversing the paradox, we do not get rid of the real dilemma that underlies it. Seeing bureaucratic organizations for what they are—impersonal social instrumentalities—helps diffuse some of the dangers posed by personifying them or otherwise imputing to them values they do not embody or possess. But the relationship between how we conceive and portray these social entities and what they "really" are is plainly enough a dialetical one: by projecting an instrumental image of the organization, and by adopting the norms and attitudes implied by it, we are not merely describing and responding to given data, but are also to a certain degree legislating it into existence; the instrumental view of the organization may therefore itself enhance some of the oppressive organizational attributes that are commonly associated with the bureaucratic organization's relentless instrumentality.[11] Whether or not this dilemma admits of any resolution, the least we must do to reduce its opposing dangers is to be acutely aware of its existence.

These comments go some way toward discharging the second task of this conclusion: to indicate the major issues not discussed in this study which ought to be addressed by a complete legal theory for bureaucratic society. Plainly, in the bureaucratic society the position-holder is a figure who deserves special attention. As I have already indicated, the concept of role-distance may be a key factor in a theory of position-holders which tries to articulate and accommodate the claims of individuality and autonomy, on the one side, and those of the organizational role, on the other. Though it would be foolhardy to attempt here any specification of the content of such a theory, it might be useful to briefly illustrate the kind of correspondence that can be envisioned between the present theory and the projected study of position-holders.

First, failure by a position-holder to maintain the appropriate role-distance presents on the individual level dangers analogous to that of goal-displacement, which we have noted on the institutional level:[12] as is well-known, an overzealous and excessively literal execution of a function that can result from total role identification may undermine the substantive goals to which that role is supposed to contribute.

Secondly, a legal theory of organizational position-holders, whatever its details, would also likely accomplish on the individual level a shift of emphasis similar to the one advocated in this study on the institutional level: de-emphasizing the traditional dividing line that separates the state from the rest of "private" society, and drawing instead a sharper line between individuals, on the one side, and organizations—including governmental ones—on the other. A theory of organizational position-holders would similarly gather together, as raising the same issues and amenable to the same legal treatment, all "detachable" roles—no matter whether governmental, corporate, or other—and juxtapose them to "primary" or "integrated" individual selves. By thus focusing on the dichotomy between self and organizational role, and viewing role-distance as a crucial variable, a theory of position-holders is likely to undermine whatever discontinuities there presently are in the law between the treatment of government officials and that of private functionaries, and thus replicate on the individual level the main thesis of Part IV of this book.

Finally, I have argued in this book that different mixtures of considerations of utility and autonomy should apply to various social entities depending on the degree of their bureaucratization and their relative proximity to the organizational pole of the O-I continuum. Again, a corresponding pattern may be observed on the individual level. The concept of role-distance may help to account for and further articulate a differential legal attitude to the scope of and the measures used in the regulation of various social roles. The view that the self can be related differently to different roles—that of mother, for example, and that of Supervisor—indicates a varying balance between individual autonomy and legal regulation in regard to these respective roles. A worked out theory would perhaps be able to establish a systematic correspondence between different role-distances and the legal norms and measures that pertain to the corresponding roles.

The other major component of a comprehensive legal theory for a bureaucratic society which is missing from the present study must be introduced with much greater caution and diffidence. By focusing on large, formal, bureaucratic organizations, I have neglected in this study the more intimate, affective, informal aspects of human association which might be designated by the term *community*. Communities, to be sure, are not particularly characteristic of the organizational society. If anything, community is squeezed out and replaced by bureaucracy. But even in the bureaucratic society (perhaps especially in it), the concept of community is of great significance both as an actuality to be found alongside formal organizations as well as inside them—and even more so as an ideal to be kept alive and born in mind in juxtaposition to the dominant bureaucratic form of social organization. It is tempting, therefore, to think of supplementing the present study by constructing a corresponding normative theory of the community. It might similarly consist of a description of an idealized community (modeled perhaps after some idealized version of the nuclear family), from which general principles regarding the appropriate legal treatment of such an entity would be derived. We would then be able to add to the individual-organization continuum considered in this book an individual-community continuum. Combining these two continua would neatly reproduce in the context of a normative theory the traditional juxtaposition of community and organization and depict the continuity between these two prototypical collective entities.[13] The general structure of the resulting theory can be schematically represented by Figure 5. The legal treatment of any specific collective entity would have to be determined by its location relative to the three continua described in this figure, that is,

Community

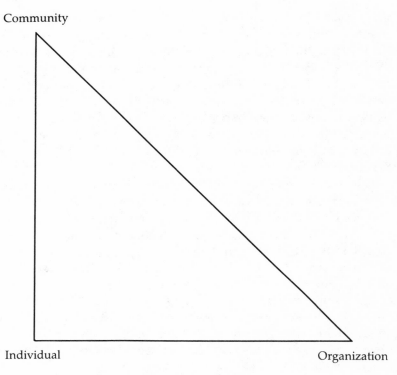

Individual   Organization

Figure 5.   Legal Entities

by the relative pull exerted by each of the three normative theories
involved—the theories that spell out, respectively, the appropriate
legal treatment of individuals, organizations, and communities.

Such a threefold structure might perhaps serve as an adequate
theoretical framework for law in organizational society. At any rate,
projecting it helps us to better understand the present study's
partial perspective. Still, I cannot leave things at that. Instead, I
must explain my hesitation in proposing this communal supplement to the present theory. My doubts have to do with a false
symmetry between organization and community which is implied
by the projected theoretical structure. Once we appreciate and
remove this fallacy, we will gain a better understanding of the O-I
dimension. I would accordingly like to suggest an interpretation of
this dimension that makes it sufficient to accommodate those social

relationships that would otherwise be placed along the added communal dimension. The point can be best made by resorting once more to the idea of role-distance.

Consider the roles of mother and Supervisor mentioned above. The Supervisor fills an organizational position, whereas the mother can be seen as playing a role within the communal framework of the family. There is, it seems to me, an important intuitive sense in which the norm of role-distance properly applies to the former role but would be utterly misplaced in the latter. In the case of social relationships held together by spiritual bonds of love, friendship, affection, or faith, fusion—not distance—is held up as the ultimate ideal. Whereas the Supervisor can successfully discharge her task while at the same time maintaining an integrated, autonomous self only if she keeps a certain remove from her role, the mother would accomplish neither—she would fail both as mother and as person—if she were to adopt a similar stance. Put somewhat differently, the point is that being a mother or father is properly part of one's self, one's self-definition as a person, in a way that being a Supervisor should not.* If so, the notion of an individual (as an object of legal treatment and a bearer of rights) must already include those deep involvements and attachments to others which are fully integrated with and thus partially constitutive of the self. Insofar as by community we mean to designate a system of such involvements and attachments, to speak of individual rights and of corresponding communal rights would be redundant: there can be no difference, in this line of argument, between what we may think of as family rights, for example, and the individual rights of the mother (or other members of the family). Put differently, insofar as the communal dimension (but not the organizational dimension) is already built into an adequate depiction of the individual, the model of aggregation—which I have rejected with respect to organizations—becomes viable in the case of the community. The normative status of the community can be exhaustively accounted

---

*There is a certain ambiguity in the use of role terms (such as "Supervisor"), which can be clarified by considering a role that displays that ambiguity with special force. A priest, for example, combines an organizational position and a spiritual mission. He can maintain role-distance relative to the former aspect of this role while fully embracing the latter.

for in terms of the rights possessed by its individual constituents. So understood, family law can be seen as the prototype of communal law, which is at the same time individual law *par excellence*.

If sound, this line of thought suggests a justification for the exclusive preoccupation of this study with formal organizations: Organizations are indeed distinctive social entities (and legal actors) in the sense that, unlike communities, they cannot be incorporated even in an expansive interpretation of individual or self. It can also now be seen that the O-I schema proposed here may turn out to be more spacious and accommodating of the variety of actual social relationships than might have been otherwise thought. This statement must, however, be understood in light of the general view of legal theory that was presented in the Introduction: To fit the wide variety of collective entities and social relationships into the O-I continuum is to coerce them into a theoretical Procrustean bed. Such an operation can be beneficial only if conducted with the limited ambitions of legal theory firmly in mind. It might be well, then, to conclude this study with a reiteration of the qualifications regarding the role and possibilities of legal theory that were spelled out in the Introduction; or better yet, with the following quotation—a useful reminder for any theoretical treatise.

But, speaking of bees, let me tell one more old story. The little Ruster, who went as a drummer at the head of the Swedish army, when in 1813 it marched into Germany, could never weary of telling stories of that wonderful land in the south. The people there were as tall as church towers, the swallows were as big as eagles, the bees as geese.

"Well, but the bee-hives?"

"The bee-hives were like our ordinary bee-hives."

"How did the bees get in?"

"Well, that they had to look out for," said the little Ruster.[14]

Notes

1. See for example the diversity of views about legal scholarship expressed in a recent symposium on this subject in 90 *Yale L. J.* no. 5 (1981).

2. Charles L. Black, Jr., "Law as an Art," *Yale Law Report,* Winter 1979–80, p. 12.

3. Oliver W. Holmes, *The Common Law* (Boston: Little, Brown, 1881; reissued by Harvard University Press, 1963), p. 5.

4. On the relation between welfare economics and utilitarianism, see Chapter 4, note 9 *infra.*

5. See Polinsky's testimony about Richard Posner, referring to his book *Economic Analysis of Law* (Boston: Little, Brown, 1972): "Although [Posner] initially concedes that his analysis has limitations, he virtually ignores them and their implications thereafter." A. Mitchell Polinsky, "Economic Analysis of Law as a Potentially Defective Product: A Buyer's Guide to Posner's Economic Analysis of Law," 87 *Harv. L. Rev.* 1655, 1657 (1974) (footnotes omitted).

6. E.g., Arthur A. Leff, "Economic Analysis of Law: Some Realism About Nominalism," 60 *Va. L. Rev.* 451 (1974).

7. See Christopher D. Stone, *Where the Law Ends: The Social Control of Corporate Behavior* (New York: Harper & Row, 1975), p. 2.

8. See, for example, Stone, *Where the Law Ends.* See also his article "Controlling Corporate Misconduct," 48 *Pub. Interest* 55 (1977); John C. Coffee, Jr., "Beyond the Shut-Eyed Sentry: Toward a Theoretical View of Corporate Misconduct and an Effective Legal Response," 63 *Va. L. Rev.* 1099 (1977); and Note, "Decision-making Models and the Control of Corporate Crime," 85 *Yale L. J.* 109 (1976). For an explicit reliance on organization theory in discussing institutional decrees, see Note, "Implementation Problems in Institutional Reform Litigation," 91 *Harv. L. Rev.* 428, 432–35 (1977). The focus in most of these studies, however, is on the

issue of the legal control of organizational behavior. Less attention is paid to other aspects of organizations' legal treatment.

9. Friedrich Kessler, "Contracts of Adhesion—Some Thoughts About Freedom of Contract," 43 *Colum. L. Rev.* 629 (1943).

10. See, for example, Lawrence Mohr, *Explaining Organizational Behavior* (San Francisco: Jossey-Bass, 1982).

CHAPTER 1

1. This is the title of Kenneth Boulding's book (New York: Harper, 1953).

2. See Robert Presthus, *The Organizational Society* (New York: Random House, 1962), especially chap. 3.

3. Peter Drucker, *Management: Tasks, Responsibilities, Practices* (New York: Harper & Row, 1973), p. ix. Charles Lindblom gives a concise description of the magnitude of this development: "Although hierarchy and bureaucracy are ancient in origin, in the contemporary world man is organized into bureaucracy as never before. In the early nineteenth century, four out of five Americans were self-employed; the number is now less than one in ten. Assuming all but the smallest corporations are bureaucratically organized, over half the gainfully employed work in bureaucracies. Another 13 million Americans work in the thousands of bureaucratic organizations that make up the federal government, fifty state governments, and 78,000 units of local government. Millions of people are also members of bureaucratically organized labor unions, employer groups, fraternal orders, veteran associations, and farm organizations. Some of these bureaucracies are enormous. By numbers employed the largest in the United States is the Defense Department with over a million civilian employees (and another 2 million in the armed forces) followed by American Telephone and Telegraph and General Motors, each with roughly 800,000. An unplanned revolution has been brought about by men who, without making a political issue out of their dimly perceived intentions, drew most of the work force out of small farming and small enterprise into the authority relations of the modern bureaucratic enterprise." Charles Lindblom, *Politics and Markets* (New York: Basic Books, 1977), p. 28.

4. For a compilation of some data on the size and concentration of American corporations, see Philip I. Blumberg, *The Megacorporation in American Society: The Scope of Corporate Power* (Englewood Cliffs, N.J.: Prentice-Hall, 1975), pp. 16–37.

5. See Christopher D. Stone, *Where the Law Ends: The Social Control of Corporate Behavior* (New York: Harper & Row, 1975), pp. 1–10; Alfred Con-

ard, *Corporations in Perspective* (Mineola, N.Y.: Foundation Press, 1976), p. 420.

6. See Introduction, p. 5 *supra.*

7. See Chapter 4, pp. 83–84 *infra* for some suggestions concerning the influence that organizations may have had on developments in various legal areas.

8. Noted examples of the early debates about the nature of corporate personality are: Arthur W. Machen, Jr., "Corporate Personality," 24 *Harv. L. Rev.* 253 (1911); Harold J. Laski, "The Personality of Associations," 19 *Harv. L. Rev.* 404 (1916); Max Radin, "The Endless Problem of Corporate Personality," 32 *Colum. L. Rev.* 643 (1932); W. Jethro Brown, "The Personality of the Corporation and the State," 21 *L. Q. Rev.* 365 (1905); Wesley N. Hohfeld, "Nature of Stockholders' Individual Liability for Corporate Debts," 9 *Colum. L. Rev.* 285 (1909); I. Maurice Wormser, "Piercing the Veil of Corporate Entity," 12 *Colum. L. Rev.* 496 (1912); George Canfield, "The Scope and Limit of the Corporate Entity Theory," 17 *Colum. L. Rev.* 128 (1917); and Judson Crane, "The Uniform Partnership Act and Legal Persons," 29 *Harv. L. Rev.* 838 (1916). For a comprehensive discussion of the various theories of corporate personality, see Frederick Hallis, *Corporate Personality* (London: Oxford University Press, 1930).

9. See Stone, *Where the Law Ends*, p. 2

10. See generally D. C. Phillips, *Holistic Thought in Social Science* (Stanford: Stanford University Press, 1976); see in particular the dispute, especially in sociology and history, concerning "methodological individualism." The issue was framed by Karl Popper in *The Open Society and Its Enemies* (Princeton, N.J.: Princeton University Press, 1950), and in *The Poverty of Historicism* (London: Routledge and Kegan Paul, 1957); and by F. A. Hayek in *Individualism and Economic Order* (London: Routledge and Kegan Paul, 1952), and in *The Counter Revolution of Science* (Glencoe, Ill.: Free Press, 1952). For some important stages in the debate that ensued, see J. W. N. Watkins, "Ideal Types and Historical Explanation," in *Readings in the Philosophy of Science*, ed. H. Feigl and M. Brodbeck (New York: Appleton-Century-Crofts, 1953), and "Historical Explanation in the Social Sciences," in *Theories of History*, ed. Patrick Gardiner (New York: Free Press, 1959), pp. 503–14; Ernst Gellner, "Holism v. Individualism in History and Sociology," ibid., pp. 488–503; Maurice Mandelbaum, "Societal Facts," ibid., pp. 476–88; K. J. Scott, "Methodological and Epistemological Individualism," in *Modes of Collectivism and Individualism*, ed. John O'Neill (London: Heinemann, 1973), pp. 215–20; Steven Lukes, "Methodological Individualism Reconsidered," in *The Philosophy of Social Explanation*, ed. Alan Ryan (Oxford: Oxford University Press, 1973), pp. 119–29.

11. In his splendid lecture "On the Nature of Legal Persons," 54 *L.Q.*

Rev. 494 (1938), Professor Martin Wolff recounts some of the "grotesque forms" that the personification of organizations has assumed throughout the ages. He cites as one example the view of John of Salisbury, the twelfth-century scholastic, who in his theory of the state "designated the prince as the head, the senate as the heart, the prince's 'assistants' as the flanks, the *praesides provinciarum* and the judges as the ears, eyes and tongue, the officials and soldiers as the hands, the Treasury and the Tax collectors . . . as the intestines and belly, the peasants and handicraftsmen as the feet, so that the misery suffered by them became the gout." Ibid., pp. 498–99. It should be noted that though we are no longer given to such "anthropomorphous extravagances" (ibid., p. 499), we still retain in our language at least one element of this account: we commonly refer to the chief executive (of a state or a corporation, for example) as the "head" of the organization. Such usage makes it natural to "impute" to the organization its "head's" state of mind—e.g., for the purpose of finding it criminally liable.

12. See, for example, Robert Hessen, *In Defense of the Corporation* (Stanford: Hoover Institution Press, 1979), p. 42: "The term corporation actually means a group of individuals who engage in a particular type of contractual relationship with each other." "When individuals join together in a voluntary venture, they neither gain nor lose any rights. Regardless of the legal form they choose for their organization—a corporation or a partnership, for example—it can only acquire and exercise those rights which its members possess as individuals—nothing more and nothing less." Ibid, p. 40. This is also the position taken by Roger Pilon, "Corporations and Rights: On Treating Corporate People Justly," 13 *Georgia L. Rev.* 1254 (1979), especially pp. 1313, 1322.

13. As the argument in this book seeks to demonstrate, rejecting the assimilation of organizations to individuals (for the purpose of their legal treatment) and insisting on viewing them as *distinctive* entities does not lead back to the so-called "concession" theories of corporate personality, which view organizations as created by the state and thus as subject to its uninhibited discretionary power. Instead, the theory that will be proposed here combines a recognition of the distinctiveness of organizations with their being right-bearing entities in ways and on grounds to be explained later. (See especially Chapter 4 and my comments on the concession theory in the conclusion, p. 200 *infra*.)

14. For a standard textbook treatment of the firm within the traditional framework of neoclassical economics, see, for example, Kelvin Lancaster, *Introduction to Modern Micro-economics* (Chicago: Rand McNally, 1969), pp. 137–79; and C. E. Ferguson, *Microeconomic Theory* (Homewood, Ill.: Richard D. Irwin, 1966), Part III.

15. See, for example, the continuum from "Individual Proprietorship," through "General" and "Limited Partnership," to "Business (or Stock) Corporation," as described under the title "Selection of Form of Business Enterprise" in a standard hornbook such as Henry Henn and John Alexander, *Laws of Corporations* (St. Paul, Minn.: West, 1983), pp. 48–138.

16. See H. H. Gerth and C. Wright Mills, eds. and trans., *From Max Weber: Essays in Sociology* (New York: Oxford University Press, 1946), pp. 196–244.

17. Gerth and Mills, eds., *From Max Weber*, p. 198.

18. For those familiar with Professor Allison's three models of organization, it may be helpful to point out that my description of the transition from the "old" to the "new" image of the corporation roughly corresponds to the transition from his model I (the Rational Actor Model) to models II (the Organizational Process Model) and III (the Governmental Politics Model). See Graham Allison, *Essence of Decision* (Boston: Little, Brown, 1971), pp. 10–30, 69–96, 144–81.

19. Adolf A. Berle, Jr. and Gardiner C. Means, *The Modern Corporation and Private Property* (New York: Macmillan, 1932).

20. See, for example, Robert A. Gordon, *Business Leadership in the Large Corporation* (Washington, D.C.: The Brookings Institution, 1945), pp. 23–45; Robert Larner, *Management Control and the Large Corporation* (New York: Dunellen, 1970); Blumberg, *The Megacorporation*, p. 89 and chap. 5. But cf. Melvin A. Eisenberg, *The Structure of the Corporation* (Boston: Little, Brown, 1976). From the separation of ownership and control, it does not follow, of course, that there are no other pressures on management to serve shareholders' interests. See Brian Hindley, "Separation of Ownership and Control in the Modern Corporation," 13 *J. L. & Econ.* 185 (1970), for the role of "the market for corporate control" in this respect; and Walter Werner, "Management, Stock Market and Corporate Reform: Berle and Means Reconsidered," 77 *Colum. L. Rev.* 388 (1977), for the role played by the capital market.

21. James Burnham, *The Managerial Revolution* (New York: John Day, 1941); Blumberg, *The Megacorporation*, pp. 145–47; John Galbraith, *The New Industrial State*, 2d ed. (Boston: Houghton Mifflin, 1971), chap. 8.

22. Blumberg, *The Megacorporation*, p. 5. See also Ralf K. Winter, *Government and the Corporation* (Washington, D.C.: American Enterprise Institute for Public Policy Research, 1978), p. 31; Galbraith, *The New Industrial State*, chap. 7; B. Manning, book review, 67 *Yale L. J.* 1477, 1482–83 (1958). But for the contrary view, one that upholds the supremacy of shareholders in the corporation, see, for example, Eisenberg, *The Structure of the Corporation*. It should be observed that there is no internal inconsistency in my reliance on certain incipient changes in the legal conception of corporations

in order to buttress a critique of the law's general attitude to them. First, corporate law, as it focuses directly and exclusively on the corporation, is more likely than other branches of law to be aware of and responsive to changing corporate economic and social realities. Secondly, the changes in the corporate lawyer's perceptions regarding the nature of the corporation to which I am alluding do not amount to an articulated and comprehensive conception that might guide the law in general (though, as my argument suggests, these changes do point toward such a conception).

23. Adolf A. Berle, Jr., *Power Without Property* (New York: Harcourt, Brace & World, 1959); idem, *The 20th Century Capitalist Revolution* (New York: Harcourt, Brace, 1954).

24. See Galbraith, *The New Industrial State*, p. 91; Blumberg, *The Megacorporation*, pp. 94–128; Michael Reagan, *The Managed Economy* (London: Oxford University Press, 1963), p. 79.

25. See, for example, Eugene Fama, *Foundations of Finance* (New York: Basic Books, 1976), chaps. 7–8.

26. "A more spacious conception of 'membership,' and one closer to the facts of corporate life, would include all those having a relation of sufficient intimacy with the corporation or subject to its power in a sufficiently specialized way." Abram Chayes, "The Modern Corporation and the Rule of Law," in Edward S. Mason, ed., *The Corporation in Modern Society* (Cambridge: Harvard University Press, 1959), p. 41.

The literature on corporate social responsibility is burgeoning. Here are just some highly selective examples: Morrell Meald, *The Social Responsibilities of Business* (Cleveland: The Press of Case Western Reserve University, 1970) (for an historical survey, see especially pp. 207–97); Charles E. Gilliland, Jr., ed., *Readings in Business Responsibility* (Braintree, Mass.: D. H. Mark, 1969), especially pp. 11–27, 79–86; James W. McKie, ed., *Social Responsibility and the Business Predicament* (Washington, D.C.: The Brookings Institute, 1974), especially pp. 1–108; Stone, *Where the Law Ends*, pp. 71–118; Neil H. Jacoby, *Corporate Power and Social Responsibility* (New York: Macmillan, 1973). Most of the pertinent cases deal with corporate contributions and donations; but in these cases, a ritualistic bow to the conventional conception of the corporation is normally made, by insisting on some connection between the donation and the business goals of the corporation, no matter how tenuous that connection may in fact be. For a more explicit judicial endorsement of the "social responsibility" view of the corporation, see *Harold Co. v. Seawell*, 472 F. 2d 1081 (1972), especially at p. 1091. And cf. the recognition by an English court of the duties of directors toward employees in *Parke v. Daily News* [1962] Ch. 927, 963.

27. Cf. the distinction between "harmonistic" and "antagonistic" models of corporation in German law. See S. Simitis: "Workers' Participation in

the Enterprise—Transcending Company Law?" 38 *M. L. Rev.* 1, 18–19 (1975).

28. James D. Thompson, *Organizations in Action* (New York: McGraw-Hill, 1967), p. 132. Cf. Dennis Thompson, "Moral Responsibility of Public Officials: The Problem of Many Hands," 74 *Am. Poli. Sci. Rev.* 905, 906 (1980), on the inadequacy of a Weberian picture of organizations as a basis for allocating responsibility within them.

29. E.g., Richard Cyert and James March, *A Behavioral Theory of the Firm* (Englewood Cliffs, N.J.: Prentice-Hall, 1963), p. 27; Fremont E. Kast and James E. Rosenzweig, *Organization and Management: System Approach*, 2d ed. (New York: McGraw-Hill, 1974), p. 42.

30. "*Resultants* in the sense that what happens is not chosen as a solution to a problem but rather results from compromise, conflict and unequal influence; *political* in the sense that the activity from which decisions and actions emerge is best characterized as bargaining along regularized channels among individual members of the [organization]." Allison, *Essence of Decision*, p. 162.

31. See Herbert Simon, *Administrative Behavior*, 3d ed. (New York: The Free Press, 1976), pp. 220–22; Gordon, *Business Leadership*, p. 321; Oliver Williamson, *Corporate Control and Business Behavior* (Englewood Cliffs, N.J.: Prentice-Hall, 1970), chap. 3; Michel Crozier, *The Bureaucratic Phenomenon* (Chicago: University of Chicago Press, 1964).

32. See Williamson's discussion (*Corporate Control*, p. 41) of the substitution of the "peak coordinator (who is an individual)" by "the process of peak coordination," which is a function carried out by a collectivity of individuals. Galbraith coined the term *technostructure* to describe "all who participate in group decision-making" in the corporation (*The New Industrial State*, p. 71). The technostructure (a term meant to be more inclusive than *management*) replaces, according to Galbraith, the individual entrepreneur as the locus of corporate decisionmaking; see ibid., pp. 70–71, and chap. 8.

33. For a summary of the changes in the economic theory of the firm, see, for example, Allison, *Essence of Decision*, pp. 72–76. See also Ira Horowitz, *Decisionmaking and the Theory of the Firm* (New York: Holt, Rinehart and Winston, 1970); Oliver Williamson, *The Economics of Discretionary Behavior: Managerial Objectives in a Theory of the Firm* (Englewood Cliffs, N.J.: Prentice-Hall, 1964); and idem, "The Modern Corporation: Origins, Evolution, Attributes," 19 *J. Econ. Lit.* 1537 (1981).

34. See, for example, Cyert and March, *A Behavioral Theory;* Robin Marris, *The Economic Theory of "Managerial Capitalism"* (New York: Free Press, 1964); Oliver E. Williamson, *Markets and Hierarchies* (New York: Free Press, 1975).

35. Though this should not diminish the credit due to Berle and Means or other modern economists, it is worth observing that Professors Jensen and Meckling quote from *The Wealth of Nations* to demonstrate that Adam Smith was already aware of incentive problems that arise when the decisions in the firm are made by managers who are not the firm's security holders. Michael C. Jensen and William H. Meckling, "Theory of the Firm: Managerial Behavior, Agency Costs and Ownership Structure," 3 *J. Financial Econ.* 305 (1976).

36. See, for example, W. J. Baumol, *Business Behavior, Value and Growth*, rev. ed. (New York: Macmillan, 1969); Marris, *Economic Theory;* Galbraith, *The New Industrial State.*

But see Milton Friedman's advocacy of the postulate of profit maximization on grounds of its predictive power in his article "The Methodology of Positive Economics," in *Essays in Positive Economics* (Chicago: University of Chicago Press, 1953), pp. 3–46.

37. The two seminal works establishing this approach are Simon, *Administrative Behavior*, especially pp. 271–75; and Cyert and March, *A Behavioral Theory*, especially pp. 28, 35–36.

38. The acknowledgment of the importance of size is reflected in the increased attention to models of oligopoly and monopoly. See Reagan's statement that "at the level of the individual firm, the pattern is one of oligopoly: a very few firms of large size account for the bulk of production in industry after industry." Reagan, *The Managed Economy*, p. 8.

39. "For any large, heavily capitalized, technologically sophisticated enterprise facing an only partly predictable future, there is no one obvious production and sales strategy that will avoid loss and maximize profits, sales, or whatever other desideratum the corporate leadership pursues. Even simple profit maximization would be complicated. Should the enterprise take all the profits it can in the immediate future? Should it moderate its ambitions now in order to build a clientele that in a longer future might make higher profits possible?" Lindblom, *Politics and Markets*, pp. 153–54. Such decisions, concludes Lindblom, "remain at the discretion not of the consumer but of the corporate executive." Ibid. On the concept of discretion in this context and its importance in the economic theory of the firm, see also Marris, *Economic Theory*, p. 46; Cyert and March, *A Behavioral Theory*, p. 20; Williamson, *Corporate Control*, chap. 3 (especially pp. 49–52) and chaps. 4, 5.

40. See, for example, Williamson's distinction between U-form and M-form corporations, and his discussion of the economic implications of this structural distinction, in *Corporate Control*, chap. 8; and in *Markets and Hierarchies*, pp. 132–54.

41. Trans. Eden Paul and Cedar Paul (New York: Free Press, 1962).

42. "In general, the weight of available evidence on private association is overwhelmingly on the side of Michels' 'law' of oligarchy." Grant McConnell, *Private Power and American Democracy* (New York: Vintage, 1970), p. 152.

43. Michels, *Political Parties*, p. 353.

44. See, for example, Philip Selznick, *The Organizational Weapon* (New York: Free Press, 1960), chap. 1; Presthus, *The Organizational Society*, p. 25.

45. James Q. Wilson, *Political Organizations* (New York: Basic Books, 1973), p. 10; see also Thompson, *Organizations in Action*, pp. 6–7.

46. Wilson, *Political Organizations* (note 45 *supra*).

47. Ibid., p. 211.

48. Ibid.

49. Cambridge: Harvard University Press, 1965.

50. Cf. Professor Hessen's view: "When individuals join together in a voluntary venture, they neither gain nor lose any rights. Regardless of the legal form they choose for their organization—a corporation or a partnership, for example—it can only acquire and exercise those rights which its members possess as individuals—nothing more and nothing less." Hessen, *In Defense of the Corporation*, pp. 60–61. See also Pilon, "Corporations and Rights," p. 1313: "Indeed, as we move along the continuum that runs from the one-man to the giant corporation, all corporate problems—but especially those of liability—become increasingly complex. Short of drawing arbitrary lines, however, the underlying theory remains the same." See also pp. 1320–26 on corporate rights.

51. Albert O. Hirschman, *Exit, Voice and Loyalty* (Cambridge: Harvard University Press, 1970).

52. The most important proponent of this view was Otto Gierke. His work is available in English under the following titles: *The Political Theories of the Middle Ages*, trans. F. W. Maitland (Cambridge, England: Cambridge University Press, 1900); *Natural Law and the Theory of Society, 1500–1800*, trans. E. Barker (Cambridge, England: Cambridge University Press, 1934); and *Associations and Law: The Classical and Early Christian Stages*, ed. and trans. S. Heiman (Toronto: University of Toronto Press, 1977).

CHAPTER 2

1. Martin Wolff, "On the Nature of Legal Persons," 54 *L. Q. Rev.* 494, 506 (1938).

2. H. L. A. Hart, *The Concept of Law* (Oxford: Clarendon Press, 1961), pp. 189–95.

3. Ibid., p. 189.

4. 70 *L. Q. Rev.* 37 (1954).

5. Ibid at 56.

6. Ibid.

7. Cf. Professor Caplow's statement that the study of organizations presupposes that "all human organizations, regardless of time, place, or cultural setting in which they occur belong to a single class of natural kind," and that "organizations have certain features which do not occur at all in other collectivities." Theodore Caplow, *Principles of Organization* (New York: Harcourt, Brace & World, 1966), pp. 6–8.

8. See Lawrence Mohr, *Explaining Organizational Behavior* (San Francisco: Jossey-Bass, 1982).

9. Different authors define organizations in terms of different items from this list—alone or in some combination. For example, Parsons focuses on goal-orientation: "*Primacy of orientation to the attainment of a specific goal is used as the defining characteristic of an organization which distinguishes it from other types of social systems.*" Talcott Parsons, *Structure and Process in Modern Societies* (Glencoe, Ill.: Free Press, 1960), p. 17. Haas and Drabek pick up permanence and complexity: "An organization is defined as *a relatively permanent and relatively complex discernible interaction system.*" J. Eugene Haas and Thomas Drabek, *Complex Organizations—A Sociological Perspective* (New York: Macmillan, 1973), p. 8. Peter Blau and W. Richard Scott's book is about *Formal Organizations* (San Francisco: Chandler, 1962). And in Robert Bonczek, Clyde Holsapple, and Andrew Whinston, *Foundations of Decision Support Systems* (New York: Academic Press, 1981), p. 28, organizations are defined as "processors of materials and information."

10. "All structuralists . . . are at one in recognizing as fundamental the contrast between *structures* and *aggregates,* the former being wholes, the latter composites formed of elements that are independent of the complexes into which they enter." ". . . The laws governing a structure's composition are not reducible to cumulative one-by-one association of its elements." Jean Piaget, *Structuralism,* trans. Chaninah Maschler (New York: Harper & Row, 1968), pp. 6–7.

11. Blau and Scott, *Formal Organizations,* p. 1.

12. "The important point is that *decision-making in the light of long run benefits presumes a concept of the institution.* The enterprise as a going concern, as a relational entity, becomes the focus of policy and strategy." Philip Selznick, *Law, Society and Industrial Justice* (New York: Russel Sage Foundation, 1967), p. 47.

13. "Even in its infancy the melding of disparate interests and purposes gives rise to a corporate long range point of view that is distinct from the intents and purposes of the collection of incorporators viewed individually." Peter A. French, "The Corporation as a Moral Person," 16 *Am. Phil. Q.* 207, 214 (1979).

14. The point here, as in regard to the other organizational properties under discussion, is that the organizational identity is not equal or reducible to the identities of any particular individuals. This is not to say that the identity of individual persons—over time or in other respects—is free of philosophical problems. Indeed, some issues analogous to those raised here in respect to organizational identity also appear in discussions of personal identity. The latter are, however, clearly beyond the scope of this study. See, for example, essays collected in John Perry, ed., *Personal Identity* (Berkeley: University of California Press, 1975), especially the essay by Derek Parfit, "Personal Identity"; and in Amelie Oksenberg Rorty, ed., *The Identities of Persons* (Berkeley: University of California Press, 1969).

15. On the role and nature of information processing in organizations, see Bonczek et al., *Foundations;* and Harold Wilensky, *Organizational Intelligence* (New York: Basic Books, 1967).

16. See Chapter 1, note 30 *supra.*

17. See Buchanan's (rather extreme) position that rationality is a property only of individuals, and that it is meaningless to attribute rationality to collective decisions. J. M. Buchanan, "Individual Choice in Voting and the Market," 62 *J. Political Econ.* 334 (1954).

18. Kenneth J. Arrow, *Social Choice and Individual Values,* 2d ed. (New Haven: Yale University Press, 1963). For a critical discussion, see R. Duncan Luce and Howard Raiffa, *Games and Decisions* (New York: John Wiley, 1957), pp. 327–70.

19. New York: W. W. Norton, 1978.

20. Professor Wolff makes a related point when he develops the notion of "a state of affairs which is a *consequence* of decisions, but yet is not itself an *object* of decision." He gives the following illustration: "A traffic jam is the consequence of thousands of individual decisions by motorists— decisions to visit the kids, to go to the store, to take in a movie, to get out of town. As a result of all those decisions, too many cars arrive simultaneously at a bridge or a tunnel or intersection which can't handle the load. But no one at all decided to cause a traffic jam. Hence the traffic jam is not properly an object of anyone's decision." Robert Paul Wolff, *The Poverty of Liberalism* (Boston: Beacon Press, 1968), pp. 87–88.

21. See Daniel C. Dennett, "Conditions of Personhood," in *Brainstorms* (Montgomery, Va.: Bradford Books, 1978), pp. 267–85, at p. 271. On the relation between organizational decisionmaking and the ascription of intentionality to organizations, cf. French, "The Corporation."

22. For a comprehensive review of various measures of organizational size, see J. R. Kimberly, "Organizational Size and the Structuralist Perspective: A Review, Critique, and Proposal," 21 *Ad. Sci. Q.* 57 (1976), and sources cited there.

23. See pp. 23–24 *supra.*

24. On the relationship between organizational size and other aspects of organizational structure, see, for example, Peter Blau, "Interdependence and Hierarchy in Organizations," 1 *Social Science Research* 1 (1972); Kimberly, "Organizational Size"; Henry Mintzberg, *The Structuring of Organizations* (Englewood Cliffs, N.J.: Prentice-Hall, 1979), pp. 230–35.

25. See generally Richard H. Hall, *Organizations: Structure and Process,* 2d ed. (Englewood Cliffs, N.J.: Prentice-Hall, 1977), pp. 152–80.

26. Chester Barnard, *The Functions of the Executive* (Cambridge: Harvard University Press, 1938), pp. 73–77.

27. Ibid., p. 88.

28. See Herbert Simon, *Administrative Behavior,* 3d ed. (New York: Free Press, 1976).

29. Ibid., pp. 12–15 and chap. 10.

30. On the processes of socialization and indoctrination which individuals undergo within organizations, adopting an organizational perspective and value system, see Philip Selznick, *Leadership in Administration* (New York: Harper & Row, 1957), pp. 17–18; Anthony Downs, *Inside Bureaucracy* (Boston: Little, Brown, 1976), pp. 233–36; Robert Presthus, *The Organizational Society* (New York: Random House, 1962), pp. 7–8, 16; and Simon, *Administrative Behavior,* p. 103. These processes are part of what I mean by organizational impersonality, which leads to its impermeability, as discussed in the following paragraphs.

31. For a definition of organizational complexity, see James Thompson, *Organizations in Action* (New York: McGraw-Hill, 1967), pp. 54–59, 79. See also Hall, *Organizations,* pp. 130–51.

32. See, for example, the discussion of decisionmaking *supra.*

33. On the quality of opaqueness as related to the multiplicity of structural "overlays" in organizations, see Henry Mintzberg, *The Structuring of Organizations,* p. 36. The connection between the complexity and the opaqueness of organizations is illustrated by the image of the "black box" in Stafford Beer, *Cybernetics and Management* (New York: John Wiley, 1959), p. 49; cf. French, "The Corporation," pp. 212–14.

34. See note 42 *infra;* also Christopher D. Stone, *Where the Law Ends: The Social Control of Corporate Behavior* (New York: Harper & Row, 1975), p. 7.

35. Blau and Scott, *Formal Organizations,* p. 5. The instrumental nature of organizations is a central theme in organization theory. See, for example, Charles Perrow, *Complex Organizations* (Glenview, Ill.: Scott, Foresman, 1972), p. 14, where he describes as "one of the dominant themes of [his] book" that "organizations must be seen as tools." This theme has already been emphasized by Weber, who defined bureaucracy as "a system of continuous activity pursuing a goal of a specified kind." Max Weber, *Basic Concepts in Sociology,* trans. H. P. Secher (New York: Citadel Press, 1962), p. 115. See also Downs, *Inside Bureaucracy,* p. 24; Amitai

Etzioni, *Modern Organizations* (Englewood Cliffs, N.J.: Prentice-Hall, 1964), p. 5. Cf. in this context Philip Selznick's distinction between "organizations" and "institutions." Organizations sometimes undergo "institutionalization," described by him as follows: "The prizing of social machinery beyond its technical role is largely a reflection of the unique way in which it fulfills personal or group needs. Whenever individuals become attached to an organization or a way of doing things as persons rather than as technicians, the result is the prizing of the device for its own sake. From the standpoint of the committed person, the organization is changed from an expendable tool into a valued source of personal satisfaction." Selznick, *Leadership in Administration*, p. 17.

36. Speaking of the legitimacy conferred on the organization by the pursuit of its goals, we may distinguish between internal and external legitimacy. Cf. Adolf A. Berle, Jr., *Power Without Property* (New York: Harcourt, Brace & World, 1959), pp. 98–110. Max Weber was especially concerned with the former: seen as a structure of authority, the bureaucracy needs a source of legitimacy to justify voluntary obedience to directives issued within the hierarchy. This legitimacy, according to Weber, is of the rational-legal kind: authority within the bureaucracy is legitimate because it is exercised in accordance with a set of rules that are rationally designed to achieve the valued goals of the organization. Max Weber, *The Theory of Social and Economic Organization*, trans. Alexander M. Henderson and Talcott Parsons (New York: Free Press, 1947), pp. 328–36.

Talcott Parsons, on the other hand, focuses on the external legitimacy of the organization: its legitimacy as an entity that makes claims on society's resources. Parsons, *Structure and Process*, pp. 20–21. According to Parsons's view, "the organization is always defined as a subsystem of a more comprehensive social system." Ibid., p. 20. Accordingly, its place or "role" within the system has to be legitimized in terms of the values of the superordinate system to which the particular organization belongs. "Since it has been assumed that an organization is defined by the primacy of a type of goal, the focus of its value system must be the legitimation of this goal in terms of the functional significance of its attainment for the superordinate system." Ibid., pp. 20–21.

37. On the divergence between *official* and *operative* goals, see Perrow, *Complex Organizations*. See generally Lawrence B. Mohr, "The Concept of Organizational Goal," 67 *Am. Pol. Sc. Rev.* 470 (1973), and sources cited in notes 38–43 *infra*.

38. See generally W. Keith Warner and E. Eugene Havens, "Goal Displacement and the Intangibility of Organizational Goals," 12 *Ad. Sc. Q.* 545 (1968); Charles Perrow, "The Analysis of Goals in Complex Organizations," 26 *Am. Soc. Rev.* 854 (1961); and sources cited in notes 39–41 *infra*.

39. Etzioni, *Modern Organizations*, p. 10. The following summary of the goal displacement phenomenon is based on Etzioni's account on pp. 10–12.

40. See Robert K. Merton, *Social Theory and Social Structure* (Glencoe, Ill.: Free Press, 1957), pp. 197 ff.

41. Philip Selznick, "An Approach to a Theory of Bureaucracy," 8 *Am. Soc. Rev.* 49 (1943); quoted by Etzioni, *Modern Organizations*, p. 12.

42. See Daniel Katz and Robert L. Kahn, *The Social Psychology of Organizations* (New York: John Wiley, 1966), p. 15; and sources cited in Chapter 1, notes 31–32 *supra*.

43. The term roughly corresponds to the sociologists' concern, initiated by Philip Selznick, with what he termed "the recalcitrance of the tools of action." See his "Foundations of the Theory of Organization," 13 *Am. Soc. Rev.* 25 (1948); and *T.V.A. and the Grass Roots* (Berkeley: University of California Press, 1949).

44. Cf. Professor Perrow's observation: "The interminable debate in the 1940's and 1950's over the old question of whether the group was more than the sum of its parts, and the almost inevitable but shaky answer of yes, is a similar illustration of this ontological problem. The current fadish term 'synergism,' indicating that something unique emerges from the interaction of discrete inputs of energy, is a reaffirmation of the reality (and superiority) of the collective character of a system." Perrow, *Complex Organizations*, p. 79.

45. Short descriptions of the open system approach to organizations can be found in Fremont Kast and James Rosenzweig, *Organization and Management: System Approach*, 2d ed. (New York: McGraw-Hill, 1974), pp. 100–25; idem, "General Systems Theory: Applications for Organizations and Management," *Academy of Management J.*, Dec. 1972, pp. 447–65; Haas and Drabek, *Complex Organizations*, pp. 83–93. For examples of writings that adopt the systems approach, see Harold Koontz and Cyril O'Connell, *Management: A Systems and Contingency Analysis of Managerial Functions* (New York: McGraw-Hill, 1976); and Ephraim Yuchtman and Stanley E. Seashore, "A System Resource Approach to Organizational Effectiveness," 32 *Am. Soc. Rev.* 891 (1967).

CHAPTER 3

1. For the view that they do, see Max Black, *Models and Metaphors* (Ithaca, N.Y.: Cornell University Press, 1962), pp. 25–47.

2. R. Boyd, "Metaphor and Theory Change: What Is 'Metaphor' a Metaphor For?" in Andrew Ortony, ed., *Metaphor and Thought* (Cambridge, England: Cambridge University Press, 1979), pp. 356–408, at p. 358.

3. Ibid.

4. D. Schön, "Generative Metaphor: A Perspective on Problem-setting in Social Policy," in Ortony, ed., *Metaphor and Thought,* pp. 254–83, at pp. 264–65.

5. M. Rein and D. Schön, "Problem-setting in Policy Research," in C. H. Weiss, ed., *Using Social Research in Public Policymaking* (Lexington, Mass.: D. C. Heath, 1977), cited in Ortony, ed., *Metaphor and Thought,* p. 265.

6. Schön, "Generative Metaphor," p. 265.

7. Ibid., pp. 266–67.

8. For a critical discussion of the role played by various metaphors in organization theory, see Jareth Morgan, "Paradigms, Metaphors, and Puzzle Solving in Organization Theory," 25 *Ad. Sci. Q.* 605 (1980).

9. See note 11 to Chapter 1 *supra.*

10. Robert Nozick, *Anarchy, State, and Utopia* (New York: Basic Books, 1974), p. 7.

11. E.g., *Spiegel v. Beacon Participations, Inc.,* 297 Mass. 398, 8 N.E. 2d 895 (1937). See Annotation in 35 ALR 2d 1167 § 9; see generally 18 *Am. Jur.* 2d § 236. Authorities differ on whether the purchase by a corporation of some of its outstanding stock constitutes a reduction of its capital. See also Arthur Nussbaum, "Acquisition by a Corporation of Its Own Stock," 35 *Colum. L. Rev.* 971 (1935). English companies cannot purchase their own stock. This was established in *Trevor v. Whitworth* (1887) 12 App. Cas. 409, H.L. See L. C. B. Gower, *The Principles of Modern Company Law,* 3d ed. (London: Stevens, 1969), p. 112.

12. Cf. Professor Conard's example of what he calls the "holderless" corporation, which is a result of modern corporation laws that "permit the corporation to 'exist' and transact business through incorporators or initial directors before shares have been issued." Alfred Conard, *Corporations in Perspective* (Mineola, N.Y.: Foundation Press, 1976), p. 160, and sources cited in note 36 there. For another possibility of a corporation without any individual owners, there is the following scenario suggested by Professor Wolff: "If the private company A, whose members are X and Y, holds all the shares in the company B, and then X and Y transfer their shares in the company A to B company—a strange proceeding, but certainly possible and said actually to have happened—this would eliminate all human beings as shareholders of the two companies and make the properties something resembling a foundation, as long as no shares are re-transferred to any human being." Martin Wolff, "On the Nature of Legal Persons," 54 *L. Q. Rev.* 494, 505 (1938).

13. Cf. this: "Insofar as new corporate development is coming to be financed from accumulated capital of corporations themselves, much of

the corporate property has no human owner at all." Julius Stone, *Social Dimensions of Law and Justice* (Stanford: Stanford University Press, 1966), p. 428. See Chapter 1, notes 23–24 *supra,* and accompanying text.

14. See Chapter 1, note 21 *supra,* and accompanying text.

15. "The genuinely automatic factory—the workerless factory that can produce output and perhaps also, within limits, maintain and repair itself—will be technically feasible long before our twenty-five years have elapsed." Herbert Simon, *The Shape of Automation* (New York: Harper & Row, 1965), p. 34.

16. These two steps—self-ownership by the corporation and automation—are also depicted in a similar story in A. Hacker, ed., *The Corporation Take-over* (New York: Harper & Row, 1964), pp. 3–5.

17. Cf. Patricia Werhane's use of the name "Robotron" to designate a corporation operated by robots in her argument against the notion that corporations are moral agents, in "Formal Organizations, Economic Freedom and Moral Agency," 14 *J. of Value Inquiry* 43 (1980), especially pp. 47–50.

18. For a nontechnical reference (such that I could follow), see Margaret A. Boden, *Artificial Intelligence and Natural Man* (New York: Basic Books, 1977).

19. Simon, *The Shape of Automation,* p. 47; see also pp. 79–91.

20. K. M. Sayre: "Philosophy and Cybernetics," in Frederick J. Crosson and Kenneth M. Sayre, eds., *Philosophy and Cybernetics* (New York: Simon and Schuster, 1967), p. 13.

21. But see a more skeptical view on the potentialities of computers in Michael Polanyi, *Personal Knowledge: Towards a Post Critical Philosophy* (Chicago: University of Chicago Press, 1974); and Hubert L. Dreyfus, *What Computers Can't Do: A Critique of Artificial Reason* (New York: Harper & Row, 1972).

22. For a brief summary of and sources about the "human relations" school in the study of organizations, see J. Eugene Haas and Thomas E. Drabek, *Complex Organizations—A Sociological Perspective* (New York: Macmillan, 1973), pp. 42–48; and Charles Perrow, *Complex Organizations* (Glenview, Ill.: Scott, Foresman, 1972), chap. 3.

23. Stafford Beer suggests the metaphor of an "intelligent machine" for a cybernetic approach to the study of organizations. See his *Cybernetics and Management* (New York: John Wiley, 1959), pp. 128 ff. Professor Ladd relies on the metaphor of a machine in his discussion of the moral status of organizations: "In a sense . . . organizations are like machines, and it would be a category mistake to expect a machine to comply with the principles of morality." John Ladd, "Morality and the Ideal of Rationality in Formal Organizations," 54 *The Monist* 488, 500 (1970).

24. It should be noted that by speaking of an *"intelligent* machine" I do not mean to confine the metaphor to a "mechanical" as opposed to an "organic" or open-system conception of organizations. Indeed, the attraction of the intelligent machine metaphor lies in part in its ability to combine the mechanical and organic imageries. Cf. Daniel Katz and Robert L. Kahn, *The Social Psychology of Organizations* (New York: John Wiley, 1966), p. 71. On the role played by these and other metaphors in organization theory, see Morgan, "Paradigms."

CHAPTER 4

1. Frank I. Michelman, "Property, Utility, and Fairness: Comments on the Ethical Foundations of 'Just Compensation' Law," 80 *Harv. L. Rev.* 1165 (1967); George P. Fletcher, "Fairness and Utility in Tort Theory," 85 *Harv. L. Rev.* 537 (1972).

2. Bruce A. Ackerman, *Private Property and the Constitution* (New Haven: Yale University Press, 1977), chaps. 3–4.

3. Fletcher, "Fairness and Utility."

4. Joseph M. Steiner: "Economics, Morality, and the Law of Torts," 26 *U. of Toronto L.J.* 227 (1967). But it may be useful to sound here Prof. Friedrich's caveat, issued in a different context, concerning the use of dichotomies: "Such pairs of contrasts are well suited to highlight an issue; it is more than doubtful that they have any close resemblance to what we find in the real world. They make for a two-party system in the intellectual arena, rather than a many sided discussion among individual seekers after truth." Carl J. Friedrich: "The Political Thought of Neo-Liberalism," 49 *Am. Pol. Sc. Rev.* 509, 524 (1955).

5. Fletcher, "Fairness and Utility."

6. Brian Barry, "And Who Is My Neighbor?" 88 *Yale L.J.* 629, 631 (1979).

7. Thomas Kuhn, *The Structure of Scientific Revolutions,* 2d ed. (Chicago: University of Chicago Press, 1970), chaps. 2, 4. See also idem, "Second Thoughts on Paradigms," in *The Essential Tension* (Chicago: University of Chicago Press, 1977), pp. 293–97, where Kuhn acknowledges that as many as twenty-two different senses of the word *paradigm* as it was introduced in *The Structure of Scientific Revolutions* have been discerned. Prof. Fletcher admits that "there is an element of fashion in using words like 'paradigm' and 'model.'" Fletcher, "Fairness and Utility," p. 540, note 12. The use of these terms coupled with an apology is itself a growing fashion, to which I here succumb.

8. See Professor Hart's eloquent testimony:

We are currently witnessing, I think, the progress of a transition from a once widely accepted old faith that some form of utilitarianism, if only we could discover the right form, *must* capture the essence of political morality. The new faith is that the truth must lie not with a doctrine that takes the maximization of aggregate or average general welfare for its goal, but with a doctrine of basic human rights, protecting specific basic liberties and interests of individuals, if only we could find some sufficiently firm foundation for such rights to meet some long familiar objections.

H. L. A. Hart, "Between Utility and Rights," 79 *Colum. L. Rev.* 828 (1979). See also Barry, "My Neighbor," pp. 630–31; and Robert Young, "Dispensing with Moral Rights," 6 *Political Theory* 63 (1978).

9. On the utilitarian basis of welfare economics, see, e.g., I. M. D. Little, *Critique of Welfare Economics*, 2d ed. (Oxford: Clarendon Press, 1957), p. 42; and A. G. Pigou, *The Economics of Welfare*, 4th ed. (London: Macmillan, 1962), p. 20. But see Prof. Richard Posner's recent attempt to challenge the orthodoxy that associates economics with utilitarianism, and set the two apart, in "Utilitarianism, Economics, and Legal Theory," 8 *J. Leg. Stud.* 103 (1979).

10. See H. L. A. Hart, "American Jurisprudence Through English Eyes: The Nightmare and the Noble Dream," 11 *Ga. L. Rev.* 969, 987–88 (1977).

11. Barry, "My Neighbor." An illustrative list of major works that mark the ascent of the paradigm of autonomy would include: John Rawls, *A Theory of Justice* (Cambridge: Harvard University Press, 1971); Robert Nozick, *Anarchy, State, and Utopia* (New York: Basic Books, 1974); Ronald Dworkin, *Taking Rights Seriously* (Cambridge: Harvard University Press, 1977); and Charles Fried, *Right and Wrong* (Cambridge: Harvard University Press, 1978).

12. All of the above-mentioned writers explicitly relate their theories to Kant. See Rawls, *Theory of Justice*, pp. 251–57; Nozick, *Anarchy*, pp. 30–31; Dworkin, *Taking Rights Seriously*, p. 198; Fried, *Right and Wrong*, pp. 33, 115.

13. Both Nozick and Fried use the metaphor of a "moral space," defined by individual rights, which surrounds and protects the person. See Nozick, *Anarchy*, p. 57; Fried, *Right and Wrong*, pp. 137–38.

14. Cf., e.g., Joel Feinberg, *Social Philosophy* (Englewood Cliffs, N.J.: Prentice-Hall, 1973), pp. 65–66.

15. This two-tiered approach to the justification of an organizational claim corresponds to the distinction between the "internal" and the "external" legitimacy of organizations suggested in Chapter 2, note 36 *supra*.

16. Cf. Jeffrie G. Murphy, "Rights and Borderline Cases," 19 *Arizona L. Rev.* 228, 230–31 (1977), for a similar use of this term.

17. Fried, *Right and Wrong*, pp. 11–12. See also p. 81: "A claim of right blocks appeal to consequences in justifying violations of a right."

18. Ibid., p. 12.

19. Dworkin, *Taking Rights Seriously*, p. 198.

20. Ibid., p. 269.

21. Ibid. This is essentially what Fried means by a right being categorical: "A claim of right is preemptory. It says that because I have this right you must do (or forbear doing) this thing irrespective of whether recognizing my right would maximize the sum of advantages." Fried, *Right and Wrong*, p. 85. For a related and useful general discussion, see Rex Martin and James Nickel, "Recent Work on the Concept of Right," 17 *Am. Phil. Q.* 165–80 (1980) (including a bibliographical list).

22. For some related discussions of the "moral agency" of corporations and other organizations, see Kenneth Goodpaster, "On Being Morally Considerable," 75 *J. Phil.* 308 (1978); idem, "Morality and Organizations," in Thomas Donaldson and Patricia Werhane, eds., *Ethical Issues in Business* (Englewood Cliffs, N.J.: Prentice-Hall, 1979), p. 114; John Ladd, "Morality and the Ideal of Rationality in Formal Organizations," 56 *Monist* 488 (1970); Peter French, "The Corporation as Moral Person," 16 *Am. Phil. Q.* 207 (1979); Patricia Werhane, "Formal Organizations, Economic Freedom and Moral Agency," 14 *J. Value Inquiry* 43 (1980); Thomas Donaldson, "Moral Agency and Corporations," 10 *Phil. in Context* 54 (1980); E. T. Michell, "A Theory of Corporate Will," 56 *Ethics* 96 (1946).

23. Fried, *Right and Wrong*, p. 20. This is also the underlying premise of Nozick's *Anarchy, State, and Utopia*, to take another example. He opens his book with the statement: "Individuals have rights and there are things no person or group may do to them (without violating their rights)." Ibid., p. ix. See also Steven Lukes, *Individualism* (Oxford: Basil Blackwell, 1973), p. 51: "In general this idea of the dignity of the individual has the logical status of a moral (or religious) axiom which is basic, ultimate and overriding, offering a general justifying principle in moral argument."

24. Amitai Etzioni, *Modern Organizations* (Englewood Cliffs, N.J.: Prentice-Hall, 1964), p. 3.

25. Cf. Ladd, "Morality," p. 508: "Since, as I have argued in some detail, formal organizations are not moral persons, and have no moral responsibilities, they have no moral rights. In particular they have no *moral* right to freedom or automony." But see other views in sources cited in note 22 *supra*.

26. However, the "intelligent machine" metaphor that I use may backfire at this point, insofar as some philosophers argue that robots may be moral agents possessed of automony rights. See, for example, Boden's (tongue in cheek?) observation that "the Kantian imperative enjoins rational beings to treat each other as ends in themselves equally worthy of moral respect, which casts doubt on the admissibility of preferring *human*

over *robot* interests." Margaret Boden, *Artificial Intelligence and Natural Man* (New York: Basic Books, 1977), p. 469. Also see a more extended argument to this effect in Laszlo Versengi, "Can Robots be Moral?" 84 *Ethics* 248–59 (1974).

27. For the view that freedom of speech is indeed an automony right, see Thomas Scanlon, "A Theory of Freedom of Expression," 1 *Phil. & Pub. Aff.* 204 (1972); and Harry Wellington, "On Freedom of Expression," 88 *Yale L.J.* 1105 (1979).

28. Obviously these allegations are not part of O_2's legal cause of action. These facts are relevant to the philosophical underpinnings of the corporation's legal claim. More specifically, these facts are relevant to the determination whether the corporation's claim to damages for *its* loss, resulting from the cutting of the cable, should enjoy the status of an autonomy right (in virtue of the losses to those various individuals).

29. See p. 35 *supra.*

30. Professors Cyert and March, who introduced the concept, explain the existence of slack within organizations as chiefly the product of the bargaining process among the various members of the coalition that constitutes the large organization. See Richard M. Cyert and James G. March, *A Behavioral Theory of the Firm* (Englewood Cliffs, N.J.: Prentice-Hall, 1963), pp. 36–38. Others emphasize the uncertainties surrounding the production function and the nonmarketability of managerial and other skills as the main reasons for organizational slack. See Harvey Leibenstein, "Allocative Efficiency Versus X-Efficiency," 56 *Am. Econ. Rev.* 392 (1966). On the role of slack in organizations, see also Anthony Downs, *Inside Bureaucracy* (Boston: Little, Brown, 1976), pp. 138–39; and Albert O. Hirschman, *Exit, Voice and Loyalty* (Cambridge: Harvard University Press, 1970), pp. 10–15.

31. On the expanding role of the "institutional investor," see Chapter 1, notes 23–24 *supra,* and accompanying text.

32. Fried, *Right and Wrong*, p. 36.

33. Ibid., p. 41.

34. Ibid.

35. Ibid., p. 40.

36. See Fried, ibid., note on pp. 202–03, and sources cited there. For a modern philosophical argument that relies on the doctrine of double effect, see Philipa Foot, "The Problem of Abortion and the Doctrine of Double Effect," 5 *Oxford Rev.* 5 (1967). See also Joseph Boyle, Jr., "Toward Understanding the Principle of Double Effect," 90 *Ethics* 527–38 (1980).

37. Thomas Nagel, "War and Massacre," 1 *Phil. & Pub. Aff.* 123, 130 (1972).

38. Ibid., p. 133.

39. See Fried, *Right and Wrong,* pp. 12, 159–60, where he argues that the immediacy of the physical harm suffices to make an injury following negligent risk-creation into a *direct* harm. The requirement of the directness of the harm, once paramount in tort law, may be understood, accordingly, as a reflection of the paradigm of autonomy. Indeed, two contemporary proponents of the autonomy paradigm in tort law, Professors Epstein and Fletcher, reaffirm in their respective theories the importance of directness. Professor Epstein takes as his point of departure for all tort liability the paradigm case of "A hit B," where the immediacy of the physical impact of injurer upon victim is the controlling element. See Richard Epstein, "A Theory of Strict Liability," 2 *J. Leg. Stud.* 151 (1973). Similarly, Prof. Fletcher associates "the now rejected emphasis on the directness and immediacy of causal links" with "the paradigm of reciprocity"—his counterpart to what I call here the paradigm of autonomy. See Fletcher, "Fairness and Utility," p. 572.

40. Fried, *Right and Wrong,* p. 133.

41. John T. Noonan, Jr., *Persons and Masks of the Law* (New York: Farrar, Straus and Giroux, 1976), p. xii.

42. Duncan Kennedy, "Legal Formality," 2 *J. Leg. Stud.* 351, 380 (1973).

43. See Fletcher, "Fairness and Utility," p. 553.

44. *Persons and Masks of the Law,* p. xii. Cf. Reinhold Niebuhr, *Moral Man and Immoral Society* (New York: Scribner, 1960).

45. Charles Fried, *An Anatomy of Values* (Cambridge: Harvard University Press, 1970), pp. 222–23. Fried continues the *personalist argument* by asking whether it applies to a stranger in distress. The answer is in the affirmative (ibid., p. 224):

If we say no to the particular stranger we are saying to him that though we can see plainly enough that he is a particular person, not just a statistical, possible person, we refuse to take that particularity into account. We will look through him—or through his individuality, at any rate—as if he were not there, and see only an abstraction. We will refuse to recognize an individuality that is there for us to recognize, and we will do it moreover in a context where that other person's life might be at stake. It is this that seems a horrible thing to do, horrible to contemplate and horrible to experience.

Though Fried himself rejects the argument here, he later changed his mind and adopted a position in line with the personalist argument. See his *Right and Wrong,* pp. 184–85.

46. Fried, *Right and Wrong,* p. 34.

47. Cf. Fried's charge that "utilitarianism in its uncompromising universality deprives all individual differences, and thus the individual himself, of moral significance. Utilitarianism posits that it is the sum total of happiness that counts, and how happiness is distributed among persons

is a secondary, and instrumental matter." Ibid., pp. 33–34; see also Hart, "Between Utility and Rights," p. 829.

48. Cf. Nozick's view (*Anarchy*, pp. 32–33):

There is no *social entity* with a good that undergoes some sacrifice for its own good. There are only individual people, different individual people, with their own individual lives. Using one of these people for the benefit of others, uses him and benefits the others. Nothing more. . . . To use a person in this way does not sufficiently respect and take account of the fact that he is a separate person, that his is the only life he has.

49. Hart, "Between Utility and Rights," p. 829.

50. A more extreme version of the nonaggregation principle is John Taurek's, in "Should the Numbers Count?" 6 *Phil. & Pub. Aff.* 293 (1977). In this article, Professor Taurek deals with what he calls "trade-off situations," in which "we must choose between bestowing benefits on certain people, or preventing certain harms from befalling them, and bestowing benefits on or preventing harms from befalling certain others," and asks "whether we should, in such trade-off situations, consider the relative numbers of people involved as something in itself of significance in determining our course of action." Ibid., p. 293. He concludes that we should not. "My way of thinking about these trade-off situations," he writes, "reflects a refusal to take seriously in these situations any notion of the sum of two persons' separate losses. . . . The discomfort of each of a large number of individuals experiencing a minor headache does not add up to anyone's experiencing a migraine. In such a trade-off situation as this we are to compare your pain or your loss, not to our collective or total pain, whatever exactly that is supposed to be, but what will be suffered or lost by any given single one of us." Ibid., p. 308. For a similar position, see G. E. M. Anscombe, "Who Is Wronged?" 5 *Oxford Rev.* 16 (1967). But see Prof. Derek Parfit's criticism of Taurek's article, in "Innumerate Ethics," 7 *Phil. & Pub. Aff.* 285 (1978). And see further correspondence from Charles Fried, and a response from Derek Parfit, in 8 *Phil. & Pub. Aff.* 393–97 (1979).

51. See Guido Calabresi, *The Costs of Accidents* (New Haven: Yale University Press, 1970), pp. 39–67, and sources cited there.

52. Nozick, *Anarchy*, p. 67.

53. Academic freedom has in fact been recognized as a First Amendment right. See, for example, *Whitehill v. Elkins*, 389 U.S. 54 (1967): *Keyishian v. Board of Regents*, 385 U.S. 589 (1967); *Shelton v. Tucker*, 364 U.S. 479 (1960). See also Thomas Emerson, *The System of Freedom of Expression* (New York: Random House, 1970), pp. 613–14.

54. See Edward Gross, "Universities as Organizations: A Research Approach," 33 *Am. Soc. Rev.* 518, 529 (1968), for an empirical finding that academic freedom ranks first among universities' goals.

55. See Gross, ibid., for a list and ranking of the multiple goals typically pursued by universities.

56. See pp. 36–37 *supra*.

57. On the tendency of organizations toward expansion and self-aggrandizement for systemic reasons, see Downs, *Inside Bureaucracy*, pp. 16–18; and Chester I. Barnard, *The Functions of the Executive* (Cambridge: Harvard University Press, 1938), p. 159.

58. Charles Fried, *Contract as Promise* (Cambridge: Harvard University Press, 1981).

59. See Nozick, *Anarchy*, p. 57.

60. Posner, "Utilitarianism," p. 125. Prof. Posner speaks specifically of a woman's right to choose her sexual partner, but the same argument is equally applicable to bodily integrity in general.

61. See, e.g., Richard A. Posner, *Economic Analysis of Law*, 2d ed. (Boston: Little, Brown, 1977), p. 28: "The legal protection of property rights has an important economic function: to create incentives to use resources efficiently."

62. Hart, "Between Utility and Rights," p. 829.

63. E. Mishan, "The Post-War Literature on Externalities: An Interpretive Essay," 9 *J. Econ. Lit.* 1 (1971).

64. See p. 35 *supra*.

65. See p. 36 *supra*.

66. Cf. Galbraith: "Autonomy may still be accorded to the corporation. This is necessary for effective administration—for efficiency. But this is a pragmatic decision and no principle is involved." John K. Galbraith, "On the Economic Image of the Corporate Enterprise," in Ralph Nader and Mark J. Green, eds., *Corporate Power in America* (New York: Grossman, 1973), p. 7.

67. See a similar typology of interactions in James S. Coleman, *Power and the Structure of Society* (New York: Norton, 1974), pp. 36–37, 51.

68. Cf. Charles Lindblom, *Politics and Markets* (New York: Basic Books, 1977), p. 37.

69. See Matthew Tobriner and Joseph Grodin, "The Individual and the Public Service Enterprise in the New Industrial State," 55 *Cal. L. Rev.* 1247 (1967). Also see Lawrence Blades, "Employment at Will v. Individual Freedom: On Limiting the Abusive Exercise of Employer Power," 67 *Colum. L. Rev.* 1404, 1416 (1967), criticizing the termination at will doctrine and arguing that "such a philosophy of the employer's dominion over his employee may have fit the rustic simplicity of the days when the farmer or small entrepreneur, who may or may not have employed others, was the epitome of American individualism. But the philosophy is incompatible with these days of large, impersonal corporate employers; it does not comport

with the need to preserve individual freedom in today's job oriented, industrial society." See also Note, "Protecting at Will Employees Against Wrongful Discharge," 93 *Harv. L. Rev.* 1816 (1980); Philip J. Levine, "Toward a Property Right in Employment," 22 *Buffalo L. Rev.* 1081 (1973); and *Ezekial v. Winkley*, 20 Cal. 3d 267, 142 Cal. Rptr. 418, 572 P. 2d 32 (1977).

70. See Friedrich Kessler, "Contracts of Adhesion—Some Thoughts about Freedom of Contract," 43 *Colum. L. Rev.* 629 (1943), especially p. 631.

71. See Ian R. Macneil, "The Many Futures of Contracts," 47 *S. Cal. L. Rev.* 691 (1974); and Stewart Macaulay, "Changing a Continuing Relationship Between a Large Corporation and Those Who Deal With It: Automobile Manufacturers, Their Dealers and the Legal System," 1965 *Wis. L. Rev.* 483. See generally, on the relations of contract law to the rise of organizations, Karl Llewellyn, "What Price Contract—An Essay in Perspective," 40 *Yale L.J.* 704 (1931); and Philip Selznick, *Law, Society and Industrial Justice* (New York: Russell Sage Foundation, 1969).

72. See Margaret Radin, "Property and Personhood," 34 *Stan. L. Rev.* 957, 992–94 (1982), and sources cited there.

CHAPTER 5

1. See note 61 *infra*.

2. Cf. Ronald Dworkin, *Taking Rights Seriously* (Cambridge: Harvard University Press, 1977), p. 83.

3. Bodily integrity (to be protected by criminal and tort law), property, and contract are standard features in both the autonomy and the utility camps. Cf., e.g., Hegel's *Philosophy of Right*, trans. T. M. Knox (London: Oxford University Press, 1967), pp. 40–46, 57–62, 66–73; and *The Works of Jeremy Bentham*, the Bowring Edition (New York: Russell & Russell, 1962), vol. 3, pp. 190–92, 203, 213. As to free speech, compare John Stuart Mill, *On Liberty*, Chapter II, with T. Scanlon, "A Theory of Freedom of Expression," 1 *Phil. & Pub. Aff.* 204 (1972).

4. See generally Léon Duguit, "Les Transformations Générales du Droit Privé," trans. and reprinted in *Rational Basis of Legal Institutions* (New York: Macmillan, 1923), pp. 315–28; Frank I. Michelman, "Property, Utility, and Fairness: Comments on the Ethical Foundations of 'Just Compensation' Law," 80 *Harv. L. Rev.* 1165, 1202–13 (1967); L. T. Hobhouse, "The Historical Evolution of Property in Fact and Idea," in Bishop of Oxford, ed., *Property, Its Duties and Rights* (London: Oxford University Press, 1913), p. 1.

5. Rudolph von Jhering, *The Struggle for Law* (Chicago: Callaghan, 1915), p. 59.

6. See generally Margaret Radin, "Property and Personhood," 34 *Stan. L. Rev.* 957 (1982), and sources cited therein.

7. Robert Nozick, *Anarchy, State, and Utopia* (New York: Basic Books, 1974).

8. The classical authoritative statement of this general view of property is in Article 17 of the "Declaration of the Rights of Man" of 1789, which begins with the words: "Property being a sacred and inviolate right. . . ." In the Anglo-American legal tradition, the classical statement of the view of property as an absolute right, resistant to considerations of social utility, is Blackstone's: "The third absolute right, inherent in every Englishman, is that of property. . . . So great moreover is the regard of the law for private property that it will not authorize the least violation of it; not even for the general good of the whole community." *Commentaries*, Book I, chap. 1, pp. 138–39. See also William Van Alstyne, "The Recrudescence of Property Rights as the Foremost Principle of Civil Liberties," 43 *Law and Contemporary Problems*, 66 (1980).

9. *Politics*, Book II, chaps. 3, 5.

10. Richard Posner, *Economic Analysis of Law*, 2d ed. (Boston: Little, Brown, 1977), p. 28. Judicial decisions are seldom, if ever, explicit about the philosophical foundations of property, yet one can sometimes trace in their tone and the language they use an implicit reliance on one or the other of the two sets of justifications. Some decisions speak of property in absolutist terms with the fervor and resoluteness which befit a most fundamental right, resistant to considerations of social utility. Consider, for example, the following statement, made in *Spann v. City of Dallas*, 235 S.W. 513 at 515 (1921): "The right to acquire and own property, and to deal with it and use it as the owner chooses, so long as the use harms nobody, is a natural right. It does not owe its origin to constitutions. It existed before them. It is a part of the citizen's natural liberty—an expression of his freedom, guaranteed as inviolate by every American Bill of Rights." Also see Justice Marshall's more recent statement in *Hudgens v. NLRB*, 424 U.S. 507, 542 (1975): "No one would seriously question the legitimacy of the values of privacy and individual autonomy traditionally associated with privately owned property." Other decisions voice a utilitarian perception of property, emphasizing its subordination to considerations of social welfare. See, e.g., the view of Chief Justice Weintraub, who, after stating that "a man's right in his real property of course is not absolute," goes on to cite with approval from *Powell on Real Property* to the effect that "an owner must expect to find the absoluteness of his property rights curtailed by the organs of society, for the promotion of the best interests of others for whom these organs also operate as protective agencies." *State v. Shack*, 58 N.J. 297, 277 A.2d 369 (1971).

11. Cf. A. D. Lindsay, "The Principle of Private Property," in *Property, Its Duties and Rights* (note 4 *supra*), pp. 77–78: "How far the rights of property vested in corporations should be the same as those vested in

individuals is a subject of too great complexity to be entered into here. . . . It demands the adjustment of various interests, each having a value of its own. . . . How to preserve the variety and initiative which the existence of associations makes possible consistently with maintaining the stability of the whole state and the freedom of individual members of each association and of the State, is perhaps the most difficult of political problems which confronts us today, and one of which there is certainly no final solution." On the transformation of the institution of private property when we move from individuals to organizations, see Philip Selznick, *Law, Society and Industrial Justice* (New York: Russell Sage Foundation, 1969), pp. 63–72. The distinction between individual and corporate property is sometimes drawn in terms of the distinction between "property for use" and "property for power." See Hobhouse, "Historical Evolution," pp. 9–23; Francis Philbrick, "Changing Conceptions of Property in Law," 86 *U. Pa. L. Rev.* 691, 726 (1938).

12. See *Marsh v. Alabama*, 326 U.S. 501 (1946); *Amalgamated Food Employees Union v. Logan Valley Plaza*, 391 U.S. 308 (1968); *Lloyd Corp. v. Tanner*, 407 U.S. 551 (1972); *Hudgens v. NLRB*, 424 U.S. 507 (1976); *Prunyard Shopping Center v. Robins*, 447 U.S. 74 (1980). For other discussions of this line of cases, see, for example, "The Supreme Court, 1971 Term: Freedom of Speech, Press and Association," 86 *Harv. L. Rev.* 122 (1972); Radin, "Property and Personhood," pp. 1008–10; and Laurence Tribe, *American Constitutional Law* (Mineola, N.Y.: Foundation Press, 1978), p. 1167.

13. 407 U.S. 551 (1972).

14. I assume that these are corporations of sufficient size and complexity that they qualify as organizations as these are described in this essay. If they are not, I am content to treat the cases as illustrative hypotheticals, with the added assumption that the landowners are organizations. In analyzing the cases, I also ignore the more technical constitutional aspects, which are not my concern here. I don't believe that this does great violence to the actual reasoning in the cases, but if someone feels differently, I would again resort to the same escape: treat the discussion as a series of hypotheticals about the proper resolution of an O-I dispute. In fact, *Hudgens v. NLRB* (note 12 *supra*) deconstitutionalized the issue (as was made clear in the concurring opinion of Justice Powell and Chief Justice Burger, on pp. 523–24) by presenting it as a matter of balancing the property right of an employer against employees' Title VII rights, a balancing that is to be performed by the NLRB. This eliminates from the resolution of such disputes the need to search for (or invent) some state action, and other complicating constitutional elements, and makes my discussion of the confrontation of the two rights involved more directly relevant.

15. *Lloyd Corp.*, pp. 572–73.

16. *Logan Valley*, p. 324.

17. *Lloyd Corp.*, pp. 565–66.

18. Cf. Theodore St. Antoine, "Color Blindness But Not Myopia: A New Look at State Action, Equal Protection, and 'Private' Racial Discrimination," 59 *Mich. L. Rev.* 993, 1014 (1961): "The owner of the small corner ice cream parlor would hardly be held to be engaged upon matters of high public interest when, acting wholly independently, he draws the color line among his employees and patrons. But a far more searching scrutiny would await any analogous policies on the part of the great nation-wide public utility."

19. See pp. 60–61 *supra*.

20. *Lloyd Corp.*, p. 581.

21. *Marsh*, p. 516.

22. 397 U.S. 728 (1970).

23. Chief Justice Burger writing for the Court, ibid., on p. 737.

24. Note 22 *supra*.

25. *The Moral Law: Kant's Groundwork of the Metaphysics of Morals*, trans. H. J. Paton (London: Hutchinson, 1948), pp. 96–97.

26. Von Jhering, *Struggle for Law*, p. 59.

27. The distinction between individual and organizational property rights (in regard to their scope, weight, and remedy) proposed in this chapter has wide-ranging ramifications that cannot be fully explored here. Just to mention one additional illustration, consider the area of eminent domain. In *Lovett v. West Virginia Central Gas Co.* (65 W.Va. 739, 65 S.E. 196 [1909]), for example, the court's rhetoric, as well as its explicit willingness to let an individual's property right override the public interest, clearly imply an autonomy perspective. In this case, the respondent gas company condemned strips of the plaintiffs' land for the purpose of laying pipelines, but then proceeded to lay those pipelines at places other than the condemned land. Lovett asked for, and got, an injunction requiring the removal of the pipelines from the land that had not yet been condemned. The company argued that "the wrong sought to be restrained is a mere technical one, that the use of lands other than those condemned has not injured Lovett, but, in fact, benefited him; . . . and that it is unreasonable and unnecessary hardship, working injury to the public to require the removal of the pipelines" (pp. 197–98). In upholding the injunction, the court said, *inter alia:* "It may be that the taking of the property is not a great injury; yet it is a taking. The landowner objects to the use of any other land than that legally taken. He has the right so to object. His motives in objecting, whatever they may be, cannot change the legal principles involved. He is entitled to be protected as to that which is his, without regard to its money value. . . . If it be true that no great value is involved, yet sure it is that a right belonging to Lovett is involved. . . ." (p. 198). "It is insisted that the bill should have been dismissed because it does not appear that the

lands occupied by the pipelines were more valuable than those con-demned. But a question of right is involved, and not a question of value" (p. 199). "It is insisted that the removal of the pipelines will, for a time, take from the public in various cities and towns the use of gas; that a removal of the lines will be a great hardship upon the company and its patrons, the public. But Lovett's rights to the undisturbed use of his property is as fixed and as sacred as are the rights of the public" (p. 200).

Whether or not this approach is sound in relation to all individual property, it would be clearly misplaced, according to the view expounded in this chapter, in the case of corporate property. Yet, in *East & West R.R. Co. v. East Tenn. & Georg. R.R. Co.* (75 Ala. 275 [1883]), the court explicitly extended the same zealous protection to corporate property, holding that in eminent domain cases where no valid condemnation of the property in dispute has yet been made, "a court of equity, without inquiring whether there is irreparable injury or injury not susceptible of adequate redress by legal remedies, will intervene for the protection of the owner. And it will intervene, though, as in the present case, the contest may be between two incorporated companies" (p. 281).

28. Cf. Professor Epstein's related analogy between property and con-tract as viewed from a libertarian perspective:

One of the first functions of the law is to guarantee to individuals a sphere of influence in which they will be able to operate without having to justify themselves to the state or to third parties: if one individual is entitled to do within the confines of the tort law what he pleases with what he owns, the two individuals who operate with those same constraints should have the same right with respect to their mutual affairs against the rest of the world.

Richard Epstein, "Unconscionability: A Critical Reappraisal," 18 *J.L. Econ.* 293, 293–94 (1975).

29. *Contract as Promise* (Cambridge: Harvard University Press, 1981).

30. Ibid., p. 16.

31. Ibid., p. 19. See also Patrick Atiyah, *The Rise and Fall of Freedom of Contract* (Oxford: Oxford University Press, 1979), pp. 1–7.

32. Anthony Kronman, "Specific Performance," 45 *U. Chi. L. Rev.* 351, 359 (1978), and n. 36 there.

33. Ibid., pp. 359–60.

34. See Chapter 4, pp. 69–71 *supra*.

35. Cf. Professor Lucas's eloquent statement of a similar point:

It is one thing for Naboth to refuse to sell his vineyard to Ahab because it is his patrimony, and he will be breaking faith with his fathers and abandoning his family traditions if he parts with it. It is quite another thing for Naboth Holdings Inc. to refuse to sell one of their properties to the Ahab Education Authority because they are holding out for a higher price. Naboth's right to retain his ancestral acres ought not to become the means whereby big business can profiteer at the expense of the community.

J. R. Lucas, *Democracy and Participation* (Harmondsworth, England: Penguin Books, 1976), p. 227.

36. Alan Schwartz, "The Case for Specific Performance," 89 *Yale L.J.* 271, 297 (1979).

37. Ibid.

38. 435 U.S. 765 (1978). For some of the literature spawned by this case, see Gary Hart and William Shore, "Corporate Spending on State and Local Referendums: *First National Bank of Boston v. Bellotti,*" 29 *Case W. Res. L. Rev.* 808 (1979); Note, "Political Contributions—*First National Bank v. Bellotti*—Another Hurdle for Shareholder Protection," 4 *J. Corporation L.* 460 (1979); Paul Chevigny, "Philosophy of Language and Free Expression," 55 *N.Y.U. L. Rev.* 157, 189–90 (1980); Francis Fox, "Corporate Political Speech: The Effect of *First National Bank of Boston v. Bellotti* upon Statutory Limitations on Corporate Referendum Spending," 67 *Ky. L.J.* 75 (1978/79); Victor Brudney, "Business Corporations and Stockholders' Rights under the First Amendment," 91 *Yale L.J.* 235 (1981); Charles O'Kelly, Jr., "The Constitutional Rights of Corporations Revisited: Social and Political Expression and the Corporation after *First National Bank v. Bellotti,*" 67 *Georgetown U.L. Rev.* 1347 (1979); Note, "The Supreme Court, 1977 Term: Corporate Political Expression," 92 *Harv. L. Rev.* 163–74 (1979); Note, "The Corporation and the Constitution: Economic Due Process and Corporate Speech," 90 *Yale L.J.* 1833 (1981); William Patton and Randall Bartlett, "Corporate 'Persons' and Freedom of Speech: The Political Impact of Legal Mythology," 1981 *Wisc. L. Rev.* 494.

39. *Bellotti*, p. 786.

40. See generally Thomas Emerson, "Toward a General Theory of the First Amendment," 72 *Yale L.J.* 877 (1963); idem, *The System of Freedom of Expression* (New York: Random House, 1970); D. Richards, "A Moral Theory of the First Amendment," 123 *U.Pa. L. Rev.* 45 (1974); T. M. Scanlon, "Freedom of Expression and Categories of Expression," 40 *U.Pitt. L. Rev.* 519 (1979); Allen Buchanan, "Autonomy and Categories of Expression: A Reply to Professor Scanlon," 40 *U.Pitt. L. Rev.* 551 (1979).

41. Thomas Jackson and John Jeffries, Jr., "Commercial Speech: Economic Due Process and the First Amendment," 65 *Va. L. Rev.* 1 (1979); C. Edwin Baker, "Commercial Speech: A Problem in the Theory of Freedom," 62 *Iowa L. Rev.* 1 (1976); and see additional sources cited in Note, "The Corporation and the Constitution: Economic Due Process and Corporate Speech," 90 *Yale L.J.* 1833, 1836, n. 19 (1981). See also *Central Hudson Gas and Electric Corp. v. Public Service Commission of N.Y.*, 447 U.S. 557 (1979); and *Virginia State Board of Pharmacy v. Virginia Citizens Consumer Council Inc.*, 425 U.S. 748 (1975).

42. See, for example, O'Kelly, "Constitutional Rights," p. 1373; and Brudney, "Business Corporations," p. 248.

43. 424 U.S. 1 (1975). See also J. Skelly Wright, "Politics and the Constitution: Is Money Speech?" 85 *Yale L.J.* 1001 (1976).

44. Ibid., p. 16.

45. Ibid., p. 21.

46. Brudney, "Business Corporations," p. 268.

47. *Bellotti*, p. 789.

48. Ibid., p. 787.

49. Note 43 *supra*, pp. 48–49.

50. *Bellotti*, pp. 790–91, citing *Buckley v. Valeo*, pp. 48–49.

51. Or an *active* derivative right—see pp. 112–13 *infra*.

52. *Bellotti*, p. 786.

53. Brudney, "Business Corporations," p. 264.

54. *Bellotti*, p. 789; Chevigny, "Philosophy of Language," pp. 189–90.

55. For the distinction between business corporations and other associations regarding the right to free speech, cf. Note, "The Corporation and the Constitution" (note 38 *supra*), p. 1857.

56. 357 U.S. 449 (1957).

57. Ibid., p. 459.

58. Cf. ibid., pp. 458–60, where the problem of standing is discussed.

59. See Chapter 2, pp. 28–30 *supra*.

60. But see some further comments on the relationship between community and the present theory, in the Conclusion, pp. 207–10 *infra*.

61. "The Constitutional privilege against self-incrimination . . . grows out of the high sentiment and regard of our jurisprudence for conducting criminal trials and investigating proceedings upon a plane of dignity, humanity and impartiality." *U.S. v. White*, 322 U.S. 694 (1943). It should therefore be resistant to considerations of utility: "What Lord Camden denominated 'an argument of utility' should not prevail now as it did not in Westminster Hall when he pronounced his great judgment against general warrants." *Wilson v. U.S.*, 221 U.S. 361, 393 (1910) (McKenna J., dissenting).

62. 201 U.S. 43 (1906).

63. 322 U.S. 694 (1943).

64. Ibid., p. 701.

65. Ibid., pp. 701–03.

66. 417 U.S. 85 (1983).

67. Ibid., p. 104.

68. Cf. *U.S. v. Cogan*, 257 F. Supp. 170, 173–74 (1966):

Heeding *White's* admonition that mechanical reference to legal categories is not the way to handle the problem, we cannot conclude that the records of all things known to the law as general partnerships are necessarily clothed with the privilege. It may be that the principle of *White* will reach partnerships with scores or hundreds of members, where the relationship is not and cannot be face-to-face, where there is an inevitable measure of bureaucratization, of defined "office" apart from particular incumbents, of permanence, "institutionalization," and action by designated agents in "representative capacities". . . . These criteria are not met here; these general partnerships are "small" and personal by any standard.

69. Cf. Philip Selznick, *Law, Society and Industrial Justice* (New York: Russell Sage Foundation, 1969), pp. 43–52.

70. See, for example, *Fineberg v. U.S.*, 393 F.2d 417 (1968); and *Hair Industry Ltd. v. U.S.*, 340 F.2d 510 (1965), where the privilege was denied to one-person corporations.

71. Not to be confused with Etzioni's use of this term in his familiar typology of organizations. See Amitai Etzioni, *Complex Organizations* (New York: Free Press, 1961), pp. 31–33.

72. George Fletcher, "Fairness and Utility in Tort Theory," 85 *Harv. L. Rev.* 537 (1972).

CHAPTER 6

1. Paul Weiler, "Two Models of Judicial Decision-making," 46 *Canadian Bar Rev.* 406 (1968); Kenneth E. Scott, "Two Models of the Civil Process," 27 *Stan. L. Rev.* 937 (1975); Abram Chayes, "The Role of the Judge in Public Law Litigation," 89 *Harv. L. Rev.* 1271 (1976); Owen M. Fiss, "Foreword: The Forms of Justice," 93 *Harv. L. Rev.* 1 (1979).

2. See Chayes, "Role of the Judge," p. 1283.

3. This model draws upon and corresponds to Weiler's "adjudication of disputes model" (see Weiler, "Two Models," p. 408); Scott's "conflict resolution model" (see Scott, "Two Models," p. 937); and Chayes's "traditional model" (see Chayes, "Role of the Judge," pp. 1282–83). Noted proponents of the view of adjudication captured by this model include Jerome Frank, *Law and the Modern Mind* (New York: Tuder, 1936); Lon Fuller, "The Forms and Limits of Adjudication," 92 *Harv. L. Rev.* 353 (1978, published posthumously); Ronald Dworkin, "Hard Cases," in *Taking Rights Seriously* (Cambridge: Harvard University Press, 1977), p. 81; and Rolf Sartorius, "Social Policy and Judicial Legislation," 8 *Am. Phil. Q.* 151 (1971).

4. See Weiler's "judicial-policy-maker model," in Weiler, "Two Models," p. 437; Scott's "behavior modification model," in Scott, "Two Models," p. 938; and Chayes's "public law litigation model," in Chayes, "Role of the Judge," pp. 1288–1304.

5. Chayes, "Role of the Judge," p. 1282.

6. Scott, "Two Models," p. 938.

7. See Weiler, "Two Models," p. 410; Chayes, "Role of the Judge," p. 1282; and Donald L. Horowitz, *The Courts and Social Policy* (Washington, D.C.: The Brookings Institution, 1977), p. 284.

8. E.g., Chayes, "Role of the Judge," p. 1302.

9. "Here the rule of decision would prescribe that a decision is justifiable if and only if it best takes into account the interests of the litigants who are currently before the court." Richard Wasserstrom, *The Judicial Decision* (Stanford: Stanford University Press, 1961), p. 114. See also Vilhelm Aubert, "Courts and Conflict Resolution," 11 *J. of Conflict Resolution* 40, 41 (1967), for a view of the judge as giving a "service" to the litigants, who are seen as his "clients."

10. Several writers have emphasized the tension between these two sets of interests. See George Fletcher, "Fairness and Utility in Tort Theory," 85 *Harv. L. Rev.* 537, 540 (1972); Horowitz, *The Courts,* p. 274; and Melvin A. Eisenberg, "Participation, Responsiveness, and the Consultative Process: An Essay for Lon Fuller," 92 *Harv. L. Rev.* 410, 413 (1978).

11. See pp. 130–34 *infra.*

12. On the status of these models, see Sartorius, "Social Policy," p. 160; Weiler, "Two Models," p. 408; Scott, "Two Models," p. 940; and Fiss, "Foreword," p. 29.

13. See Horowitz, *The Courts,* pp. 4–9; Weiler, "Two Models," p. 438; and Chayes, "Role of the Judge," p. 1282.

14. Dworkin, "Hard Cases"; Sartorius, "Social Policy."

15. See Fiss, "Foreword," p. 36, where he rejects Chayes's historical view about the transition from *arbitration* to *regulation:* "The function of adjudication, whether in the nineteenth century or twentieth century, . . . has not been to resolve disputes between individuals but to give meaning to our public values."

16. E.g., Fuller, note 3 *supra.*

17. E.g., Dworkin, "Hard Cases"; and Sartorius, "Social Policy." This is also the import of Prof. Fletcher's rhetorical question: "The courts face the choice. Should they surrender the individual to the demands of maximizing utility? Or should they continue to protect individual interests in the face of community needs?" Fletcher, "Fairness," p. 573. Prof. Mishkin calls for restraint in deviating from the conventional mode of adjudication. See Paul J. Mishkin, "John Randolph Tucker Lecture: Federal Courts as State Reformers," 35 *Wash. and Lee L. Rev.* 949, 950, and passim (1978).

18. Roscoe Pound, "The Theory of Judicial Decision—Part III," 36 *Harv. L. Rev.* 940 (1923); Fiss, "Foreword"; and Chayes, "Role of the Judge."

19. See Joseph Raz, "Legal Principles and the Limits of Law," 81 *Yale L. J.* 823, 848–51 (1972), where he criticizes Dworkin's position that judges never "act on their own beliefs as legislators do" (p. 850), but rather decide cases always on the basis of preexisting, objectively given, principles. Dr. Raz calls this position a "dangerous myth" that takes literally and legitimizes a misleading rhetoric that judges sometimes use.

20. Pound, "Theory," p. 954. He argues that the judge should adopt a utilitarian orientation, and criticizes the preoccupation with "rights," which tend to take unjustified precedence over "policies" (pp. 954–55). On the relationship between the rights-policies distinction and the two models of adjudication, see my discussion on pp. 139–44 *infra.*

21. See Fiss, "Foreword," p. 2.

22. E.g., Horowitz, *The Courts,* p. 47: "There is tension between two different judicial responsibilities: deciding the particular case and formulating a general policy." See also, on the tension between the two functions of adjudication in the context of administrative law, Lillian R. Altree, Note, "Administrative Sanctions: Regulation and Adjudication," 16 *Stan. L. Rev.* 630 (1964).

23. Martin Shapiro, "Courts," in F. Greenstein and N. Polsby, eds., 5 *Handbook of Political Science,* 321, 374 (1975).

24. Ibid., p. 349. See also pp. 333, 347.

25. Cf. Roscoe Pound's noted attempt to devise different judicial decisionmaking strategies, depending on the subject matter of the litigation: Pound, "Theory," pp. 951–52, 957.

26. On the relationship between what I call the regulation model and the rise of large organizations, see Fiss, "Foreword," p. 35. Chayes also links some of the changes he detects in the nature of adjudication to organizations (Chayes, "Role of the Judge," p. 1291) and to "the emergence of the group as the real subject or object of litigation" (ibid., p. 1292).

27. This is, of course, not to say that the division of labor between the two models proposed here resolves the tension or competition between them. Few propositions about important social problems can claim the neatness and finality connoted by a "resolution," and the present suggestion is certainly not one of them. Still, the difference that organizations make to the nature of adjudication is substantial, and focusing on the interplay between the two models will prove, I hope, to be an illuminating way to bring that difference out. It should also be emphasized that the discussion that follows touches only upon some, not all, aspects of adjudication, giving in this way only a partial image of it. The discussion makes various tacit presuppositions, the exposition and elaboration of which would make the argument unduly cumbersome. Only by way of example, I will mention here the fact that the role of statutes is completely ignored in what follows. See a similar approach in Wasserstrom, *The Judicial Decision,* p. 8. This is not meant to challenge (or to affirm) the supremacy of legislation in judicial decisionmaking. I only assume (as does most of the literature about adjudication) that legislation (as well as other authoritative sources) leave a sufficiently broad leeway for judicial discretion and creativity, where the judge's own conception of his role and the goals that he

should pursue become important determinants of his decisionmaking. Cf. Cardozo: "It is when the colors do not match, when the references in the index fail, when there is no decisive precedent, that the serious business of the judge begins." Benjamin N. Cardozo, *The Nature of the Judicial Process* (New Haven: Yale University Press, 1921), p. 21.

28. "The threshold question raised by the division of view on this appeal is whether the court should resolve the litigation between the parties now before it as equitably as seems possible; or whether, seeking promotion of the general public welfare, it should channel private litigation into broad public objectives. A court performs its essential function when it decides the rights of parties before it. Its decision of private controversies may sometimes greatly affect public issues. . . . But this is normally an incident to the court's main function to settle controversy." *Boomer v. Atlantic Cement Co.*, 26 N.Y. 2d 219, 222; 257 N.E. 2d 870, 871 (1970).

29. "Just because a public law decision affects so wide a group, the court may believe it inappropriate, in determining liability, to base its decision on the issues raised by those few members of the group who happen to be in the court room. In such cases, therefore, the judge may subordinate the norm of settling the dispute that has been put to him, on the basis of the issues put to him, in favor of the function of making rules that are responsive to public needs." Eisenberg, "Participation," pp. 427–28.

30. In describing the *traditional model* (his counterpart to my arbitration model), Chayes ("Role of the Judge," p. 1283) lists as one of its elements that "the impact of the judgment is confined to the parties."

31. Cf. Professor Wilhelm Aubert's attempt to define the nature of international dispute-settlement by attending to the difference between the behavorial attributes of individuals (the subjects of municipal adjudication) and those of states (the actors on the international scene). He writes: "Insofar as international law deals with the relationship between states, the legal subjects have an entirely different motivational structure from human organisms. Nations do not behave as individuals do. They are units of a different order. Many of the points [about adjudication] discussed above refer to psychological mechanisms characteristic of human beings. These may or may not have application also to nations. But it does not follow from a legal definition of a state as a legal subject that it takes on the real characteristics of the units after which its legal form has been shaped." Aubert, "Courts," p. 47. It is somewhat ironic that Professor Aubert himself treats municipal adjudication as if it applied to individuals only, failing to realize that it, too, often deals with "units of a different order" from individuals, namely organizations.

32. For a definition and discussion of the twin concepts of

"presentation" and "futurizing," see Ian R. Macneil, "The Many Futures of Contracts," 47 *S. Cal. L. Rev.* 691, 800–04 (1974).

33. See Note, "The Wyatt Case: Implementation of a Judicial Decree Ordering Institutional Change," 84 *Yale L.J.* 1338 (1975); Note, "Implementation Problems in Institutional Reform Litigation," 91 *Harv. L. Rev.* 428 (1977); Note, "The Remedial Process in Institutional Reform Litigation," 78 *Colum. L. Rev.* 784 (1978); Mishkin, "Tucker Lecture," p. 959; Fiss, "Foreword," pp. 44–58; Theodore Eisenberg and Stephen Yeazell, "The Ordinary and the Extraordinary in Institutional Litigation," 93 *Harv. L. Rev.* 465 (1980); Colin Diver, "The Judge as Political Powerbroker: Superintending Structural Change in Public Institutions," 65 *Va. L. Rev.* 43 (1979).

34. Cf. Professor Stone's recommendation that "the society shall have to locate certain specific and critical organizational variables, and, where feasible, reach into the corporation to arrange them as it itself deems appropriate. . . . What I have in mind is a legal system that, in dealing with corporations, moves toward an increasingly direct focus on the *processes of corporate decisionmaking.*" Christopher Stone, *Where the Law Ends: The Social Control of Corporate Behavior* (New York: Harper & Row, 1975), pp. 120–21.

35. "A system of judiciary law (as every candid man will readily admit) is nearly unknown to the bulk of the community, although they are bound to adjust to the rules or principles of which it consists. . . . [T]hose portions of the law which are somewhat complex . . . are by the mass of the community utterly unknowable. . . . Unable to obtain professional advice, or unable to obtain advice which is sound and safe, men enter into transactions of which they know not the consequences. . . ." John Austin, cited in Jerome Frank, *Courts on Trial* (Princeton: Princeton University Press, 1949), pp. 283–84. See also Duncan Kennedy, "Form and Substance in Private Law Adjudication," 89 *Harv. L. Rev.* 1685, 1699 (1976).

CHAPTER 7

1. A related link between various formal aspects of judicial decisionmaking and substantive philosophical orientations can be found in George Fletcher, "Fairness and Utility in Tort Theory," 85 *Harv. L. Rev.* 537 (1972); Ronald Dworkin, "Hard Cases," in *Taking Rights Seriously* (Cambridge: Harvard University Press, 1977), p. 81; Duncan Kennedy, "Form and Substance in Private Law Adjudication," 89 *Harv. L. Rev.* 1685 (1976).

2. E.g., Dworkin, "Hard Cases." His thesis is that judicial decisionmaking should always maintain its distinctive style, and that judges should never, even in "hard cases," act as legislators.

3. For a good general discussion, see Arthur Goodhart, "Precedent in

English and Continental Law," 50 *L.Q. Rev.* 40 (1934). For a more philosophical discussion of the doctrine of precedent, see Richard Wasserstrom, *The Judicial Decision* (Stanford: Stanford University Press, 1961), chaps. 3–4.

4. See, for example, Paul Weiler, "Two Models of Judicial Decisionmaking," 46 *Canadian Bar Rev.* 406, 413 (1968); and Abram Chayes, "The Role of the Judge in Public Law Litigation," 89 *Harv. L. Rev.* 1281, 1283 (1976).

5. But cf. Dworkin's suggestion that "perhaps an assumed, overriding goal like utility is best advanced if courts make rules on the basis of *present* community standards, principles and policies . . . without reference to their utility, and legislatures and other institutions test the utility of such principles and policies, substituting others if they find the incumbents wanting." Ronald Dworkin, "Does Law Have a Function?" 74 *Yale L.J.* 640, 648 (1965). Note, however, that while Dworkin suggests that this might be the case, he offers no grounds for believing that it is so.

6. The following quotation illustrates the common identification of the particularity of the judicial decision with its individuality: "*Any lawsuit tends to focus on the particular.* The nature of the litigation heightens the impact of specific wrongs which are presented in immediate and graphic terms. *This emphasis on the individual's point of view* is precisely one of the strengths of the judicial forum." Paul J. Mishkin, "John Randolph Tucker Lecture: Federal Courts as State Reformers," 35 *Wash. and Lee L. Rev.* 949, 964 (1978) (emphasis added).

7. Roscoe Pound, "A Theory of Judicial Decision—Part III," 36 *Harv. L. Rev.* 940 (1923).

8. Wasserstrom, *Judicial Decision,* chap. 7.

9. Dworkin, "Hard Cases." Dworkin's *rights thesis* generated considerable discussion. For some noted critiques, see Joseph Raz, "Legal Principles and the Limits of Law," 81 *Yale L.J.* 823 (1972); idem, "Professor Dworkin's Theory of Rights," 26 *Political Studies* 123 (1978); Kent Greenawalt, "Policy, Rights, and Judicial Decision," 11 *Ga. L. Rev.* 991 (1977); H. L. A. Hart, "American Jurisprudence Through English Eyes: The Nightmare and the Noble Dream," 11 *Ga. L. Rev.* 969 (1977). For Dworkin's reply to some of these criticisms, see his article "Seven Critics," 11 *Ga. L. Rev.* 1201. I do not mean to enter this debate between Dworkin and his critics. I take Dworkin's position as expressing one of the features of the arbitration model and examine the relevance of Dworkin's arguments, taken on their own terms, to organizational litigation.

10. On the principles—policies distinction and its relevance to adjudication—see also Harry H. Wellington, "Common Law Rules and Constitutional Double Standards: Some Notes on Adjudication," 83 *Yale L.J.* 221 (1973).

11. Dworkin, *Taking Rights Seriously*, p. 85.

12. Ibid.

13. Ibid., p. 269.

14. Ibid., p. 198.

15. Ibid., p. 199.

16. Ibid., p. 89.

17. Ibid., p. 86.

18. About the relationship between predictability achieved by fixed rules and the ideal of individual autonomy, see Duncan Kennedy, "Legal Formality," 2 *J. Leg. Stud.* 351, 371 (1973).

19. On Dworkin's own doubts as to the applicability of the rights thesis in an organizational context, see his reply to critics in *Taking Rights Seriously* (paperback ed.), p. 345.

20. See Marc Galanter, "Why the 'Haves' Come Out Ahead: Speculations on the Limits of Legal Change," 9 *Law & Soc. Rev.* 95, 100 (1974).

21. This difference between individuals and organizations in their respective interest in the outcome of litigation bears on the issue of prospective overruling, as pointed out in Note, "Prospective Overruling and Retroactive Application in the Federal Courts," 71 *Yale L.J.* 907, especially 945 n. 192 (1962).

22. Cf. Vilhelm Aubert, "Courts and Conflict Resolution," 11 *J. of Conflict Resolution* 40, 45 (1967).

23. Cf. ibid., p. 46.

24. See Lawrance Ross, *Settled Out of Court: The Social Process of Insurance Claims Adjustment* (Chicago: Aldine, 2d ed. 1980).

25. J. J. C. Smart and Bernard Williams, *Utilitarianism: For and Against* (Cambridge, England: Cambridge University Press, 1973), p. 95.

26. Ibid., p. 99.

27. Ibid., p. 117.

28. See a consideration and a rejection of the "role theory" of the judge's moral responsibility in Kennedy, "Form and Substance," pp. 1772–73. Cf. Thomas Nagel, "Ruthlessness in Public Life," in *Mortal Questions* (Cambridge, England: Cambridge University Press, 1979); and Bernard Williams, "Politics and Moral Character," in *Moral Luck* (Cambridge, England: Cambridge University Press, 1981), especially pp. 63–66.

29. See pp. 66–69 *supra*.

30. See Wasserstrom, *Judicial Decision*, p. 141; and Arthur A. Leff, "Economic Analysis of Law: Some Realism about Nominalism," 60 *Va. L. Rev.* 451, 460–61 (1974).

31. See Chapter 4, pp. 69–71 *supra*.

32. Charles Fried, *An Anatomy of Value* (Cambridge: Harvard University Press, 1970), pp. 222–23.

33. "If the doctrine of precedent has any significant meaning, it would seem necessarily to imply that rules are to be followed *because they are rules* and not because they are 'correct' rules." Wasserstrom, *Judicial Decision*, p. 52.

34. Commentators tend to be skeptical about the actual contribution of the doctrine of *stare decisis* to uniformity and predictability. See, for example, Jerome Frank, *Courts on Trial—Myth and Reality in American Justice* (Princeton: Princeton University Press, 1949), pp. 268–70, 282–85; Chayes, "Role of the Judge," pp. 1287–88; Wasserstrom, *Judicial Decision*, pp. 60–66, and sources cited there.

35. This is probably what Chief Justice Stone meant by saying that a precedent should be overruled only if "the evil of a decisional error exceeds the evil of an innovation." *United States v. South Eastern Underwriters Association*, 332 U.S. 533, 594 (1944). (Cited in Wasserstrom, *Judicial Decision*, p. 49.)

36. It might seem possible to ground the method of precedent in the value of enforcing preexisting expectations. This, however, appears to be circular: one would have a sound expectation to a particular decision based on a prior one only if one assumed the court's commitment to the method of precedent. At any rate, the rejoinder to such an argument in favor of *stare decisis* would be along the same lines as my argument under the heading of *past orientedness* which underlines the difference between individual and organizational expectations. See pp. 139–44 *supra*.

37. But see quite a different approach in Prof. Shapiro's attempt to account for the doctrine of *stare decisis* in terms of communication theory: Martin Shapiro, "Toward a Theory of Stare Decisis," 1 *J. Leg. Stud.* 125 (1972).

38. Dworkin, *Taking Rights Seriously*, p. 113.

39. Ibid., pp. 180–83; 272–78.

40. Ibid., p. 227.

41. Cf. Kennedy, "Form and Substance," p. 1737. This idea received a vivid expression in an old contract case: "A man may do what he will with his own, having due regard to the right of others, and if he chooses to erect a monument to his caprice and folly on his premises, and employs and pays another to do it, it does not lie with a defendant who has been so employed and paid for building it, to say that his own performance would not be beneficial to the plaintiff." *Chamberlain v. Parker*, 45 N.Y. 569 (1871). But the *locus classicus* of this moral sentiment is still, it seems to me, Bartleby's defiant response to his employer's urgings: "At present I would prefer not to be a little reasonable." Herman Melville, "Bartleby, Scribner," in *The Complete Stories of Herman Melville*, ed. Jay Leyda (New York: Random House, 1949), p. 26.

42. Cf. Prof. Fiss's argument for abandoning the passive posture of the judge in structural reform litigation, in Owen Fiss, "Foreword: The Forms of Justice," 93 *Harv. L. Rev.* 1, 24–27 (1979).

43. This was probably the experience of Justice Robinson, who proclaimed to disregard precedent completely and insisted on deciding each case on its merits. See Andrew A. Bruce, "Judicial Buncombe in North Dakota and Other States," 88 *Central L.J.* 136; "Judge Robinson's Reply," 88 *Central L.J.* 155; and Note, "Rule and Discretion in the Administration of Justice," 33 *Harv. L. Rev.* 972 (1920).

CHAPTER 8

1. For a description of the void in legal and political philosophy regarding the role of corporations and other organizations, see Walter Goedecke, "Corporations and the Philosophy of Law," 10 *J. of Value Inquiry* 81 (1976).

2. Bruce Ackerman, *Social Justice in the Liberal State* (New Haven: Yale University Press, 1980).

3. Ronald Dworkin, *Taking Rights Seriously* (Cambridge: Harvard University Press, 1977).

4. Robert Nozick, *Anarchy, State, and Utopia* (New York: Basic Books, 1974).

5. John Rawls, *A Theory of Justice* (Cambridge: Harvard University Press, 1971).

6. E.g., Dworkin's statement: "I count legal persons as individuals, so that corporations may have rights. . . ." *Taking Rights Seriously*, p. 91 n. 1. And see Rawls, who includes "associations (states, churches, or other corporate bodies)" alongside individuals as parties in the "initial situation," but then excludes them without a comment or explanation from the "original position." *A Theory of Justice*, p. 146.

7. For some general accounts of pluralism, see Francis Coker, *Recent Political Thought* (New York: Appleton-Century, 1934); K. C. Hsiao, *Political Pluralism* (New York: Harcourt, Brace, 1927); Robert Dahl, *Pluralist Democracy in the United States* (Chicago: Rand McNally, 1967); Michael P. Smith, "Pluralism Revisited," in Michael P. Smith et al., *Politics in America: Studies in Policy Analysis* (New York: Random House, 1974). The term *political pluralism* is sometimes used to designate the "normative" pluralism associated with the views of thinkers such as Otto von Gierke in Germany, Lèon Duguit in France, Harold Laski and J. N. Figgis in England, and M. P. Follett in America. My use of the term is broader, in that it includes all those who take seriously the political role of organizations, whether or not they also look upon them favorably, as the "normative pluralists" did. On

the distinction between "normative" and "empirical" (or "descriptive") pluralists, see Smith, "Pluralism Revisited," p. 4.

8. Note 4 *supra.*

9. Ibid., p. ix.

10. Ibid., p. 26.

11. Ibid., p. 149.

12. Ibid., p. 57. The kernel of this argument was already made by Mill in the last chapter of *The Principles of Political Economy.* One of the exceptions to his "non-interference" principle ("Laissez-faire . . . should be the general practice: every departure from it, unless required by some great good, is a certain evil") arises when a business is conducted in the form of a *joint stock company.* The assumption that a person will know, better than the state, his own best interests is no longer relevant in that case, when the management of the business is vested in someone other than the owner. As Robert Wolff points out, what to Mill seemed a minor exception to his libertarian rule, threatens (or, depending on one's taste, promises) under contemporary conditions to devour the entire rule: "Since virtually the entire American economy is now controlled by joint stock corporations we may conclude that Mill would endorse a program of strict government management of private business. The premises of individualism quite naturally entail this collectivist conclusion: all that is required is a recognition of the changed circumstances in which the major portion of the economic activity of the nation is conducted." Robert Paul Wolff, *The Poverty of Liberalism* (Boston: Beacon Press, 1968), p. 43.

13. Nozick, *Anarchy,* p. 169.

14. Ibid., p. 172.

15. Ibid., p. 170.

16. Ibid., p. 171.

17. Ibid., p. 169.

18. Ibid.

19. That Nozick's conception of coercion pertains only to the "strong" sense is supported by his treatment of the concept in his article "Coercion," in Peter Laslett et al., eds., *Philosophy, Politics and Society,* 4th series (New York: Harper & Row, 1972).

20. See, for example, Prof. Klein's confidence on this point: "The process I am concerned with is one that . . . endows General Motors with the capacity to bear the burden of the tax—just as if the corporation were a human being. This last stage of the process is reification/animism to the point of nonsense. It is a process of pure magic in which the burden of the tax falls on no one. . . . The payment by General Motors, however, is bound to have important adverse economic effects on some real people, and these effects are what matters most when a corporate tax is imposed

or increased." William A. Klein, "Income, Taxation and Legal Entities," 20 *UCLA L. Rev.* 13, 53–54 (1972). In what follows, I try to show that no magic is involved in challenging the self-evidence of the proposition in the text.

21. See pp. 64–66 *supra*.

22. For a lucid, nontechnical, though somewhat dated text, see Richard Goode, *The Corporation Income Tax* (New York: John Wiley, 1951). For more recent reviews of the literature, see Peter Mieszkowski, "Tax Incidence Theory: The Effects of Taxes on the Distribution of Income," 7 *J. Econ. Lit.* 1103 (1969); George F. Break, "The Incidence and Economic Effects of Taxation," in Alan S. Blinder et al., *The Economics of Public Finance* (Washington, D.C.: The Brookings Institution, 1974).

23. "The one conclusion about which there does seem to have developed an informed consensus is that the problem of tracing any of the various consequences of the tax is exceedingly complex, involving virtually endless interrelationships between narrower, but still thorny and unresolved problems from almost every subfield of economics." William A. Klein, "The Incidence of the Corporation Income Tax: A Lawyer's View of a Problem in Economics," 1965 *Wis. L. Rev.* 576, 578.

24. He will find in opposition, e.g., M. A. Adelman, "The Corporate Income Tax in the Long Run," 65 *J. Pol. Econ.* 151 (1957); and A. Harberger, "The Incidence of Corporation Income Tax," 70 *J. Pol. Econ.* 215, 234 (1962).

25. See J. Stiglitz, "The Corporation Tax," 5 *J. Pub. Econ.* 303 (1976).

26. Strictly speaking, my argument defends only an ongoing regime of corporate tax. Within such a regime, no individual may have a valid claim that she would have been better off without the tax. The argument is, however, exposed to the "first generation" objection: the shareholders at the time when the tax is imposed for the first time are, in fact, going to bear its burden. The value of their shares is actually likely to drop. The initial imposition of the tax would therefore be illegitimate on Nozick's premises. This objection can be met in two ways. First, in the spirit of the "hypothetical explanations" used both by Nozick and in this discussion, we may imagine that the tax is imposed for the first time only on "ownerless corporations," i.e., on corporations that own all their stock. Consequently, when individuals buy shares in such corporations for the first time, they already buy them *within* the regime of corporate tax, paying the adjusted price. Secondly, and more importantly, as a matter of fact we do already live under a regime of corporate tax. While Nozick's objection to other taxes does entail a call for abolishing them (which gives the political bite to his philosophical discussion), no such conclusion follows from his possible objection to the initial imposition of corporate tax. A revocation of the tax will not rectify the historical injustice done to the "first generation," but it will, on the other hand, create a new injustice. A

revocation of the tax will merely mean a windfall profit to the current owners of the shares, and a relative decline in the value of other kinds of investments. Since the revocation of the tax benefits other individuals than those disadvantaged by its imposition, it compounds rather than offsets the initial injustice (if such there were).

27. See Goode, *Corporation Income Tax*, p. 30.

28. On the problem of the "free rider" as a rationale for governmental action, see Mancur Olson, *The Logic of Collective Action* (Cambridge: Harvard University Press, 1965).

29. That Nozick holds this position is strongly implied by his discussion where he deals with free-rider situations (*Anarchy*, pp. 93–95, 265–68).

30. For a criticism of Nozick's argument, see Elliott Abramson, "Philosophization Against Taxation: Why Nozick's Challenge Fails," 23 *Arizona L. Rev.* 753 (1981).

31. E.g., Note, "The Relation and Integration of Individual and Corporate Income Taxes," 94 *Harv. L. Rev.* 717 (1981); and Klein, "Income."

32. Prof. Merriam should probably be credited for awakening the interest of political scientists in the concept of private governments. See Charles E. Merriam, *Public and Private Government* (New Haven: Yale University Press, 1944). The concept has since become quite widespread. See, for example, Grant McConnell, *Private Power and American Democracy* (New York: Alfred A. Knopf, 1966; Vintage Books edition, 1970), chap. 5; Sanford A. Lakoff, ed., *Private Government* (Glenview, Ill.: Scott, Foresman, 1973).

33. See his *Law, Society and Industrial Justice* (New York: Russell Sage Foundation, 1969).

34. Sanford Lakoff, "Private Government in the Managed Society," in Lakoff, ed., *Private Government*, p. 225.

35. Henri S. Kariel, *The Decline of American Pluralism* (Stanford: Stanford University Press, 1961), p. 259.

36. Cf. John K. Galbraith, *American Capitalism—The Concept of Countervailing Power* (Boston: Houghton Mifflin, 1952), chap. 10.

37. "Since the facts make clear that mass organizations—whether national corporations, national unions or national professional associations—cannot be relied on to protect the individual against repression by his own group, the state itself is his sole resort. . . . Against large scale groups, only the state can maintain or create rights for the protection of the individuals." *The Decline of American Pluralism*, pp. 258–59. This unique position of the state, as the sole protector of individual rights in an organizational setting, results, claims Kariel, from the fact that its "source of power is independent of mass organizations" and that it is "representative of non-incorporated, disassociated interests." Ibid. On the role of the state as protector of individual rights against organizations, see also Wolfgang

Friedmann, *The State and the Rule of Law in a Mixed Economy* (London: Stevens, 1971), p. 20; and James Weinstein, *The Corporate Ideal in the Liberal State 1900–1918* (Boston: Beacon Press, 1968).

38. For a detailed suggestion for expanding those protections, see David Ewing, *Freedom Inside the Organization: Bringing Civil Liberties to the Workplace* (New York: Dutton, 1977).

39. See, e.g., Philip Taft, *Rights of Union Members and the Government* (Westport, Conn.: Greenwood Press, 1975).

40. See, for example, Professor Arthur Miller's vigorous attack on the "orthodox constitutional theory and doctrine [which] recognize the existence of two entities: government and the individual person. Nothing intermediate is envisaged." Whereas "the most important social unit, despite the original theory of the Constitution, has become the pluralistic social group." *The Modern Corporate State* (Westport, Conn.: Greenwood Press, 1976); the quotations are from pp. 27 and 19, respectively.

41. Alexander Pekelis long ago made a strong case for extending constitutional rights to the protection of individuals against private organizations. See his "Private Governments and the Federal Constitution," in the collection of his essays *Law and Social Action*, ed. Milton Konvitz (Ithaca, N.Y.: Cornell University Press, 1950), p. 91. Prof. Berle introduced the theme of "constitutionalizing" the corporation; see: Adolf A. Berle, Jr., "Constitutional Limitations on Corporate Activity—Protection of Personal Rights from Invasion Through Economic Power," 100 *U. Penn. L. Rev.* 933, 943 (1952). This theme was further developed by a number of other writers, e.g., Arthur S. Miller, "Toward Constitutionalizing the Corporation," 80 *W. Va. L. Rev.* 187 (1978); and W. Willard Wirtz, "Government by Private Groups," 13 *La. L. Rev.* 440 (1953).

42. See, for example, Theodore J. St. Antoine, "Color Blindness But Not Myopia: A New Look at State Action, Equal Protection, and 'Private' Racial Discrimination," 59 *Mich. L. Rev.* 993, 1011 (1961); Jesse H. Choper, "Thoughts on State Action: The 'Government Function' and 'Power Theory' Approaches," 1979 *Wash. U.L.Q.* 3, and cases cited there. Certain developments in the law may, however, be seen as marking a movement in the general direction recommended here, while alleviating the need for a strained application of the state action doctrine. There is, for one thing, an important body of law that protects basic individual rights against private entities as well as against the government on the basis of both federal and state civil rights statutes (especially in the area of racial discrimination). In the absence of such a protection, one can observe an increasing reliance on state constitutions and their interpretation by some state Supreme Courts as establishing rights against private entities even when state action cannot be found. See, for example, *Robins v. Pruneyard Shopping*

Center, 23 Cal.3d 899, 592 P.2d 341, 153 Cal. Rptr. 854 (1979), *aff'd sub nom. Pruneyard Shopping Center v. Robins,* 447 U.S. 74 (1980); and Note, "Private Abridgment of Speech and the State Constitutions," 90 *Yale L.J.* 165 (1980).

43. L. T. Hobhouse, "The Historical Evolution of Property in Fact and in Idea," in *Property, Its Duties and Rights,* ed. Bishop of Oxford (London: Oxford University Press, 1913), p. 1.

44. See, for example, Prof. Holland's argument that under the conditions of industrialized capitalist society, private property defeats the values of individual autonomy which it purports to protect. H. S. Holland, "Property and Personality," in *Property, Its Duties and Rights,* ibid., p. 169. This comes quite close to the Marxist critique of private property. For a recent statement of the Marxist position, see George Brenkert, "Freedom and Private Property in Marx," 8 *Phil. & Pub. Aff.* 122 (1979).

45. *Santa Clara County v. Southern Pac. R.R.,* 118 U.S. 394 (1886); *Gulf, Colorado & Santa Fe Railway v. Ellis,* 165 U.S. 150 (1897). This application of constitutional protections to corporations was subject to recurrent objections by some justices, notably, in recent times, Justices Douglas and Black. See, for example, Justice Douglas's dissent (joined by Justice Black) in *Wheeling Steel Corp. v. Glander,* 337 U.S. 562 (1949), where he points out that the applicability of the Fourteenth Amendment to corporations has never been discussed by the Court: "There was no history, logic or reason given to support that view." Ibid., p. 576. He goes on to say (ibid., p. 581):

It may be most desirable to give corporations this protection from the operation of the legislative process. But that question is not for us. It is for the people. If they want corporations to be treated as humans are treated, if they want to grant corporations this large degree of emancipation from state regulation, they should say so.

46. *Lochner v. New York,* 198 U.S. 45 (1905). For other important cases belonging to this era, see, for example, *Coppage v. Kansas,* 236 U.S. 1 (1915); and *Adair v. U.S.,* 208 U.S. 161 (1908). For a critical discussion of these cases, see Lawrence Blades, "Employment at Will v. Individual Freedom: On Limiting the Abusive Exercise of Employer Power," 67 *Colum. L. Rev.* 1404, 1417 (1967).

47. That in the nineteenth century and the beginning of this one individualistic rhetoric and individual rights were used by the Supreme Court to protect and promote large enterprise has been argued by several writers. See, for example, John W. Ward, "The Ideal of Individualism and the Reality of Organization," in Earl Cheit, ed., *The Business Establishment* (New York: John Wiley, 1964); and Charles Lindblom, *Politics and Markets* (New York: Basic Books, 1977), p. 191. For related historical accounts, see, e.g., James W. Hurst, *Law and the Conditions of Freedom in the Nineteenth Century United States* (Madison: University of Wisconsin Press, 1956); Gabriel

Kolko, *The Triumph of Conservatism* (New York: Free Press, 1963); Morton J. Horowitz, *The Transformation of American Law 1780–1860* (Cambridge: Harvard University Press, 1977). Among the most famous (and by now notorious) cases that illustrate the point are *Lochner v. N.Y.* and *Adair v. U.S.* (see note 46 *supra*). Professor Kessler makes a similar charge with respect to private law: "Freedom of contract enables enterprises to legislate by contract and, what is even more important, to legislate in a substantially authoritarian manner without using the appearance of authoritarian forms. Standard contracts in particular could thus become effective instruments in the hands of powerful industrial and commercial overlords, enabling them to impose a new feudal order of their own making upon a vast host of vassals." Friedrich Kessler, "Contracts of Adhesion: Some Thoughts About Freedom of Contract," 43 *Colum. L. Rev.* 629, 642 (1943).

48. It is interesting to note that contemporary social conditions have evoked in a number of writers a feudal imagery; some of them use the term *neo-feudalism* to describe current social reality. See, for example, Theodore J. Lowi, *The End of Liberalism* (New York: W. W. Norton, 1969), p. 102; Hans Morgenthau, *The Purpose of American Politics* (New York: Alfred A. Knopf, 1960), pp. 279–92; and Charles A. Reich, "The New Property," 73 *Yale L.J.* 733, 768 (1964). The term, however, is used by the various authors with somewhat different connotations. The meaning that I attach to it is spelled out in the text.

49. See, for example, Harold Laski, "The Pluralistic State," in *Foundations of Sovereignty* (New York: Harcourt, Brace, 1921), pp. 232–49.

50. Laurence Tribe, *American Constitutional Law* (Mineola, N.Y.: Foundation Press, 1978), p. 876.

51. *Kedroff v. St. Nicholas Cathedral*, 344 U.S. 94 (1952); M. D. Howe, "Foreword: Political Theory and the Nature of Liberty," 67 *Harv. L. Rev.* 91 (1953); Tribe, *American Constitutional Law*, ibid.

52. "Recapitulated here is an ancient paradox of liberalism: to destroy the authority of intermediate communities and groups in the name of freeing their members from domination destroys the only buffer between the individual and the state, and risks enslaving the individual to the state's potential tyranny. But the paradox is also a dilemma: submerging persons in the intermediate communities and groups that seek dominion over their lives creates the risk that individuals will remain at the mercy of hierarchical and subjugating social structures." Tribe, *American Constitutional Law*, p. 898.

53. Prof. Friedmann is among those who view the tension between the role of the state and that of organizations in diachronic terms: "We are witnessing another dialectic process in history: the national sovereign state—having taken over effective legal and political power from the social

groups of the previous age—surrenders its power to the new massive social groups of the industrial age." Wolfgang G. Friedmann, "Corporate Power, Government by Private Groups, and the Law," 57 *Colum. L. Rev.* 155, 165 (1957).

54. Robert Horn, *Groups and the Constitution* (Stanford: Stanford University Press, 1956), p. 154.

55. From among the authors whose views have been cited in this chapter, see, for example, Dworkin's statement that "representative democracy is widely thought to be the institutional structure most suited, in a complex and diverse society, to the identification and achievement of utilitarian policies" (*Taking Rights Seriously*, p. 276); and Kariel's position, whose emphasis on the state's role in protecting individual rights is similarly based on a conception of the state "whose source of power is independent of mass organizations, [and] which is representative of nonincorporated, disassociated interests" (*Decline of American Pluralism*, p. 259).

56. This is, of course, not to say that there aren't severe difficulties with aggregating individual preferences through voting. One such conspicuous difficulty has been mentioned before: Arrow's impossibility theorem. See Kenneth Arrow, *Social Choice and Individual Values*, 2d ed. (New Haven: Yale University Press, 1963).

57. The term *corporate state* has become quite widespread. See, for example, Daniel Fusfeld, "The Rise of the Corporate State in America," 6 *J. Econ. Issues* 1 (1972); Roberto Unger, *Knowledge and Politics* (New York: Free Press, 1975), p. 175; and Miller, *The Modern Corporate State*. The usage, however, connotes different things for different writers. The meaning I attach to the term is indicated in the text.

58. See, e.g., Arthur Bentley, *The Process of Government* (Chicago: University of Chicago Press, 1908); Earl Latham, *The Group Basis of Politics* (Ithaca, N.Y.: Cornell University Press, 1952); and David Truman, *The Governmental Process* (New York: Alfred A. Knopf, 1953).

59. On the political power of corporations in America, see generally Fusfeld, "Rise of the Corporate State"; Theodore K. Quinn, *Giant Business: Threat to Democracy* (New York: Exposition Press, 1953); Edwin M. Epstein, *The Corporation in American Politics* (Englewood Cliffs, N.J.: Prentice-Hall, 1969); Andrew Hacker, ed., *The Corporation Takeover* (New York: Harper & Row, 1964); Ralph Nader and Mark J. Green, eds., *Corporate Power in America* (New York: Grossman, 1973); Richard J. Barker, *The American Corporation* (New York: E. P. Dutton, 1970); Maurice Zeitlin, *American Society, Inc.*, 2d ed. (Chicago: Rand McNally, 1977); Morton Mintz and Jerry S. Cohen, *Power, Inc.* (New York: Bantam Books, 1977); Mark V. Nadel, *Corporations and Political Accountability* (Lexington, Mass.: D. C. Heath, 1976). The important political role played by business corporations is, of

course, not a uniquely American phenomenon. See, for example, Chitoshi Yanaga's study: *Big Business in Japanese Politics* (New Haven: Yale University Press, 1968).

60. The following account in terms of the three "channels" draws particularly on Carl Kaysen, "The Corporation: How Much Power? What Scope?" in E. Mason, ed., *The Corporation in Modern Society* (Cambridge: Harvard University Press, 1959); Lindblom, *Politics and Markets*, pp. 152–55, 170–213; Michael Reagan, *The Managed Economy* (London: Oxford University Press, 1963), pp. 99–120; and see also sources cited in note 59 *supra*.

61. The best-known philosophical elaboration of this theme is Herbert Marcuse, *One-Dimensional Man* (Boston: Beacon Press, 1964).

62. See William H. Whyte, Jr., *The Organization Man* (New York: Simon and Schuster, 1956).

63. This is, of course, a deliberately one-sided presentation of the literature on corporate political power. The view described in the text is sufficiently weighty to justify an examination of its legal, normative implications, challenging the prevailing, complacent view of majoritarian politics which underlies much legal thinking. This, however, is not to say that the views represented by the corporate state model do not have learned dissenters, who think the talk of the "corporate state" is misplaced or at least greatly exaggerated. See, for example, Neil H. Jacoby, "Myths of the Corporate Economy," in J. Fred Weston, ed., *Large Corporations in a Changing Society* (New York: New York University Press, 1974), p. 129; Richard A. Posner, "Power in America: The Role of the Large Corporation," in Weston, ed., ibid., p. 103; and Ralf K. Winter, *Government and the Corporation* (Washington, D.C.: American Enterprise Institute, 1978), p. 27.

64. The concept of "double counting," as a defect in the workings of majoritarian democracy, has been used by Dworkin in a different context. See *Taking Rights Seriously*, pp. 234–38, 275–78. While it is doubtful that Dworkin succeeds in identifying a genuine case of "double counting" (see H. L. A. Hart, "Between Utility and Rights," 79 *Colum. L. Rev.* 828, 838–46, [1979]), the notion is a useful one and describes well one of the problems associated with corporations impinging upon majoritarian democracy, as discussed in the text.

65. Cf. Reagan, *The Managed Economy*, p. 132; and E. E. Schattschneider, *The Sovereign People* (New York: Holt, Rinehart & Winston, 1961), chap. 7.

66. Which individual values and preferences are "free" or "authentic" and which are "manipulated" or "falsified" is, of course, a difficult issue that is beyond the scope of the present discussion.

67. See p. 36 *supra*.

68. See Martin Shapiro, *Freedom of Speech: The Supreme Court and Judicial Review* (Englewood Cliffs, N.J.: Prentice-Hall, 1966), passim; and *The Supreme Court and Administrative Agencies* (New York: Free Press, 1968), pp. 206–07.

CHAPTER 9

1. *Law in the Modern State*, trans. Frida and Harold Laski (New York: B. W. Huebsch, 1919), p. 240.

2. On decentralization and loss of central control in government, see, e.g., Michael D. Reagan, *The Managed Economy* (London: Oxford University Press, 1963), pp. 222–33. Professor Dahl points out that "the national government is one out of more than ninety thousand governments of all kinds existing within the boundaries of the United States." Robert Dahl, *Pluralist Democracy in the U.S.* (Chicago: Rand McNally, 1967), p. 171. Cf. Graham T. Allison, *Essence of Decision: Explaining the Cuban Missile Crisis* (Boston: Little, Brown, 1971), p. 67: "A government consists of a conglomerate of semi-feudal, loosely allied organizations, each with a substantial life of its own."

3. See Grant McConnell, *Private Power and American Democracy* (New York: Alfred A. Knopf, 1966), chaps. 6–9; and John K. Galbraith, *The New Industrial State*, 2d ed. (Boston: Houghton Mifflin, 1971), p. 234. For a discussion of this phenomenon in a legal theoretical context, see Roberto M. Unger, *Knowledge and Politics* (New York: Free Press, 1975), pp. 175 ff. See also the discussion of the erosion of the public/private distinction in Gerald Frug, "The City as a Legal Concept," 93 *Harv. L. Rev.* 1059, 1128–41 (1980), and sources cited there.

4. E.g., the Communication Satellite System, discussed in this context by Reagan, *The Managed Economy*, p. 190.

5. See ibid., pp. 191–94; Galbraith, *New Industrial State*, p. 316.

6. Public utilities are the obvious example.

7. See pp. 116–17 *supra*.

8. For a more detailed analysis of various parameters of the judicial stance, see Bruce Ackerman, *Private Property and the Constitution* (New Haven: Yale University Press, 1977), pp. 49–56.

9. See pp. 60–61 *supra*.

10. See, for example, Martin Shapiro, *Law and Politics in the Supreme Court* (New York: Free Press, 1964); idem, *The Supreme Court and Administrative Agencies* (New York: Free Press, 1968); and James Freedman, *Crisis and Legitimacy: The Administrative Process and American Government* (Cambridge, England: Cambridge University Press, 1978).

11. Cf. Ronald Dworkin, *Taking Rights Seriously* (Cambridge: Harvard University Press, 1977), p. 199.

12. See pp. 36–37 *supra*.

13. Title VII (Equal Employment Opportunity) of the 1964 Civil Rights Act, P.L. 88-352, 78 Stat. 253.

14. See pp. 74–77 *supra*.

15. Cf. Note, "Preventing Unnecessary Intrusions on University Autonomy," 69 *Cal. L. Rev.* 1538, 1546–51 (1981).

16. For a general discussion of the relationship between antitrust legislation and labor law, see Milton Handler and William Zifchak, "Collective Bargaining and the Antitrust Laws: The Emasculation of the Labor Exemption," 81 *Colum. L. Rev.* 459 (1981); Robert Gorman, *Basic Text on Labor Law* (St. Paul, Minn.: West, 1976), pp. 621–38; and Lawrence Sullivan, *Handbook on the Law of Antitrust* (St. Paul, Minn.: West, 1977), pp. 723–31.

CONCLUSION

1. Cf. Robert Hessen, *In Defense of the Corporation* (Stanford: Hoover Institution Press, 1979), pp. 1–22, for a relatively recent critique of the concession theory. However, as mentioned before, Professor Hessen's rejection of this theory leads him to espouse the aggregate view of the corporation and embrace its normative implications—the equation of corporate rights with the individual rights of shareholders. See Chapter 1, note 50 *supra*.

2. Though it is not my aim here to take issue with any specific piece written within the general critical mode described in the text, I should mention as an example of the genus one recent comprehensive radical attack on bureaucracy launched from a legal point of view: Gerald Frug, "The Ideology of Bureaucracy in American Law," 97 *Harv. L. Rev* 1276 (1984).

3. This was one of the explicit messages of Chapter 8.

4. See Erving Goffman, "Role Distance," in *Encounters* (Indianapolis: Bobbs-Merrill, 1961), pp. 85–152. Though I derive the core meaning of this concept from Goffman, my usage as described in the text deviates from his.

5. See Chapter 5, pp. 114–16 *supra*.

6. The general theme of having the institutional level "reflected" on the individual level is, of course, a familiar one in the history of sociology. For the importance of the concept of "role" in mediating the two levels, see Peter Berger and Thomas Luckmann, *The Social Construction of Reality* (Garden City, N.Y.: Doubleday, 1966), pp. 78–79.

7. Cf. Erving Goffman, *Asylums: Essays on the Social Situation of Mental Patients and Other Inmates* (Garden City, N.Y.: Doubleday, 1961), p. 314.

8. Erving Goffman documents various modes of evasion and insubordination by patients in mental hospitals and interprets this behavior in relation to the concept of role-distance in his essay "The Underlife of a Public Institution: A Study of Ways of Making Out in a Mental Hospital," ibid., pp. 171–320.

9. On the propensity of roles acquired in secondary socialization to be "put on" in a manipulative manner, cf. Berger and Luckmann, *Social Construction of Reality*, p. 172.

10. Goffman, *Encounters*, p. 130.

11. Cf. Charles Taylor, "Neutrality in Political Science," in Peter Laslett and W. G. Runciman, eds., *Philosophy, Politics and Society*, 3d series (Oxford: Blackwell, 1967), pp. 25–57.

12. See the discussion of goal-displacement in Chapter 2, pp. 36–37 *supra*.

13. The relationship of these comments to Tönnies's distinction between *Gemeinschaft* and *Gesellschaft* is too obvious to ignore and too complicated to spell out here. It must therefore only be acknowledged. See Ferdinand Tönnies, *Community and Society* (*Gemeinschaft und Gesellschaft*), trans. Charles Loomis (East Lansing, Mich.: Michigan State University Press, 1957). See Loomis's own attempt to elaborate and apply the distinction, in Charles Loomis and J. Allan Beegle, *Rural Sociology* (Englewood Cliffs, N.J.: Prentice-Hall, 1957). Of particular relevance here is his essay "The Division of Labor, the Community, and Society," in Charles Loomis, *Social Systems: Essays in Their Persistence and Change* (Princeton, N.J.: D. Van Nostrand, 1960). For short surveys of related dichotomous typologies of social structure, see the essay by Charles Loomis and John McKinney, "The Application of Gemeinschaft and Gesellschaft as Related to other Typologies," in the above-cited English translation of Tönnies's work, pp. 12–29; and Horace Miner's article, "Community-Society Continua," in *International Encyclopedia of the Social Sciences* (New York: Macmillan and Free Press, 1968), vol. 3, pp. 174–80.

14. Selma Largerlöf, *The Story of Gösta Berling*, trans. Pauline Bancroft Flach (Garden City, N.Y.: Doubleday, 1898), pp. 472–73. The quoted parable is followed by this comment: "Dear Reader, must I say the same? The giant bees of fancy have now swarmed about us for a year and a day; but how they are going to come into the bee-hive of fact, that they really must find out for themselves."

Index

Designer:	Betty Gee
Compositor:	Interactive Composition Corporation
Text:	10/13 Palatino
Display:	Palatino
Printer:	Braun-Brumfield, Inc.
Binder:	Braun-Brumfield, Inc.